OBAMABOMB

A Dangerous and Growing National Security Fraud

Fred Fleitz

Second edition – Updated September 25, 2016

Center for Security Policy Press

Obamabomb: A Dangerous and Growing National Security Fraud is published in the United States by the Center for Security Policy Press, division of the Center for Security Policy

First edition: July 6, 2016
Second edition: September 25, 2016

THE CENTER FOR SECURITY POLICY
1901 Pennsylvania Avenue, NW, Suite 201, Washington, DC 20006
Phone: (202) 835-9077 | Email: info@securefreedom.org
For more information, please see securefreedom.org

Book Design by Adam Savit
Cover Design by J.P. Zarruk

Table of Contents

Executive Summary

The Obama administration claims the July 2015 nuclear agreement with Iran (the Joint Comprehensive Plan of Action or JCPOA) is a great victory for President Obama's foreign policy that reduced the threat from the Iranian nuclear program and will help bring Iran into the community of nations. As the agreement approaches its one-year anniversary in mid-2016, Obama officials are defending it as successful by citing International Atomic Energy Agency (IAEA) reports that Iran has fully complied with the accord.

The author argues based on a close examination of the JCPOA and developments afterward, the Iran nuclear deal is a dangerous agreement which has caused and will continue to cause serious damage to American, Middle East and international security.

- **Timeline to an Iranian Nuclear Bomb Will Shorten During Deal.** Although supporters of the JCPOA say it will keep Iran one year away from a nuclear weapon for at least 10 years, the truth is that this agreement arranged for merely a short-term extension of the timeline to an Iranian nuclear bomb through easily reversible steps by Iran and dangerous U.S. concessions that will allow Iran to significantly shorten the timeline to a nuclear weapon while the nuclear agreement is in effect. President Obama has admitted that the timeline to an Iranian nuclear bomb will shrink "almost down to zero" by "year 13, 14, 15" of the nuclear agreement.

- **Dangerous U.S. Concessions on Uranium Enrichment and Heavy-Water Reactor.** U.S. concessions allowing Iran to enrich uranium, develop advanced enrichment centrifuges, and operate a plutonium-producing heavy-water reactor while the JCPOA is in effect not only threatens the security of the Middle East by enabling an Iranian nuclear weapons program, but also harms global nuclear nonproliferation efforts by undermining key nonproliferation principles, to lead other states to pursue uranium enrichment, heavy-water reactors and plutonium separation facilities.

- **Misleading Claims About Plutonium-Producing Reactor.** Obama officials claim Iran's under-construction Arak heavy-water reactor will be redesigned so it cannot produce weapons-grade plutonium. This is false. Although

1

this reactor was disabled and is being redesigned, when operational it will produce a weapons-worth of plutonium every four years. If Iran modifies this reactor and changes its fueling, it will produce enough plutonium for a nuclear bomb every two years. Iran will also gain expertise in the construction and operation of heavy-water reactors due to the JCPOA redesign.

- **Weak Verification and Dumbed Down IAEA** Iran Reports. The JCPOA's verification provisions are much weaker than its supporters claim. The agreement's supposedly tough verification measures are limited to Iran's declared nuclear sites and supply chain. A convoluted process to allow IAEA inspectors access to undeclared Iranian nuclear sites will probably never be used because of disagreements among P5+1 states and the threat of Iranian withdrawal from the agreement if it is sanctioned for refusing to allow inspectors to visit such sites. Iran has placed military sites off-limits to IAEA inspectors but has not been held accountable for this by the IAEA or the United States. The IAEA also has "dumbed-down" its reporting on Iran's nuclear program since January 2016 which makes it difficult for IAEA member governments, the U.S. Congress and the American people to assess whether Iran is complying with the nuclear deal.

- **Obama White House Used Deceptive Campaign to Sell a Bad Iran Deal.** Because the president and his senior advisors knew that they could never sell to the American people and the U.S. Congress such a weak a nuclear deal based on the dangerous concessions they made to Iran, Obama officials pursued and promoted this agreement through an unprecedented campaign of stealth and deception. This included the National Security Council running a press "echo chamber" to manipulate and mislead the news media about the nuclear deal. Other tactics included false claims such as "the only alternative to the nuclear deal is war with Iran," smearing opponents of the deal as warmongers, censoring press coverage and possibly using the NSA to spy on congressional opponents of the agreement.

- **Secret Side Deals to Hide Concessions from Congress.** The Obama administration resolved Iran's 11th hour resistance to finalizing the JCPOA by quietly removing two crucial issues from the agreement – ballistic missiles and Iran's past nuclear weapons work (also known as the Possible Military Dimensions of Iran's nuclear program or PMD) – and then falsely claimed these issues were still part of the nuclear deal in public statements and testimony to Congress. The PMD issue was moved into a secret side deal between the IAEA and Iran which Obama officials claim they never read. Both issues angered Congress and are examples of how the Obama administration tried to conceal and mislead lawmakers and the American public about controversial U.S. concessions made to negotiate the JCPOA. Other secret side deals have been discovered, including granting Iran exemptions to receive sanctions relief, $1.7 billion in ransom secretly sent to Iran by the United State to free U.S. prisoners paid in cash, and the dumbing-down of the IAEA's reports on Iran's nuclear program.

- **December 2015 IAEA PMD Report Found Nuclear Weapons Work Continued At Least Until 2009.** A December 2, 2015 IAEA report on the Possible Military Dimensions of Iran's nuclear program found Iranian nuclear weapons-related research continued until at least 2009. A leading arms control group believes "there is no way to know whether this research was terminated" because of Iran's poor record of cooperation with IAEA investigations and use of secret nuclear facilities. Ordinarily such findings would require follow-up IAEA investigations; however, the United States instead joined other IAEA members on December 15, 2015 to unanimously vote to close the IAEA's Iran PMD "file."

- **Huge Expansion in Iran's Nuclear Program from 2009-2013 Probably Intended to Increase Tehran's Leverage in Nuclear Talks.** Iran's nuclear program expanded more between 2009 and 2013 than at any other time in its history. The number of Iranian centrifuges surged from about 5,400 in January 2009 to about 19,000 in August 2013. Although Iran did not have enough enriched uranium (in the form of reactor-grade uranium hexafluoride or UF6) to make even one nuclear weapon in December 2008, President Obama said in July 2015 that Iran could make between eight and 10 nuclear weapons from its enriched uranium stockpile. This surge in Iran's nuclear program probably was intended to increase Iranian leverage in nuclear talks and make its nuclear infrastructure, especially uranium enrichment, too big to give up.

- **Sanctions Did Not Bring Iran to the Bargaining Table.** Many experts and some politicians believe Iran was brought to the bargaining table by crippling U.S. and EU sanctions. It is more likely Iran came to the bargaining table to have sanctions lifted without giving up its nuclear program and that the primary factors that led to the start of talks to get a final nuclear agreement were (1) Iranian leaders had sufficiently increased the size of its nuclear program to begin negotiations and (2) a letter sent to Supreme Leader Khamenei by then-Senator John Kerry in 2011 on behalf of the Obama administration led to major U.S. concessions on uranium enrichment and the investigation of Iran's past nuclear weapons-related work in exchange for a nuclear agreement.

- **The Nuclear Talks Destroyed Crucial WMD and Counterterrorism Sanctions Against Iran.** The nuclear talks with Iran dismantled important UN, EU and U.S. sanctions against Iran, many of which were put in place in response to its ballistic missile program and sponsorship of state terrorism. Although the Obama administration claims U.S. terrorism-related sanctions remain in place, the JCPOA lifted UN and EU sanctions against Iranian terrorist organizations and individuals. UN missile sanctions against Iran were replaced during nuclear talks by a new formulation that is much weaker that Russia claims is not legally binding. Furthermore, most of the tough sanctions imposed on Iran over the last 10 years probably can never be re-imposed even in the event of gross violations of the JCPOA by Iran.

- **The Iran Deal is a Product of President Obama's Radicalism and Incompetence.** The JCPOA is the product of the radical and naïve foreign policy views of President Barack Obama, who sees Iran more as a victim of past U.S. policies than a rogue state and state sponsor of terror. Obama's incompetent policies have been exacerbated by an incredibly incompetent NSC staff. The Obama administration primarily pursued this agreement not to stop or slow Iran's nuclear program, but due to misguided assumptions that it would somehow bring Iran into the community of nations, help make it a partner to fight the terrorist group ISIS[1] and even promote peace and stability in the Middle East. A surge in belligerent and destabilizing behavior by Iran since the JCPOA was announced has disproved these assumptions and led to bipartisan calls in Congress for new sanctions against Iran.

- **The Iran Deal has Weakened American Influence and Prestige.** The JCPOA contributed to a global perception of U.S. weakness under President Obama, especially in the Middle East. This probably encouraged Iran to increase its presence in Syria and Iraq after the JCPOA was announced and to increase tensions in the Persian Gulf in 2016 by harassing U.S. Navy ships and threatening to shoot down U.S. Navy planes. Russia also significantly increased its military support of Syria's Assad regime in September 2015 and began airstrikes against rebel fighters, including many supported by the United States. Russia appears to be using the power vacuum in the region caused by Obama's policies to advance its own influence at the expense of the United States.

- **The Obama Administration is Trying to Grant Iran More Concessions.** Despite increased belligerent and destabilizing behavior by Iran since the announcement of the JCPOA, the Obama administration has been working to provide Tehran with additional concessions because Iranian leaders claim Iran receives inadequate benefits from the nuclear deal. As a result, Obama officials in the spring of 2016 were seeking to grant Iran at least partial access to the U.S. financial system and dollarized financial transactions. This move violates promises the administration made to Congress during the summer of 2015. It also goes against recent warnings by the Financial Action Task Force that Iranian banks are a threat to the global financial system due to their financing of terrorism and a 2011 Treasury Department finding designating Iran as "a jurisdiction of primary money laundering concern." Although a congressional outcry over the issue of financial access appeared to cause the Obama administration to backtrack on this effort, there were reports in May 2016 that Obama officials were trying to give Iran a "backdoor" to the U.S. financial system.

- **Next President Should Tear Up Deal. Tough Renegotiation Second Best Option.** Because of the JCPOA's major flaws, dangerous U.S. concessions made to negotiate it, the threat the deal poses to U.S. and international security and the deceptive tactics the Obama administration used to promote the agreement, the best way for the next president to deal with this agreement is to tear it up on his or her first day in office. Presumptive Democratic presidential candidate Hillary Clinton has pledged to support the nuclear deal and will never take such action. Presumptive Republican presidential candidate Donald Trump has harshly criticized the JCPOA as one of the worst agreements ever negotiated, yet he has pledged to renegotiate it if he wins the 2016 election. Chapter 21 provides a list of requirements Mr. Trump should use if he chooses to renegotiate the JCPOA as president.

Foreword

In July 2015, the worst diplomatic "agreement" in my lifetime – and, arguably, in American history – was reached by President Obama with the Islamic Republic of Iran. It has forced on the world an arrangement that assures that the Iranian mullahs will get nuclear weapons, later if not sooner. In the meantime, it enriches them and enables them to engage in jihad, terrorism and subversion.

While this agreement has been described as a multilateral one, it would never have happened – or at least not in its present, disastrous form – without the insistence of President Obama and his separate, appeasing negotiating track with the Iranians. This is why the Center for Security Policy has nicknamed it "the Obamabomb deal."

In this book, the Center's Senior Vice President for Policy and Programs, Fred Fleitz, dissects what is in the agreement and the threat it poses to American and international security. Drawing upon his analytic skills honed over twenty-five years in the intelligence community and other senior governmental positions, Mr. Fleitz examines the many misrepresentations and manipulations perpetrated by Obama officials to sell this agreement. He also discusses major vulnerabilities and flaws with the deal that have been largely ignored by the mainstream media.

The reason this so-called agreement was not submitted to the Senate as a treaty as required by the U.S. Constitution is obvious. For one thing, it was never signed by any of the parties. It is utterly unverifiable and unenforceable. It undermines our allies. It will exacerbate nuclear proliferation, not preclude it. And on and on.

As a result, majorities in both houses of Congress and the vast majority of the American people objected to this accord and, if given the chance, would have rejected it. But they were not given the chance.

It is our hope that this book will be a valuable resource for Americans and their elected representatives to reverse or, at a minimum, limit the damage caused by the Obamabomb deal.

Frank J. Gaffney, Jr.
President
Center for Security Policy
July 5, 2016

1. Introduction

The main reason everyone agrees that Iran cannot be trusted is that it has consistently chosen not to keep previous international agreements. It has, most relevantly, ignored its obligations under the Non Proliferation Treaty, and consistently denied reasonable requests for access and information by inspectors from the International Atomic Energy Agency. That's why supporters of the agreement are quick to say that it is not based on trust of Iran but on the pact's verification provisions. But when you look at those provisions, it is clear that they are full of holes big enough to drive a covert nuclear weapons program through.

Former Senator Joseph Lieberman
July 19, 2015[2]

In January 2014, Deputy National Security adviser Ben Rhodes told liberal special interest group members visiting the White House that a nuclear deal with Iran would be a legacy achievement for President Obama's second term just like the Affordable Care Act (nicknamed by its critics "Obamacare") was for the first term.

This comparison was ironic given the how controversial both efforts were and how they were forced through Congress with no Republican support.

House Speaker Nancy Pelosi said before Congress voted on Obamacare: "We have to pass the bill so you can find out what is in it." No member of Congress read the 2,700-page Obamacare bill before it passed in March 2010. Similarly, Congress was kept in the dark about the talks which produced the July 2015 nuclear deal with Iran (the Joint Comprehensive Program of Work or JCPOA) and were not provided with secret side deals to the JCPOA even though this was required by law.

The Obama administration used deceptive campaigns of exaggerations and falsehoods to push both the Iran deal and Obamacare. The White House said under Obamacare, health care costs would go down and Americans could keep their own doctors. Both claims have proved to be false. The White House claims the Iran deal will reduce the threat from Iran's nuclear program even though Iran has kept almost its entire nuclear infrastructure and continues to enrich uranium. Comedian Jay Leno jokingly compared the two initiatives in November 2014 when he joked President Obama told the Iranians, "if you like your uranium, you can keep your uranium."

The Center for Security Policy thus nicknamed the JCPOA the "Obamabomb" deal because it is a legacy agreement of President Obama that is just as deceptive as Obamacare. The main difference is that while Obamacare may destroy the American healthcare system, the Obamabomb deal may lead to a nuclear-armed Iran that could attack America and its allies with nuclear weapons.

Defenders of the JCPOA have argued that because the JCPOA is a multilateral agreement, a future president cannot discard it without the consent of other parties to the agreement, especially America's European allies. The Obamabomb label reflects the reality that the JCPOA is actually a signature Obama initiative and a U.S.-Iran agreement that was later endorsed by other states. Key concessions to reach this deal were made in secret U.S.-Iran meetings before the 2014-1015 multilateral talks that ultimately produced the JCPOA began. Some of these secret talks reportedly included Obama senior adviser Valerie Jarrett. The most senior level negotiations on the agreement in 2014 and 2015 took place in one-on-one meetings between U.S. Secretary of State John Kerry and Iranian Foreign Mohammad Javad Zarif.

The summer 2015 debate in Washington over the Obamabomb deal was one of the most divisive since the 2010 fight over Obamacare. It also was one of the most acrimonious political battles ever over an American foreign policy initiative on what that may be worst international agreement in U.S. history.

For me, the most stunning thing about the 2015 fight in Washington over the nuclear deal was how the positions of President Obama and his Democratic supporters in Congress shifted from a prior position of "no deal is better than a bad deal" to "it's this deal or war with Iran." Based on statements by congressional Democrats acknowledging the JCPOA's serious flaws but who voted for it anyway, it's clear to me that their position on the agreement became "a bad deal is better than no deal." You can read some of these statements in Chapter 16.

The nuclear agreement with Iran was incredibly unpopular when Congress voted on it in September 2015. Both houses of Congress voted against the agreement. Like Obamacare, the Obamabomb deal received zero Republican support, and at the time, only 21% of the American people supported it.

There are new concerns in Congress about the nuclear agreement because of increased destabilizing and belligerent activities by Iran, including ballistic missile tests, threats to Israel and Iran's increased support to the Assad regime in Syria. Congress also is alarmed at reports the Obama administration is planning to make new concessions to Iran, including granting it greater access to the U.S. financial system because Iranian leaders believe their country has not received sufficient benefits from the nuclear accord.

Despite continuing opposition to the nuclear agreement in the United States, as the agreement approached its one-year anniversary in July 2016, the Obama administration is celebrated the deal as a great success that reduced the threat from the Iranian nuclear program. It made this claim by stressing that the IAEA has found Iran to be full compliance with the agreement. It did not mention several controversial secret side deals that helped clinch the agreement, including secret concessions granted to Iran so it would be eligible to receive $150 billion in sanctions relief in January 2016.

Getting to the truth on the nuclear deal has been difficult because of aggressive efforts by Obama administration to exaggerate and mislead the public and the secretive way Obama officials negotiated the deal. These efforts have been aided by reporters who either don't know enough to challenge administration spin about the agreement or are simply in the tank with the Obama administration. Also helping push the White House line on the nuclear deal is a large number of arms control and international security experts who fully understand the weaknesses of the nuclear accord but have pushed it for partisan reasons or because they hold radical views on U.S. foreign policy and the Iranian nuclear program.

Questions about the Obamabomb deal that Americans deserve answers to include:

- How could the Obama administration agree to a deal to stop or slow Iran's nuclear weapons program that actually shortens the timeline to an Iranian nuclear bomb by allowing Iran to continue to enrich uranium, experiment with advanced enrichment centrifuges and operate a heavy-water reactor?

- Why was Congress kept in the dark about the nuclear talks?

- Why did the Obama administration refuse to provide Congress the secret side deals to the JCPOA?

- Why did the United States vote at the IAEA in December 2015 to close the IAEA's investigation of Iran's nuclear weapons activities when an IAEA report said Iran did not fully cooperation with its investigation of this matter and found evidence that Iranian nuclear weapons research continued at least until 2009?

- Why was the JCPOA not submitted as a treaty for Senate ratification?

- Why does the JCPOA exclude Iran's ballistic missile program?

- Why did the Obama administration support the JCPOA when it lifts sanctions from Iranian terrorists and terrorist organizations?

- How could the Obama administration agree to give Iran over $150 billion in sanctions relief that it is certain to spend on terrorism, WMD programs and destabilizing the Middle East?

- Why is the Obama administration currently trying to provide Iran with additional sanctions, including access to the U.S. financial system?

It is my hope this book will help Americans better understand the serious threats posed by the Obamabomb deal and demand answers to these and other unanswered questions about the agreement. I do not want to promote hysteria or a "bomb Iran" approach to this serious security issue. I do, however, want to stress that it is crucial to deal with regimes like Iran with resolve and from a position of strength. Weak American policies, disputes with our allies, and political bickering in Washington benefit rogue states that consistently defend their WMD programs with resolve. I do not want war with Iran but I also am frustrated with some politicians and groups in Washington who reflexively reject the idea that the use of military force by the United States might be necessary to stop Iran's nuclear effort and have allowed Iran to exploit American diplomatic initiatives to win concessions and buy time to advance its nuclear program.

The analysis in this book is based on my 25 years working in national security positions with the United States government, including as a CIA analyst, as a senior advisor and Chief of Staff to Under Secretary of State for Arms Control and International Security John Bolton, and as a senior professional staff member with the House Permanent Select Committee on Intelligence. I followed Iran and North Korea closely in all of these jobs and had access to compartmented, highly classified intelligence on their nuclear programs.

I have been privileged to continue my analysis of the Iranian nuclear program with the Center for Security Policy which I joined in 2014. I am very grateful to Center President Frank Gaffney for offering me this opportunity and for his many years of support and friendship. I am also grateful to the Center's staff for their support in helping me prepare this publication.

Fred Fleitz
September 25, 2016

2. The Radical Worldview of Barack Obama

Chuck Hagel was right: The Obama administration's policy on Iran's nuclearization is containment, not prevention. The secretary of defense let that one slip at his confirmation hearings in January, and the media played it as a stumble by an intellectually overmatched nominee. But it wasn't a stumble. It was a gaffe—an accidental, embarrassing act of Washington truth telling—by a guy who doesn't do insincerity nearly as well as his boss.

Brett Stephens, Wall Street Journal, December 9, 2013

A Radical and Naïve President

Understanding the origins of the nuclear deal with Iran requires understanding that it is the product of a radical and naïve U.S. president

Barack Obama assumed the presidency determined to be an "anti-Bush" president by ending partisan bickering in Washington through a "post-partisan" style of leadership. By rejecting his predecessor's supposed "go it alone" militarism by initiating a foreign policy that would improve America's global reputation, Obama sought to promote world peace though multilateralism and diplomacy.

The Nobel Prize Committee was so sure Obama would be a transformational world leader that the committee in October 2009 awarded him the Nobel Peace Prize "for his extraordinary efforts to strengthen international diplomacy and cooperation between peoples" even though the president had only been in office for nine months and had no diplomatic, military, or internationally noteworthy accomplishments.

Barack Obama made clear when he ran for president his strong disagreements with President Bush's foreign policy which he claimed got the United States into an unjustified war with Iraq and alienated the world through belligerent U.S. rhetoric and unilateral actions. But Obama's world view went beyond this standard liberal view of the Bush administration: he was driven by a radical view of America's role in the world which sees American interventions overseas as inherently destabilizing.

Obama has made statements indicating that he believes U.S. superpower status is unfair to the rest of the world and prefers America becoming an equal member of a multipolar international order. This may be why he dismissed the idea of "American exceptionalism" in 2009 when he said at a NATO summit in Strasbourg, France: "I believe in American exceptionalism, just as I suspect that the Brits believe in British exceptionalism and the Greeks believe in Greek exceptionalism."

This also explains why President Obama has repeatedly apologized to the world for prior U.S. policies, especially the policies of the George W. Bush administration. This included an apology for American "arrogance" during an April 2009 speech in France, apologizing to Latin American states in April 2009 for "dictating terms" to them; apologizing for the Bush administration's war on terror in a May 2009 speech in Washington, DC, and apologizing to the Muslim world in April 2009 in speeches he gave in Cairo and Istanbul. The Istanbul and Cairo speeches enraged Obama's American critics and were mocked as being part of an Obama "apology tour." Mr. Obama has also repeatedly publicly apologized for the detention facility in Guantanamo Bay, Cuba, including during an April 2009 speech to the Turkish Parliament.

Concerning Obama's apologies to the Muslim world, a February 2016 Wall Street Journal editorial put it best: "Mr. Obama has typically addressed the issue of Islam by apologizing for Western behavior (2009 in Cairo) or analogizing Islamic State to the Christian Crusades (2015 National Prayer Breakfast)."[3]

Instead of discussing Iran's sponsorship of terrorism and its status as the world's leading state-sponsor of terror in his annual speeches to the UN General Assembly, President Obama has expressed regret for past U.S. policies toward Iran and suggested a moral equivalence between U.S. backing for a 1953 coup which installed Shah Mohammad Reza Pahlavi and the 1979 seizure of the U.S. embassy in Tehran.

Although Obama's maladroit criticisms of the foreign policy of prior U.S. presidents to international audiences increased his popularity abroad, it was received poorly in the United States and exacerbated his lousy relations with congressional Republicans. Obama's apologies to the Muslim world were criticized by the GOP as appeasement and a projection of U.S. weakness.

Frequently, the president depicts anyone who tries to discuss the threat from radical Islam as a bigots or Islamophobe. He has refused to discuss radical Islam as a global ideology at war with modern society, one that is driving ISIS, al-Qaeda and even home-grown radical Islamist terrorism. The president and presumptive

Democratic presidential candidate Hillary Clinton have been harshly criticized by presumptive Republican presidential candidate Donald Trump over their refusal to use the term "radical Islam." Mr. Obama disparaged this term in the aftermath of the June 12, 2016 Orlando nightclub shootings by calling it a Republican "talking point."

Senior cabinet officials have said that terrorist groups like ISIS and al-Qaeda are not "Islamic" and often asserting that anyone who makes this claim legitimizes these groups and insults the majority of the world's Muslims who reject them. Obama has repeatedly suggested that the Guantanamo Bay, Cuba detention facility is an important recruitment tool for ISIS and al Qaeda although he has never cited any evidence for this.

President Obama has frequently dismissed the threat to Americans from terrorism as exaggerated compared with the risk of dying from handguns, car accidents, and falling in bathtubs. Mr. Obama also has downplayed the threat from ISIS, including by calling it a "JV" terrorist group and boldly stating on November 13, 2015 – the day before 137 were killed in the Paris ISIS attacks - that the terror group had been "contained."

These kinds of incomplete and incoherent foreign policy notions are not new to the president, who managed to criticize Israel in the same speeches in which he apologized to Muslim audiences. In a stunning April 2016 interview in The Atlantic, Obama even blamed European states for not doing enough about the post-2011 security situation in Libya and "freeloading" off U.S. Libya policy. The Atlantic article also outlined that the president advised the Saudi Arabian government to "share the neighborhood" with Iran.

Obama's insistence that the most pressing national security challenge to the United States is climate change has also been ridiculed by his critics who claim it is a sign of his incompetence and lack of awareness.

Obama's reluctance to criticize radical Islam and Islamist regimes has led to many to believe that he has a personal bias toward Islam – possibly due to the years he spent as a youth in Indonesia – and therefore has pursued policies aligning the United States with Islamist states and against Israel. Obama's speeches apologizing for American policies to Muslim audiences, his decision to meet with radical American Islamist groups but not moderate ones, and his tendency to lecture Americans on Islamophobia after Islamist terrorist attacks instead of discussing the root cause of these attacks – radical Islam – has added to criticism that some kind of pro-Muslim bias has driven his foreign policy.

My view is that Obama's foreign policy is based on his uninformed and radical views of U.S. global dominance. I believe these views were heavily influenced by his decades-long ties to far-left radicals such as the Reverend Jerimiah Wright, Bill Ayers, Father Michael Pfleger, Bernadine Dohrn and probably Louis Farrakhan. But it is impossible to dismiss the pro-Muslim bias of Obama's ideology that I believe is driven by both personal factors and far left ideologues.

Left Wing Foreign Policy Experts Who Influenced Obama's Iran Policy

Understanding Barack Obama's thinking about Iran and its nuclear program also requires an understanding of the views of liberal national security experts who influence the thinking of Obama officials and the Democratic Party.

I start this discussion with a question often asked on the left (and sometimes on the right): *Why can't Iran and North Korea have nuclear weapons?* After all, the United States, the United Kingdom, France, Russia, China, Israel, Pakistan and India have them. Why can't the possession of nuclear weapons by Iran and North Korea be seen as rational decisions to ward off attacks by the United States, especially in light of the overthrow of Iraqi President Saddam Hussein in 2003 and Western military assistance to the Libyan rebels that led to the overthrow of Libyan leader Muammar Qadaffi in 2011?

Some on the right and many on the left in the United States have made such arguments. For example, Congressman Ron Paul (R-Texas) wrote on his House website on December 20, 2009:

> However, being surrounded by nuclear powers one can understand why they [Iran] might want to become nuclear capable if only to defend themselves and to be treated more respectfully. After all, we don't sanction nuclear capable countries. We take diplomatic negotiations a lot more seriously, and we frequently send money to them instead. The non-nuclear countries are the ones we bomb. If Iran was attempting to violate the non-proliferation treaty, they could hardly be blamed, since US foreign policy gives them every incentive to do so.4

Some experts on the left have argued that Iran's nuclear weapons program is justifiable because of Israel's nuclear arsenal and its refusal to become a party to the Nuclear Nonproliferation Treaty. Some of these arguments have been made in concert with growing anti-Semitic and anti-Israel rhetoric on the left, including the radical Boycott, Divestment and Sanction (BDS) movement, an international effort

16

by anti-Israel leftists to punish Israel because of its supposed occupation of Palestinian lands.

Paul Pillar, a former CIA officer who teaches at Georgetown University, contended in a March/April 2012 *Washington Monthly* article titled "We Can Live With a Nuclear Iran" that the threat from an Iranian nuclear bomb has been overhyped.[5] Pillar believes "an Iranian nuclear weapon would not be an existential threat to Israel and would not give Iran a license to become more of a regional troublemaker."

Joseph Cirincione is President of the Ploughshares Fund, a liberal arms control think tank that heavily lobbied for the JCPOA and was named to a high-level State Department arms control advisory board by Secretary of State Hillary Clinton. Cirincione believes Israel's nuclear weapons program is the cause of Iran's nuclear program and that Iran would be encouraged to abandon pursuing nuclear weapons if Israel gave up its program.[6]

The late Kenneth Waltz, a well-known professor of international relations at Columbia University, justified an Iranian nuclear bomb in a July/August 2012 *Foreign Affairs* article titled "Why Iran Should Get the Bomb."[7] According to Waltz, fears about Iran getting a nuclear bomb are unfounded because history shows that nuclear weapons stabilize regional tensions by creating a balance of power. He also noted that there has never been full-scale nuclear war between two nuclear-armed states.

Waltz believed Pakistan and India possessing nuclear weapons is a concern because of longtime hostility between them, the instability of the Pakistani government, and the substantial presence of radical Islamist terrorist groups in Pakistan, including al Qaeda. But he pointed out there are no indications that either Pakistan or India will ever use nuclear weapons against the other because to do so would invite a devastating nuclear counterattack. Moreover, both states have tried to normalize relations and are not actively provoking other neighbors, Europe, and the United States.

Although Waltz argued similar circumstances would limit the threat from an Iranian nuclear bomb, I disagree this applies to Iran.

It is foolish to argue that an Iranian nuclear bomb could be a stabilizing factor in the Middle East or that there is some element of unfairness that Israel has a nuclear arsenal but Iran does not. After all, Iran is a state sponsor of terror which regularly threatens to wipe the state of Israel off the map. Israel is surrounded by enemies and has never staged an offensive war or threatened neighboring states.

The India/Pakistan argument made by Waltz does not apply to Iran's nuclear program for these reasons and because Iran is a fanatical Islamist theocracy whose leaders may be willing to risk the catastrophic and possible nuclear retaliation of a first-strike because of their apocalyptic beliefs. Israeli Prime Minister Benjamin Netanyahu explained this issue and his concerns about Iran's nuclear program in a 2009 Atlantic interview:

> You don't want a messianic apocalyptic cult controlling atomic bombs. When the wide-eyed believer gets hold of the reins of power and the weapons of mass death, then the entire world should start worrying, and that is what is happening in Iran.[8]

It is not hard to picture Pillar and Cirincione meeting with senior Obama officials as they pursued a nuclear agreement with Iran. These are the type of experts who have the ears of liberal Democrats and almost certainly the ears of Obama, Kerry and Clinton on the Iranian nuclear program.

Influenced by the radical views of these experts and others, I believe President Obama sought a nuclear agreement with Iran primarily to improve U.S.-Iran relations and to make Iran a U.S. partner for stability in the Middle East. I don't believe he cared if a nuclear agreement actually froze or reduced Iran's nuclear program.

In comments cited in a May 5, 2016 New York Times article, David Samuels revealed that Leon Panetta, who served as President Obama's Secretary of Defense and CIA Director, has doubts whether President Obama actually wanted to halt Iran's pursuit of nuclear weapons. Panetta told Samuels when he was Secretary of Defense: "And you know my view, talking with the president, was: If brought to the point where we had evidence that they're developing an atomic weapon, I think the president is serious that he is not going to allow that to happen." Samuels then wrote:

> Panetta stops. "But would you make that same assessment now?" I ask him. "Would I make that same assessment now?" he asks. "Probably not."[9]

Because the president could not publicly disclose his actual highly controversial reasons and strategy for a nuclear deal with Iran, he frequently made misleading and false statements for public consumption on Iran and his objectives for a nuclear agreement, including that he would not tolerate Iran getting a nuclear weapon and criticism of Iran for threating Israel, for its human right record and for destabilizing the Middle East. Obama's statements on his intentions for a nuclear deal included:

- When campaigning for president in 2007, Obama told an American Israel Public Affairs Committee conference that "the world must work to stop Iran's uranium-enrichment program."

- On October 22, 2012, during a presidential debate with Mitt Romney, Mr. Obama said: "Our goal is to get Iran to recognize it needs to give up its nuclear program and abide by the U.N. resolutions that have been in place. . . . But the deal we'll accept is — they end their nuclear program. It's very straightforward."

- In December 2013 at a Brookings Institution forum, President Obama said: "They don't need to have an underground, fortified facility like Fordow in order to have a peaceful nuclear program. They certainly don't need a heavy-water reactor at Arak in order to have a peaceful nuclear program. They don't need some of the advanced centrifuges that they currently possess."

Obama officials were faced with a dilemma. None of the above statements or others made by Mr. Obama and his Obama officials were even close to their actual policy on the Iranian nuclear issue. Though Obama officials repeatedly claimed they would not permit Iran to get the bomb, the truth was that they were so desperate to get a nuclear agreement that they were prepared to make whatever compromises necessary to get one. They knew a nuclear agreement was possible if the United States made concessions to Tehran allowing it to keep most of its nuclear infrastructure, giving it a pass on resolving questions about possible nuclear weapons-related activities (the PMD issue) and lifting U.S. and international sanctions. But Obama officials realized such concessions would be widely unpopular in the United States and with America's allies in the Middle East. To get a deal making these concessions, the administration used an unprecedented strategy of secrecy and deception.

Secrecy was a central element of the Obama administration's negotiating strategy to prevent members of Congress, Israel and Saudi Arabia from trying to stop the agreement. Private diplomacy between the United States and Iran began in 2009 with Oman acting as a mediator on the release of U.S. and Iranian prisoners. These secret discussions eventually were used to open the door to other issues such as the

Iran nuclear program and the release of Iranians from American and European prisons. These secret talks continued into 2013.

The Obama strategy to get a nuclear agreement with Iran included a massive deception campaign to defend the negotiations with Iran and to sell the final agreement. This included misrepresenting dangerous concessions such as allowing Iran to continue to enrich uranium as a false narrative about the talks. As explained previously, a May 5, 2016 *New York Times* profile of national security advisor Ben Rhodes discussed how he manipulated young, uninformed journalists and made use of an echo chamber of arms control and liberal think tank experts to promote President Obama's nuclear diplomacy with Iran. Rhodes' efforts were assisted by large expenditures by liberal groups, some of which were funded by liberal philanthropist George Soros.

Obamabomb Deal Driven by an Incompetent National Security Council Staff

Mr. Obama has been vulnerable to radical views on national security from people like Pillar, Cirincione, Ayers and others because of his lack of national security experience and his refusal to name highly qualified national security experts as senior advisers, many of which would challenge him. Obama, who ran for president as a "community organizer," received some exposure to national security issues when he served on the Senate Foreign Relations Committee during his four years in Congress. However, since Obama declared his candidacy for president in February 2007 after only two years in the Senate, he had little time to do committee work.

Obama's national security team may be the weakest of any modern president and lacks senior experienced experts who have influence with Mr. Obama. While Obama named or retained some experienced national security experts with gravitas such as Leon Panetta as CIA Director and Secretary of Defense and Robert Gates and Chuck Hagel who also served as Obama's Secretary of Defense, they were largely ignored since Obama's foreign policy has been run by former campaign aides and congressional staffers in the National Security Council. Gates, Hagel and Panetta complained about this in their memoirs. Ashton Carter, who succeeded Gates as Secretary of Defense in 2015, reportedly has little influence with the White House.

Gates and Panetta expressed frustration in their memoirs and in statements to the news media on how junior NSC staffers run Obama's foreign policy. Gates complained about how Mr. Obama centralized power and operational activities of the government in the White House to an unparalleled degree. Gates also has slammed junior NSC staffers for the incompetence and for going outside the chain of command and directly contacting combatant commanders.[10]

Panetta has made similar comments about the Obama NSC staff and how they assume where the president will be on issues and resist allowing senior officials to present their positions to him. Panetta told David Samuels:

> "There were staff people who put themselves in a position where they kind of assumed where the president's head was on a particular issue, and they thought their job was not to go through this open process of having people present all these different options, but to try to force the process to where they thought the president wanted to be," he says. "They'd say, 'Well, this is where we want you to come out.' And I'd say '[expletive], that's not the way it works. We'll present a plan, and then the president can make a decision.' I mean, Jesus Christ, it is the president of the United States, you're making some big decisions here, he ought to be entitled to hear all of those viewpoints and not to be driven down a certain path."[11]

Incredibly, Panetta also told Samuels that he never saw copies of letters that President Obama secretly sent to Iranian Supreme Leader Khamenei between 2009 and 2012 on improving relations between the two countries and beginning negotiations to resolve concerns about Iran's nuclear program.

Excluding Gates, Panetta and Hagel from critical national security initiatives such as holding secret bilateral talks with Iran denied the president the benefit of their decades of experience and valuable constructive criticism. I believe the exclusion of these experienced national security experts from the White House's efforts to strike a nuclear deal with Iran was deliberate because they would have opposed Obama's radical agenda to get a nuclear deal that did not stop Iran's nuclear program. Panetta called for Congress to back the deal in a September 2015 op-ed after he left government but conceded that "the Iran deal would appear to reward Tehran for defying the world, make funds available for its extremist activities and generally make it stronger militarily and economically. Although the agreement provides for a temporary delay in Iran's nuclear enrichment capability, it allows Tehran to retain its nuclear infrastructure and obtain sanctions relief. The risk is that Iran could become an even bigger threat to the region."[12]

21

Samuels also wrote about how Rhodes admitted to misleading the news media and the American people to sell a nuclear deal to Iran. Specifically, Rhodes said that the administration circulated a false narrative that a rare opportunity for a nuclear agreement with Iran arose after the election of the supposedly moderate Iranian President Hassan Rouhani in 2013. According to Samuels, Rhodes promoted the fiction that this created a significant split in the Iranian regime and that the Obama administration reached out to a new moderate camp in Iran who wanted peace with their neighbors and United States.

The purpose of Rhodes' "moderate Rouhani" ruse was to distract the news media, Congress and the American people from the huge concessions the United States had offered to Tehran. The truth was that in 2011, the U.S. made these critical concessions that resulted in the JCPOA. Rhodes and the administration also knew Rouhani answers to Supreme Leader Khamenei and that his election was not in fact the start of a new, more moderate Iranian government.

Rhodes bragged to Samuels that he manipulated the news media into publishing stories supporting the White House on the Iran talks. Rhodes said he made use of "legions of arms control experts [who] began popping up at think tanks and on social media" and became "sources for hundreds of clueless reporters." According to Rhodes, this crop of newly minted experts acted as cheerleaders for the nuclear deal and, like ventriloquists' dummies, "were saying things that validated what we had given them to say."

I'm familiar with many of these newly minted, no-nothing nuclear experts quoted by the press in support of the Iran deal. Many others, however, understood how weak an Iran nuclear deal would be and were aware of the huge concessions the U.S. was offering. This includes people and organizations Rhodes singled out, such as liberal writer Laura Rozen, the Ploughshares Fund, and the Iran Project. In all likelihood, the reason these experts did not speak out against the nuclear deal was because they shared President Obama's radical views on how to improve Iranian behavior and strengthen U.S.-Iran relations.

Samuels raised serious questions about Rhodes' qualifications which reflect poorly on how Barack Obama has conducted his foreign policy. Samuels wrote that Rhodes is "according to the consensus of the two dozen current and former White House insiders I talked to, the single most influential voice shaping American foreign policy aside from Potus himself." He noted that Rhodes's "lack of conventional real-world experience of the kind that normally precedes responsibility for the fate of nations – like military or diplomatic service, or even a master's degree in international relations, rather than creative writing – is still startling." Samuels also wrote that Rhodes said he is so close to the president that "I don't know anymore where I begin and Obama ends"

A bigger problem is Rhodes' boss, National Security Adviser Susan Rice, who has been widely criticized for being out of her depth at the NSC and for unwittingly serving as the scapegoat for the cover-up of the 2011 Benghazi consulate attacks. *Foreign Policy* CEO/Editor David Rothkopf made these scathing remarks in a 2014 interview with *Atlantic* writer Jeffrey Goldberg about Rice's performance at the NSC and Obama's tendency to surround himself with incompetent advisers who are "true believers:"

> If Obama had any material management or foreign-policy experience prior to coming in to office or if he had the character of our stronger leaders on these issues—notably a more strategic than tactical orientation, more trust in his team, less risk aversion, etc.—she would be better off, as would we all. But his flaws are compounded by a system that lets him pick and empower those around him. So, if he chooses to surround himself with a small team of "true believers" who won't challenge him as all leaders need to be challenged, if he picks campaign staffers that maintain campaign mode, if he over-empowers political advisors at the expense of those with national-security experience, that takes his weaknesses and multiplies them by those of the team around him.

> And whatever Susan Rice's many strengths are, she is ill-suited for the job she has. She is not seen as an honest broker. She has big gaps in her international experience and understanding—Asia. She is needlessly combative and has alienated key members of her staff, the cabinet, and overseas leaders. She is also not strategic and is reactive like her boss. So whereas the system does have the capability of offsetting the weaknesses of a president, if he is surrounded by strong advisors to whom he listens and who he empowers to do their jobs, it can also reinforce and exacerbate those weaknesses—as it is doing now.[13]

Although not a member of the president's National Security Council staff, Valerie Jarrett, a senior White House advisor who holds the title of "Assistant to the President for Public Engagement and Intergovernmental Affairs," reportedly played an important role in the president's Iran diplomacy. According to the *Times of Israel*, Jarrett, an Iranian American who is reportedly is the president's closest adviser, conducted secret talks in Iran in 2012. The White House denied this report.[14] Lt. General William Boykin, a former deputy Undersecretary of Defense for Intelligence, told Newsmax TV in February 2015 his views about Jarrett's alleged role in the Iran talks:

There are many who are now saying that [Jarrett] is really the architect of this non-treaty with the Iranians, which ultimately will result in the Iranians having a nuclear program, and America having to accept a nuclear-armed Iran. Yeah, she's a powerful influence on [Obama].[15]

If true, this report is troubling since Jarrett is a Chicago political operative with no national security experience.

Many in Washington have been aware of the incompetence of President Obama's national security advisers and called on him to fire them and hire experienced experts after several of the presidents numerous foreign policy setbacks.

Leslie Gelb, President Emeritus of the Council of Foreign Relations and a former New York Times columnist, strongly criticized Obama's NSA staff for President Obama's failure to join other world leaders who attended a memorial march in Paris after the January 2015 Charlie Hebdo terrorist attacks. Gelb said this gaffe "demonstrated beyond argument that the Obama team lacks the basic instincts and judgment necessary to conduct U.S. national security policy in the next two years." As a result, Gelb recommended that

> Mr. Obama will have to excuse most of his inner core, especially in the White House. He will have to replace them with strong and strategic people of proven foreign policy experience. He'll also need to seed the Defense and State Departments with new top people serving directly as senior advisers to the secretaries. And he also will need to set up regular consultations—not the usual phony ones—with the two key Senate leaders in this field, Foreign Relations Committee Chairman Bob Corker and Armed Services Committee Chairman John McCain, two people who can really improve his decisions and bolster his credibility.[16]

This was a stunning rebuke coming from Gelb, a cardinal member of the liberal foreign policy establishment in the United States.

President Obama ignored this advice, perhaps because he prefers to be surrounded by inexperienced advisers who make him look like, as Robert Gates has put it, "the smartest guy in the room." This is how a sophomoric individual such as Ben Rhodes reportedly became the single most influential voice shaping American foreign policy aside from President Obama.

Due to incompetence, radical ideologies, a weak staff and an obsession with being seen as a president who ended wars and did not get the United States into new foreign conflicts, Obama's national security record has been a fiasco. He severely mishandled the withdrawal of U.S. troops in Iraq and Afghanistan and the political crises in Syria and Libya. He allowed the birth of ISIS and a surging radical Islamist insurgency that has staged terrorist attacks around the globe, including in the United

States. Lastly, Mr. Obama has fumbled relations with Russia, China, Canada, Japan, and other important nations and allies. Instead of admitting that his policies have played a significant role in all of these international mishaps, the President continues to maintain a deplorable level of arrogance towards his drastic incompetence and political radicalism, all of which are the very foundations of the Obamabomb Iran deal.

3. Iran Rebuffs Obama Administration's Initial Push for a Nuclear Deal

And so my national security team is currently reviewing our existing Iran policy, looking at areas where we can have constructive dialog, where we can directly engage with them. And my expectation is in the coming months we will be looking for openings that can be created where we can start sitting across the table, face to face, diplomatic overtures that will allow us to move our policy in a new direction.

President Barack Obama
White House press conference
February 9, 2009

Barack Obama indicated from the beginning of his presidency his determination to get a nuclear deal with Iran. Although Iran agreed to participate in new diplomatic efforts with the United States during the first five years of the Obama presidency, it also began a major build-up in its nuclear program and continued its terrorist activities, including attempting to conduct a terrorist attack in Washington, DC.

Obama in 2009 was so eager to get a landmark nuclear agreement with Iran that he said on January 26, 2009, in his first sit-down interview as president, (which he symbolically gave to the pan-Arab TV network al-Arabiya) "If countries like Iran are willing to unclench their fist, they will find an extended hand from us." This offer followed up on statements by Obama during the presidential campaign that he planned a starkly different approach to the Iranian nuclear program, including proposing to meet unconditionally with Iran's leaders. (Obama also offered to meet unconditionally with the leaders of Syria, Venezuela, Cuba and North Korea.)

The Obama administration will dispute that Mr. Obama was obsessed with getting a nuclear agreement with Iran and will point out that the President made many statements declaring he would not let Iran get a nuclear weapon and criticized Tehran for illicit nuclear activities and sponsorship of terrorism. Indeed, the *Washington Free Beacon* noted in an April 10, 2015 article that President Obama pledged at least 28 times since he first ran for the White House in 2008 that he would not tolerate Iran getting a nuclear weapon.[17]

In February 2009, Obama named veteran diplomat Dennis Ross to head up diplomatic talks with Iran. In his 2016 book "Altered Egos: Hillary Clinton, Barack Obama and the Twilight Struggle Over American Power," *New York Times* columnist Mark Landler writes that Salem ben Nasser al-Ismaily, an Omani businessman and emissary of Omani Sultan Qaboos bin Said, met with Ross in May 2009 to present a written offer drafted by Ismaily and his Iranian contacts to negotiate with the Obama administration on a range of issues, from the nuclear program to Iran's support for Hezbollah. Ismaily also assured Ross he could bring the Iranians to the negotiating table. [18]

Ismaily told Ross that one of his Iranian contacts was the head of an Iranian religious trust with close ties to Supreme Leader Khamenei. Ross informed Secretary Clinton of his meeting with Ismaily who told him to keep talking with the Omani.

Landler wrote that Obama also sent two secret letters to Iranian Supreme Leader Khamenei in 2009. The first proposed the possibility of a new start between the two countries and drew a long, querulous response. The second, which proposed direct talks on the nuclear issue, received no response.[19]

There is no certainty that the offer from Iran conveyed by Ismaily was actually sent on behalf of the Iranian government. If it was, Iran's behavior from 2009-2013, which included a large increase in its nuclear program, indicates Iranian leaders were not interested at the time in negotiating a nuclear agreement. My view is that if this letter was genuine, it probably represented the Iranian government's interest in exploiting President Obama's more conciliatory approach to the country without altering its policies or giving up its nuclear program.

In April 2009, Obama officials announced the United States would participate in P5+1 talks with Iran. In March 2009, President Obama sent an unusually cordial New Year's greeting to Iran in which he referred to it as "the Islamic Republic of Iran, the first time a U.S. president used this reference. In September 2009, President Obama called Foreign Minister Rouhani to express his interest in improving relations and a diplomatic solution to international concerns about Iran's nuclear program.

After Iran ignored a September 2009 deadline to respond to President Obama's offers of diplomatic engagement, Secretary of Defense Gates sent a secret three-page memo to top White House officials warning that the administration did not have an effective long-range strategy for dealing with Iran's steady progress towards acquiring nuclear weapons, according to the *New York Times*.[20]

While Obama officials were busy trying to seduce Iran into agreeing to a nuclear accord, Senate Foreign Relations Committee Chairman John Kerry (who became President Obama's second Secretary of State on February 1, 2013) pitched in by telling the *Financial Times* in June 2009 that Iran had a right to uranium enrichment under the NPT and condemned the Bush administration's for not agreeing to this.[21] As I will explain in Chapter 7, Kerry reportedly made this offer to Iran in secret talks in 2011 although he denies this.

Secret diplomacy began in 2009 between the United States and Iran with Oman (via Salem ben Nasser al-Ismaily) acting as a mediator on the release of U.S. and Iranian prisoners. These secret talks later became a "back channel" that was used to discuss other issues such as the Iranian nuclear program and the release of Iranians from American and European prisons. These secret talks continued into 2013.[22]

Outrage from the U.S. Congress in September 2009 after U.S., French and British officials revealed that Iran had constructed a secret uranium enrichment plant (the Fordow facility) inside a mountain to protect it from U.S. and Israeli airstrikes forced the Obama administration in October 2009 to propose a "fuel swap" agreement in which Iran would receive fuel plates for its Tehran Research Reactor (TRR) (which Iranian officials claim is used to produce medical isotopes) if it shipped the majority of its low-enriched uranium to a neutral third-country. Built by the United States in 1957, the TRR runs on uranium enriched to 19.75% U-235.

The fuel-swap proposal was the subject of multilateral talks and several counterproposals until it died in early 2011 because Western states would not agree to Iran's preconditions that they recognize Iran's "right" to enrich uranium and drop sanctions before formal talks on the Iranian nuclear program could be held. Iran also began enriching uranium to about 20% U-235 in February 2010 which indicated its lack of seriousness in pursuing the fuel swap.

A Rude Awakening

Obama officials were surprised to learn in the first months of the administration that America's enemies and adversaries had no intention of altering their policies because of America's new "transformational" president. They also came to realize that despite Mr. Obama's outreach to the Muslim world and "apology tour" speeches in Cairo and Istanbul, Islamist terrorist groups like al-Qaeda, Hamas, and Hezbollah were not about to end their hostility and acts of terrorism against the United States and its allies.

Iran and North Korea had similar reactions to the new Obama administration in 2009: they both stepped up their belligerent behavior and rhetoric. North Korean tested a long-range missile on April 5, 2009 that experts believed was a test of an ICBM capable of delivering a nuclear warhead against the United States. On May 25, 2009 North Korea conducted its second nuclear test.

Similarly, Iran tested short-range missiles in March 2009 and medium range missiles in May, September and December 2009.

Iranian security forces violently put down mass protests that broke out after the fraudulent June 2009 elections that returned incumbent Mahmoud Ahmadinejad to power. The Obama administration was criticized when France took the lead in condemning this crackdown because the White House worried that U.S. criticism of the Iranian government would undermine its effort to convince Tehran to agree to talks on a nuclear agreement.

Iran jailed three American hikers who accidently wandered into Iranian territory in July 2009 and charged them of espionage. One was released on humanitarian grounds after being held by Iran for 14 months. The other two were released on September 21, 2011. The hikers were released due to mediation by the Sultan of Oman who also paid their bail of $500,000 each.

In 2011, Obama officials announced an Iranian plot to assassinate the Saudi ambassador to Washington by bombing a Washington, DC restaurant. In 2013, Canadian officials accused an al-Qaeda cell operating out of Iran of planning to blow up a train en route to New York City from Toronto.

Iranian President Ahmadinejad further irritated the Obama administration and Congress in January 2012 when he visited four states in the Western hemisphere most hostile to the U.S. – Venezuela, Cuba, Nicaragua and Ecuador – to meet with their leaders and jointly condemn America. This trip came at a time of growing tensions over Iran's surging nuclear program.

North Korean and Iranian leaders both appeared to view President Obama's willingness to take a more conciliatory approach to U.S. differences over their WMD programs – and his interest in meeting with their top officials – not as an opportunity to improve relations with Washington but as a chance to get generous concessions from the West without giving up their WMD programs. This was the result of a fundamental misunderstanding by senior Obama officials on how the leadership of rogue states like Iran and North Korea view the United States.

These states do not hate the United States simply because of who sits in the Oval Office.

These rogue states did not hate the United States because George W. Bush was president. Iran and North Korea hate the United States regardless of which political party holds the White House because they hate America and all that it stands for regardless of who is leading it. Iran also hates the United States and modern society because it is a radical Shiite theocracy that wants to institute a global Islamic caliphate and impose Shariah law upon the world's population. Obama officials failed to realize that the only real difference Iran and North Korea saw between Bush and Obama was Mr. Obama as a weaker and more malleable U.S. president who would give them whatever they wanted in negotiations.

The Obama administration hoped to get a nuclear agreement with Pyongyang but its belligerence and obstreperousness made this impossible. The May 2009 North Korean nuclear test prevented any diplomatic progress with the North until a February 29, 2012 agreement to freeze its missile and nuclear programs in return for food aid. Pyongyang broke this agreement several weeks later by announcing it would test a long-range rocket which it claimed was a space-launch vehicle.

U.S.-North Korea relations deteriorated again in 2013 when North Korea conducted its third nuclear test on February 13, 2013 and North Korean officials threatened all-out war against the United States, including a preemptive nuclear strike. Obama officials began another attempt to engage the North in talks on its nuclear program in the fall of 2015. These were aborted after North Korea conducted its fourth nuclear test on January 6, 2016. U.S.-North Korean relations sank further after the North launched another supposed space launch vehicle on February 7, 2016. After these provocations led the Security Council on March 2, 2016 to impose new sanctions on North Korea, North Korean leaders reiterated their threats to attack the United States with nuclear weapons and conducted more missile tests.

Iranian behavior and rhetoric also was belligerent and hostile during the early years of the Obama administration but not at the extreme level of North Korea.

While this allowed path for diplomacy, it was a path Iranian leaders made sure was entirely on their terms.

The Obama administration's initial outreach to get nuclear deals with Iran and North Korea went nowhere because it did not understand the nature these regimes and their hatred of the United States. However, Iran's resistance to Obama's diplomatic overtures was different than North Korea's – it was prepared to deal, but only after it improved its negotiating position by massively increasing its nuclear program.

4. Iran's Nuclear Program Surges, 2009-2013

Figure 1: July 2015 Arm Control Association map of Iranian nuclear facilities

One of the most serious but rarely discussed Obama foreign policy setbacks is the drastic increase in Iran's nuclear program which expanded more between 2009 and 2013 than at any other time in its history.

The number of Iranian centrifuges surged from about 5,400 in January 2009 to about 19,000 in August 2013. According to the Institute for Science and International Security, Iran had produced about 1,010 kg of reactor-grade uranium by January 31, 2009 – just enough for one nuclear weapon because of the addition of 209 kg of enriched uranium since November 2008. (Note that the terms "reactor-grade uranium" and "20% enriched uranium" in this book refer to enriched UF6.)[23] By November 2013, Iran had produced 10,357 kg of reactor-grade enriched uranium

33

and 410 kg of 20% enriched uranium. In August 2015, Iran's stockpile of low-enriched uranium totaled about 15,000 kg which President Obama said was enough to make about 8-10 nuclear weapons. I disagree with this assessment because experts believe 1,100 kg of reactor-grade UF6 is enough for one nuclear weapon, 15,000 kg was enough for about 13-14 bombs.[24]

Figure 2 shows how the number of Iranian centrifuges grew between January 2007 when Iran began installing them until November 2013 when it agreed to freeze the number of installed and operational centrifuges. This chart illustrates how the number of installed centrifuges surged from just over 5,000 in January 2009 when Barack Obama became president to about 19,000 in November 2013. The chart also shows how the number of operational centrifuges enriching to reactor-grade (up to 5% U-235) went from about 3,000 in January 2009 to about 9,000 in November 2013.

Figure 2: IAEA Chart on Increase in Number of Iranian Nuclear Centrifuges, January 2007-November 2013[25]

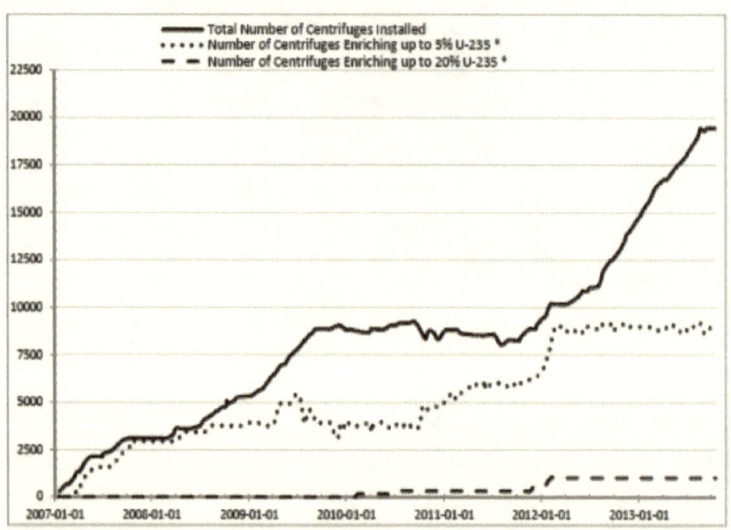

Note 1: Centrifuges involved in R&D activities are not included.
*Not all of the centrifuges fed with UF₆ may have been working.

Figure 3 illustrates the increase in Iran's enriched uranium stockpile from November 2008 to November 2013. This chart shows that Iran did not have enough enriched uranium to make any nuclear weapons in November 2008 but had enough to make at least eight by November 2014 using "available" reactor-grade enriched uranium – enriched uranium that had not been converted from enriched UF6 into fuel plates or uranium dioxide powder. This reactor-grade enriched uranium could be converted into weapons-grade enriched uranium in three to six weeks. Per President Obama's July 2015 statement that Iran had enough enriched uranium to make 8 to 12 nuclear weapons, the number of weapons Iran could make based on this chart would represent these figures if all available enriched UF6 and enriched uranium converted into other forms was further enriched.

Figure 3: Increase in Iran's Low-Enriched Uranium and the Number of Nuclear Weapons It Could Make From This Enriched Uranium, 2008-2013

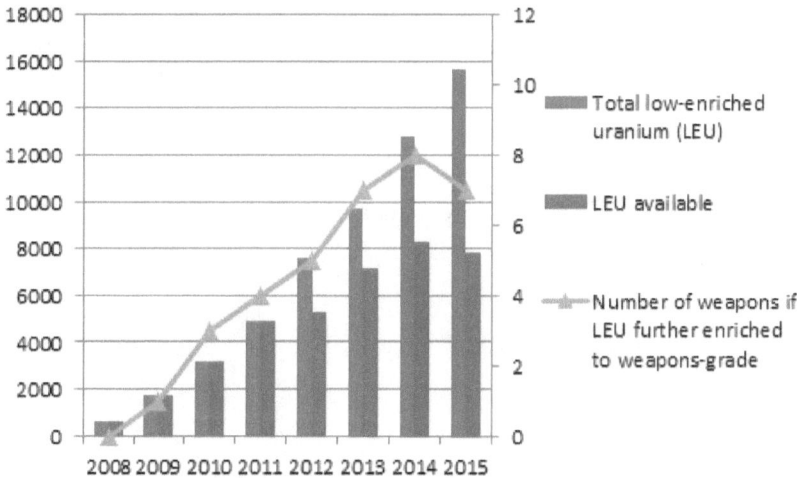

The 2009 revelation of the secret Fordow Fuel Enrichment Plant also indicated that Iran was not interested in a nuclear agreement at the time. Iran reportedly began to build this facility covertly in 2007. This was seen by many experts as part of Iran's nuclear weapons program because it was a secret facility that appeared to have been constructed to be impervious to airstrikes by the United States and Israel. Experts were even more alarmed when it was learned this facility would be used to enrich uranium to 20% U-235, supposedly to fuel the Tehran Research Reactor.

Iran began enriching uranium to the 20% level in February 2011 at Natanz. On June 8, 2011, Iranian officials announced they intended to triple the rate of 20% enriched uranium production using more advanced centrifuge designs. Iran began enriching at the 20% level at Fordow in December 2011.

In light of President Obama's repeated offers to agree to a deal that addressed international concerns about Iran's nuclear program favorable to Tehran – including ending crippling economic sanctions – why did Iranian leaders choose to significantly expand its nuclear program in violation of UN Security Council resolutions from 2009 to 2013 instead of trying to strike an agreement with Mr. Obama when he entered office in 2009?

I believe the reason for the surge in Iran's nuclear program was because Iranian officials concluded, due to President Obama's eagerness for a nuclear agreement, that they could get a favorable agreement whenever they were ready. As a result, Iran initiated a huge expansion of its nuclear program in 2009 to establish as much nuclear capacity as possible before it struck a deal with the United States to freeze this program. By expanding key parts of its nuclear program – especially its centrifuge effort – Iranian diplomats could argue in nuclear talks that these programs were too big to give up. As a result, Iran kept much more nuclear capacity in the 2015 JCPOA agreement than it would have if it had struck a deal in 2009.

5. The Possible Military Dimensions Problem

They have to do it. It will be done. If there's going to be a deal; it will be done. ... It will be part of a final agreement. It has to be.

> Secretary of State John Kerry pledging that the "possible military dimensions" of Iran's nuclear program will be addressed in a nuclear deal with Iran.

> PBS NewsHour interview
> April 6, 2015

The surge in Iran's nuclear program in violation of UN Security Council resolutions was not the only obstacle to negotiating a nuclear deal – there also was the issue of prior Iranian nuclear activities that appeared related to nuclear weapons development. The IAEA refers to such activities as the "possible military dimensions" of Iran's nuclear program or PMD.

Resolving the PMD issue is crucial to negotiating a meaningful nuclear agreement with Tehran because PMD activities represent a roadmap for inspectors to verify an agreement since they indicate the types of nuclear weapons-related research in Iran was engaged in and where this research was taking place.

William Tobey, a senior fellow with Harvard University's Kennedy School of Government and a former Department of Energy official, explained in a June 15, 2015 *Wall Street Journal* op-ed the importance of resolving PMD issues to verify a nuclear agreement with Iran:

> For inspections to be meaningful, Iran would have to completely and correctly declare all its relevant nuclear activities and procurement, past and present. Veteran CIA nuclear-verification expert John Lauder recently told me that data declarations are "most important because they help set the stage for all other measures." As former IAEA chief inspector Olli Heinonen told the New York Times last year: "You don't need to see every nut and bolt, but you are taking a heck of a risk if you don't establish a baseline of how far they went."[26]

Wendy Sherman, who headed the U.S. delegation to the nuclear talks for the United States, indicated during a December 2013 Senate hearing that resolving PMD questions was essential to a good nuclear agreement with Iran:

There are three places in the agreement that speak to the possible military dimensions of Iran's program. In the first paragraph, it talks about having the comprehensive agreement address all remaining concerns. That is a reference to their possible military dimensions. It talks about the need to address past and present practices, which is the IAEA terminology for possible military dimensions, including Parchin... So we have had very direct conversations with Iran about all of these. They understand completely the meaning of the words in this agreement, and we intend to support the IAEA in its efforts to deal with possible military dimensions, including Parchin.[27]

The PMD issue has plagued diplomacy with Tehran over its nuclear program since the National Council of Resistance of Iran (NCRI), an Iranian opposition group located in Iraq, made the first public revelations about Iran's covert nuclear activities in 2003. Resolving PMD issues became more urgent in July 2005 because of what the IAEA learned about possible covert Iranian nuclear weapons work from the "Laptop Documents," a large cache of documents acquired by the CIA in November 2004 by a walk-in source. (The IAEA's term for the Laptop Documents is the "Alleged Studies Documentation.")

The Laptop Documents included information on designing a nuclear warhead, modifying a Shahab missile to carry a nuclear warhead, and indicated aid to Iran's nuclear program from the A.Q. Khan nuclear proliferation network as well as a former Russian nuclear scientist.

The laptop documents reportedly were part of the "AMAD Plan," a comprehensive program of research on nuclear weapons led by Iranian physicist and senior member of the Islamic Revolutionary Guard Corps Mohsen Fakhrizadeh in his role as head of Iran's Physics Research Center (PHRC). In a May 27, 2014 editorial, the Wall Street Journal provided this description of the AMAD program:

> The AMAD Plan was charged with procuring dual-use technologies, developing nuclear detonators and conducting high-explosive experiments associated with compressing fissile material, according to Western intelligence agencies. The AMAD Plan's most intense period of activity was in 2002-03, according to the IAEA, when current President Hassan Rouhani headed Iran's Supreme National Security Council before becoming its chief nuclear negotiator.[28]

According to the unclassified key judgments of the 2007 National Intelligence Estimate on Iran's nuclear program, the AMAD plan was stopped abruptly in 2003 in response a halt order by top Iranian officials. IAEA reports confirmed the halt order but also said nuclear weapons-related work was restarted, although not as the comprehensive as the efforts that was in place until 2003.

According to a November 2011 IAEA report, some AMAD Plan projects were later resumed, and Fakhrizadeh retained his principal organizational role. The November 2011 IAEA report said, "The Agency is concerned because some of the activities undertaken after 2003 would be highly relevant to a nuclear weapon programme."[29] A December 2015 IAEA report said Iran's nuclear weapons-related work continued at least until 2009. [30]

Prior to July 2015, Iran provided a limited amount of cooperation to IAEA inquiries about PMD questions and mostly provided explanations that were meaningless or deceitful. Iran's general position on the PMD issue is that its nuclear program is entirely peaceful, there is no evidence it has ever pursued nuclear weapons, and that PMD allegations are fabrications by Iran's enemies. As I will explain in Chapter 18, Iran's cooperation with the IAEA's final PMD investigation in the fall of 2015 was as bad if not worse than what it provided to previous investigations.

November 2011 IAEA Report on the "Laptop Documents"

On November 8, 2011, the IAEA presented its most definitive report to date indicating Iran had conducted a wide-ranging program to construct nuclear weapons. This report has been referred to as the IAEA "dossier" on the possible military dimensions of the Iranian nuclear program.

The report reflected the leadership of the Agency's new Director General, Yukiya Amano, who succeeded pro-Iran Director General Mohamed ElBaradei on December 1, 2009. Although ElBaradei mostly overcame his initial reluctance to accept the Laptop Documents as genuine, he still limited how much the Agency could use them to evaluate the Iranian nuclear program. Amano did not share this concern, which allowed the November 2011 report on Iran to become the most damaging IAEA assessment to date on the possible military dimensions of Iran's nuclear program.

The November 2011 report followed up on former IAEA Director General Mohamed ElBaradei's 2007 "Work Plan" proposal which was intended to resolve the IAEA's outstanding PMD questions by the end of 2007. By February 2008, the IAEA had resolved all of the Work Plan issues except for most issues related to the Laptop Documents. The Work Plan process broke down in September 2008 after Iran cancelled meetings with the IAEA and visits by IAEA inspectors to nuclear sites.

Months before the release of the November 2011 report, the IAEA attempted to negotiate an agreement with Iran to obtain answers to outstanding PMD Issues related to the Laptop Documents. Fereyedoun Abbasi, head of the Atomic Energy Agency of Iran, responded to this effort with a May 26, 2011 letter stating that Iran would be "prepared to receive relevant questions" on its nuclear activities from the IAEA if it declared the Work Plan had been fully implemented and if the Agency agreed to end its special monitoring of the Iranian nuclear program and start implementing safeguards inspections "in a normal manner." The IAEA rejected this request but tried through October 2011 to convince Iran to cooperate with its PMD investigation.[31]

The November 2011 IAEA report represented a significant setback for President Obama's efforts to get a nuclear agreement with Iran since it included serious allegations of Iranian nuclear weapons-related activities which Tehran refused to explain and needed to be addressed before concluding a nuclear agreement.

The report also represented a significant change in the way the IAEA presented the Iranian nuclear issue – it no longer had "suspicions" about Iranian nuclear weaponization; it now had hard intelligence from "more than ten Member States."

In the November 2011 report, the IAEA expressed "serious concerns" that Iran had conducted research on the construction of a nuclear warhead and that this research could still be ongoing.[32] The report said a structured nuclear weapons effort was in place until 2003 and that some of this work continued after 2003 which it said "would be highly relevant to a nuclear weapon programme."[33]

A source close to the IAEA said about the report to the London Guardian, "What is striking is the totality and breadth of the information. Virtually every component of warhead research has been pursued by Iran."[34] According to the report, this included the following general activities relevant to the development of a nuclear explosive device:

- Efforts, some successful, to procure nuclear related and dual use equipment and materials by military related individuals and entities.

- Efforts to develop undeclared pathways for the production of nuclear material.

- The acquisition of nuclear weapons development information and documentation from a clandestine nuclear supply network.

- Work on the development of an indigenous design of a nuclear weapon including the testing of components.[35]

The report noted that while some of these activities have civilian as well as military applications, others are specific to nuclear weapons. The report's annex spelled out the below 12 specific activities as indicators of nuclear explosive development by Iran. These 12 activities became a list of PMD questions that Iran was supposed to resolve (but failed to do so) before concluding the July 2015 JCPOA agreement. This PMD list also was addressed in a July 2015 agreement between Iran and the IAEA that resulted in an IAEA investigation in the fall of 2015 and a December 2015 report. This report is discussed in Chapter 18.

- Program management structure: the bureaucratic structure, including government officials and agencies that oversaw Iran's nuclear weapons development.

- Procurement activities: the channels, including covert nuclear channels such as the A.Q. Khan Network that Iran used to obtain goods, services and technology for use in a nuclear weapons program.

- Nuclear material acquisition: efforts by Iran to secure a source of uranium and to convert products of enrichment into metal for use in a warhead.

- Nuclear components for an explosive device, including evidence that Iran had undergone preparatory work for the fabrication of uranium metal components for a nuclear weapon.

- Detonator development: the development of "exploding bridge wire detonators" suitable for use in a nuclear weapon.

- Initiation of high explosive and associated experiments, including testing done in 2003, as well as experimental research on high explosives carried out past 2003.

- Hydrodynamic experiments: testing the theoretical design of a nuclear weapon with surrogate materials for nuclear components.[36] The 2011 report alleged that Iran had used a bus-sized steel chamber at its Parchin military base for hydrodynamic testing to develop an implosion device. This confirmed a report first raised by ABC News in August 2004 that explosive testing had taken place at Parchin related to the development of nuclear warheads.[37]

- Modelling and calculations: computer modelling of nuclear weapons cores.

- Neutron initiator: work to manufacture a device for the core of a nuclear weapon, suitable for initiating a fissile chain reaction.

- Conducting a test: logistical arrangements made for testing a nuclear weapon.

- Integration into a missile delivery vehicle: research to determine how to mount a nuclear payload into a Shahab missile to serve as a nuclear weapon delivery system.

- Fuzing, arming and firing system: research done into developing firing systems for a nuclear weapon.[38]

In addition, the November 2011 IAEA report indicated the Agency's belief that Iran had acquired a nuclear weapon design, possibly a design more advanced than the Chinese design Libya obtained from A.Q. Khan:

> In an interview in 2007 with a member of the clandestine nuclear supply network, the Agency was told that Iran had been provided with nuclear explosive design information. From information provided to the Agency during that interview, the Agency is concerned that Iran may have obtained more advanced design information than the information identified in 2004 as having been provided to Libya by the nuclear supply network.[39]

The report also said Iran had tried to develop a "multipoint initiation system" which the IAEA said "can be used to reshape the detonation wave into a converging smooth implosion to ensure uniform compression of the core fissile material to supercritical density."[40] According to the Institute for Science and International Security, this was a reference to the "R265 shock generator system, which is a round multipoint initiation system that would fit inside the payload chamber of the Shahab 3 missile tri-conic nose cone." The Institutes's report said the IAEA obtained this information from several governments but did not refer to the Iranian codename "R265" in its reports.[41] According to the Washington Post, David Albright, the Institute for Science and International Security's president, assessed at the time that the R265 was an important technological breakthrough for Iran's nuclear weapons program and that "Iran needed outside assistance in designing the generator and testing its performance.[42]

After consultations with experts, the IAEA produced a chart assessing various possible applications of what appeared to be research by Iran for a ballistic missile nuclear warhead. This chart, reproduced below as Figure 4, indicates that the purpose of this research likely was the development of a nuclear warhead for an Iranian missile.

Figure 4: IAEA Chart on Analysis of Information on Iranian Missile Nose Cone Project[43]

	BIOLOGICAL	CHEMICAL	HIGH EXPLOSIVE	E M P	SATELLITE	NUCLEAR
Applicable Mass and Dimensions						
Contains a HV generator box						
Airburst <3000'						
Multiple Detonators Present						
No Capability for Release of Chamber from Capsule or Load from Chamber and no Antenna(s)						
Presence of 400m Shaft in Test Sketch						
Total Package Taken as a Whole						

LIKELY POSSIBLE UNLIKELY IMPOSSIBLE

One of the most alarming aspects of the report was an allegation that Iran contracted in the 1990s with a foreign nuclear scientist who had worked with explosive technology in the nuclear program of his country to assist Iran develop a high explosives initiation system and explosive testing at Iran's Parchin military base. [44] According to the report, this scientist was in Iran from 1996-2002. Although the IAEA did not provide the name of this scientist, press reports identified him as Vyacheslav Danilenko, a Ukrainian engineer who worked for three decades with the USSR's Chelyabinsk-70 nuclear weapons facility. Danilenko reportedly was hired by

Iran's Physics Research Centre which was headed by Iranian nuclear scientist Mohsen Fakhrizadeh.[45]

According to the Washington Post, the IAEA met with Danilenko who acknowledged his role in assisting explosive tests in Iran but claimed he thought his work was limited to assisting civilian engineering projects.[46]

Another alarming issue the in the November 2011 report was indications that Iran had received assistance from the A.Q. Khan Network [although the Khan Network was not explicitly named]. The 2007 document the Agency acquired on constructing uranium hemispheres resembled similar materials provided by this network to Libya that the Libyan government turned over to the United States in 2003. Concerning the 2007 uranium metal document, the IAEA said:

> The uranium metal document is known to have been available to the clandestine nuclear supply network that provided Iran with assistance in developing its centrifuge enrichment capability, and is also known to be part of a larger package of information which includes elements of a nuclear explosive design. A similar package of information, which surfaced in 2003, was provided by the same network to Libya. The information in the Libyan package, which was first reviewed by Agency experts in January 2004, included details on the design and construction of, and the manufacture of components for, a nuclear explosive device.[47]

The November 2011 IAEA report outlines that other documents suggested support from the Khan network, possibly including providing Tehran with an advanced nuclear weapons design.

> In addition, a Member State provided the Agency experts with access to a collection of electronic files from seized computers belonging to key members of the network at different locations. That collection included documents seen in Libya, along with more recent versions of those documents, including an up-dated electronic version of the uranium metal document.

> In an interview in 2007 with a member of the clandestine nuclear supply network, the Agency was told that Iran had been provided with nuclear explosive design information. From information provided to the Agency during that interview, the Agency is concerned that Iran may have obtained more advanced design information than the information identified in 2004 as having been provided to Libya by the nuclear supply network.[48]

Although the November 2011 IAEA report contained information that mostly had been previously revealed, it was considered a bombshell since it represented the Agency's case that an Iranian nuclear weapons program may be continuing. A November 8, 2011 New York Times article reflected the significance of the report at the time:

> United Nations weapons inspectors have amassed a trove of new evidence that they say makes a "credible" case that "Iran has carried out activities relevant to the development of a nuclear device," and that the project may still be under way.
>
> The long-awaited report, released by the International Atomic Energy Agency on Tuesday, represents the strongest judgment the agency has issued in its decade-long struggle to pierce the secrecy surrounding the Iranian program. The findings, drawn from evidence of far greater scope and depth than the agency has previously made public, have already rekindled a debate among the Western allies and Israel about whether increased diplomatic pressure, sanctions, sabotage or military action could stop Iran's program.[49]

The report also was significant for three other reasons. Primarily, it was carefully written to answer critics who were prepared to dismiss it as a false case against a rogue state WMD program similar to what the Bush administration had against Saddam Hussein's WMD program before the 2003 Iraq War.

Secondly, the 2011 report repudiated the controversial 2007 National Intelligence Estimate that said Iran's nuclear weapons program was halted in 2003. While this NIE was accepted without question by the left and the arms control establishment, most conservatives rejected it as a politicized analysis by the U.S. Intelligence Community to undermine the Bush administration's Iran policy. Both former CIA Director James Schlesinger and Harvard law professor Alan Dershowitz denounced this NIE as "stupid intelligence;"[50] however, many arms control experts refused to acknowledge that the 2011 IAEA report disproved the 2007 Iran NIE and instead made unpersuasive arguments at the time that the report supported it. (Obama officials and many arms control experts made the same arguments after a December 2015 IAEA PMD report that also disproved the 2007 Iran NIE.)

Lastly, the report provided detailed and compelling evidence and analysis that Iran had been developing nuclear warheads to be carried by ballistic missiles.

As part of the November 24, 2013 Joint Plan of Action, the IAEA and Iran agreed on November 11, 2013 to a new arrangement to resolve outstanding PMD issues known as the Framework for Cooperation. The purpose of this agreement was to encourage Iran to take some preliminary steps to cooperate with the IAEA leading to the resolution of the 12 PMD issues identified in the 2011 IAEA report. This agreement and a related investigation are discussed in Chapter 18.

Between January 2014 and June 2014, Obama officials on several occasions discussed the importance of Iran cooperating with the framework agreement and that Iran would be required to fully explain PMD-related issues as part of a nuclear agreement. Under Secretary of State Wendy Sherman testified about this Iran-IAEA PMD agreement to the U.S. Senate in February 2014:

> "We have required that Iran come clean on its past actions as part of any comprehensive agreement."[51]

IAEA officials made several attempts to resolve outstanding PMD questions with Iran under the framework agreement. However, by July 2015, Iran had only resolved one of 12 outstanding questions and refused to allow this issue to be part of a final nuclear agreement. This created a serious problem for the Obama administration given its previous promises that resolving PMD questions was a prerequisite for a nuclear deal. As I explain below, despite the seriousness of unresolved PMD issues and statements by Obama officials that Iran would be required to explain them as part of a nuclear agreement, the Obama administration ultimately agreed to drop these contentions to get a nuclear deal.

6. Sanctions Increase Despite Obama Administration Opposition

At your request, we engaged in an effort to come to a bipartisan agreement that I think is fair and balanced. And now you come here and vitiate that very agreement. So that says to me in the future that when you come to me and ask me to engage in a good-faith effort, you should have said, we want no amendment, not that you don't care for that amendment. Now, having said that, let me just say, everything that you say in your testimony undermines the credibility of your opposition to this amendment.

Senator Robert Menendez complains about the Obama administration
undermining a 2011 bill to impose sanctions on the Central Bank of Iran
Senate Foreign Relations Committee hearing
December 1, 2011[52]

The surge in Iran's nuclear program that began in 2009 led the U.S. Congress and the European Union to pass a series of sanctions against Iran that significantly slowed its economy, especially in 2012 and in the first half of 2013. Most sanctions passed by Congress were opposed by Obama officials who contended they were counterproductive to convincing Iran to agree to negotiations on its nuclear program. However, the Obama administration later backed and took credit for sanctions that originated in Congress and claimed they brought Iran to the negotiating table.

In 2009, the Obama administration halted the Bush administration's efforts to slowly step up sanctions against Iran by targeting trade related to its WMD programs as well as measures aimed at Iran's financing of terrorism.

This conciliatory approach became difficult to defend by the end of 2009 due to the surge in Iran's nuclear program and the revelation of the secret Fordow uranium enrichment plant. As a result of the criticism of Obama's Iran policy by congressional Republicans and some Democrats over these developments, the administration in late 2009 was forced to order the Treasury Department to resume implementing some new sanctions against Tehran. In addition, the U.S. increased arms sales to Gulf states and its naval presence in the Persian Gulf.

Yet the Obama administration remained reluctant to enforce existing sanctions and resisted congressional efforts to pass new ones. Despite the president's opposition, Congress passed four acts of sanctions against Iran during the Obama administration:

- The Comprehensive Iran Sanctions, Accountability, and Divestment Act of 2010 which passed the Senate 99-0 and the House 408-8. This act amended previous sanctions on Iran by greatly expanding the list of activities in the Iranian energy sector that could be sanctioned.

- The 2011 Menendez-Kirk Amendment to the National Defense Authorization Act for Fiscal Year 2012 which passed the Senate 100-0. This amendment increased financial sanctions against Iran by prohibiting access to the U.S. financial system for any foreign financial institution that the president determined had conducted or facilitated significant financial transactions with the Central Bank of Iran or any other designated Iranian financial institution.

- The Menendez-Wicker Amendment to the Iran Threat Reduction and Syria Human Rights Act of 2012 which passed the House 421-to-6 and the Senate in a voice vote. This amendment expanded sanctions in several areas, including sanctions against SWIFT, the international financial messaging service used by banks to facilitate global payment transactions, and other financial message services to further cut off Iran from the global financial system.

- A Menendez-Kirk-Lieberman amendment to the National Defense Authorization Act for Fiscal Year 2013, the Iran Freedom and Counter-Proliferation Act of 2012, which passed the Senate 94-0. This amendment imposed sanctions on Iran's energy, shipping, and shipbuilding and port sectors.

The Obama administration opposed and tried to weaken and delay all of these sanctions bills. This led Senator Jon Kyl to complain in 2010, "The president must drop his obstruction of and halt his efforts to water down the tough new sanctions on Iran that Congress is considering."[53] Obama officials especially opposed the 2011 Menendez-Kirk and the 2012 Menendez-Wicker Amendments which they claimed would undermine diplomatic efforts, alienate U.S. allies and cause Iran to become more resistant to negotiations on its nuclear program.

Congress, alarmed at Iran's surging nuclear program, ignored the administration's objections and passed these sanctions by wide margins.

Foundation for the Defense of Democracies Executive Director Mark Dubowitz, an expert on Iran sanctions, said in prepared testimony to a hearing of the Senate Committee on Banking, Housing, and Urban Affairs on January 27, 2015 that Congressional pressure forced the both Obama administration and the EU to drop its objections to the 2012 SWIFT sanctions against Iran:

> As a result of congressional legislation targeting SWIFT, EU regulators instructed SWIFT to remove specified Iranian banks from the SWIFT network. It was congressional pressure, and an unwillingness by Congress to accept arguments advanced by Obama Administration officials that such action would undercut the multilateral sanctions regime, which finally persuaded the Obama Administration and EU officials to act. [54]

Many other bills were proposed but not approved on the Iran nuclear question between 2010 and 2015. Two of the most important were the Nuclear Free Iran Act of 2013 and its successor the Nuclear Free Iran Act of 2015. The first bill was proposed by Senators Kirk, Schumer, and Menendez; the second by Kirk and Menendez.

Both bills were proposed because of concerns over the direction of the nuclear talks with Iran and were intended to pressure Iranian leaders to negotiate in good faith and comply with their commitments. These bills included "deferred triggers" that would kick in if Iran had not reached an agreement by certain deadlines.

The 2013 Kirk-Schumer-Menendez bill reflected the rejection by a large number of members of Congress of compromises made by the Obama administration to negotiate the Joint Plan of Action (JPA). The 2013 bill demanded changes to U.S. policy on a nuclear agreement by insisting that Iran halt all uranium enrichment, comply with all UN Security Council resolutions, resolve all outstanding PMD questions and agree to robust verification, including continuous on-site inspection and monitoring of all suspect nuclear facilities. In addition, this bill called for the dismantlement of Iran's nuclear infrastructure including enrichment and reprocessing capabilities and facilities. The president threatened to veto the Kirk-Schumer-Menendez bill. It failed to pass when it received only 59 votes in the Senate – one short of a filibuster-proof majority.

The demands in the 2013 bill on the US requirements for a final nuclear agreement with Iran were far removed from the Obama administration's position, especially on uranium enrichment. In addition, the bill reflected the challenge the

Obama administration faced to sell certain concessions it would eventually make to negotiate the JCPOA. The final nuclear agreement did not meet any of the requirements listed above in the 2013 Kirk-Menendez-Schumer Bill

The 2015 bill was similar to its 2013 predecessor although it was somewhat watered-down. This bill reflected frustration by members of the Senate at the time that the nuclear talks, which were supposed to have concluded by mid-2014, appeared to be going nowhere.

The Obama administration successfully fended off both bills by urging Congress to "give diplomacy a chance." It also noted that Iranian officials warned they would pull out of the nuclear talks if the United States implemented new sanctions. Obama and Iranian officials continue to make similar arguments today in response to proposals by Senators Kirk, Menendez, Rubio, Cruz and many members of the U.S. House to implement new sanctions in response to Iranian missile tests, continued sponsorship of terrorism, and support of the Assad regime in Syria.

A February 17, 2012 *Los Angeles Times* article accused the Obama administration of taking a "back seat" on sanctions against Iran.[55] While this article noted that the administration claimed it had imposed dozens of sanctions since 2009, it also noted that Obama officials tried to "carefully calibrate their effect" and scrambled to keep up with the pace set by Congress and the Europeans. According to the article, the Obama administration at first resisted sanctions pushed by Congress and Europe before embracing them as inevitable and was ultimately trying to avoid the appearance of "following from behind" on sanctions.

Hillary Clinton claims in her memoirs,[56] as well as frequently saying in campaign speeches, that she and President Obama worked closely with Congress to impose tough sanctions against Iran that brought it to the negotiating table. Her memoirs do not mention (and I doubt she will discuss in her campaign speeches) the fact that the State Department actually fought against, and tried to undermine, all of the sanctions Congress passed while she was Secretary of State.

Despite the Obama administration's resistance to passing new sanctions against Iran, it implemented several sanctions on its own. This included an important finding by the Treasury Department in November 2011 that relied on section 311 of the Patriot Act, which determined that the entire nation of Iran was "a jurisdiction of primary money laundering concern," noting Iran's sponsorship of terrorism, pursuit of WMD and "use of deceptive financial practices to facilitate illicit conduct and evade sanctions."[57] Although the Obama administration promised Congress in testimony on the JCPOA during the summer of 2015 that it would not lift these terrorism-related sanctions, it was learned in the spring of 2016 that the administration was planning to give Iran a "back door" to the U.S financial system that appeared to violate the Treasury Department's November 2011 determination. This issue is discussed in Chapter 20.

Other Obama administration sanctions against Iran included:

- On July 28, 2011, the U.S. Treasury Department imposed financial sanctions on six individuals believed to be al Qaeda operatives in Pakistan, Kuwait, Qatar, and Iran. Treasury officials accused a Syrian operating in Iran named Ezedin Abdel Aziz Khalil, also known as Yasin al-Sura, of being a "prominent Iran-based al Qaeda facilitator" operating in Iran under an agreement between al Qaeda and the Iranian government.

- Sanctions in October 2011 by the Treasury Department against five individuals believed responsible for an Iranian plot to assassinate the Saudi ambassador to the United States at a Washington DC restaurant. Although Obama officials at first called for sanctions against Iran's central bank due to this incident, it backed away from this idea the following month, claiming that such sanctions would disrupt international oil markets and undermine chances to negotiate a nuclear agreement. As stated earlier, Congress ignored these concerns and passed its own sanctions against Iran's central bank in late 2011.

- Sanctions in February 2014 by the Treasury Department against three Iranian revolutionary guard officers for providing support to the Afghan Taliban.

The European Union ignored pleas by the Obama administration to forgo implementing sanctions between 2010 and 2013 and passed a series of restrictive measures against Iran. These sanctions included:

- Sanctions against transfers of uranium enrichment technology.

- An asset freeze on a list on individuals and organizations believed to be helping advance the Iranian nuclear program and a ban on them from entering the EU.

- A ban on any transactions with Iranian banks and financial institutions.

- A ban on the import, purchase and transport of Iranian crude oil and natural gas.

- An EU ban on oil imports which began on July 1, 2012 which had a significant effect on the Iranian economy and caused Iranian oil exports to fall to 700,000 barrels per day in May 2013 from about 2.2 million barrels per day in 2011.

The UN Security Council passed its only sanctions resolution during the Obama administration against Iran on June 9, 2010, Resolution 1929. This resolution imposed financial sanctions against Iran, permitted inspections of ships and aircraft suspected of transporting WMD or missile-related cargoes (when in port, not on the high seas), and barred investment in Iranian nuclear facilities, including enrichment plants and uranium mines. This resolution also called on states not to assist Iran's ballistic missile program.

Did increased American and EU sanctions force Iran to come to the bargaining table and agree to the November 2013 interim nuclear agreement? Obama officials, many members of Congress and foreign policy expert believe this was the case. The problem with this assessment is that Iran's nuclear program increased at a steady pace despite growing sanctions, Moreover, the Iranian government agreed to the November 2013 deal despite the fact that Iran's economy had stabilized by mid-2013 due to the election of President Hassan Rouhani who proved to be a far better manager than his predecessor Mahmoud Ahmadinejad. The improvement of the Iranian economy under Rouhani probably indicates that although sanctions hurt the Iranian economy, the main reason for its economic problems was massive mismanagement, corruption and an inability to reconcile a market economy with the radical ideology of the country's theocratic rulers. In addition, the effectiveness of U.S. sanctions had significantly weakened by the fall of 2013 due to waivers granted by the Obama administration.

Mark Dubowitz said in his prepared testimony to a January 2015 Senate Committee on Banking, Housing, and Urban Affairs hearing:

> The Obama administration provided "a financial lifeline to Iran in the form of sanctions relief. As a result, Iran's economy has stabilized and is on a modest recovery path after a deep, sanctions-induced recession in 2012 and 2013. This has reduced Iranian regime fears of another economic crisis and increased economic resilience against future pressure.[58]

Dubowitz added his call for "deadline-triggered sanctions" aimed at ensuring the success of the nuclear talks. This proposal was very similar to what Senators Kirk and Menendez proposed in their 2015 bill.

My view is that the Iranian government came to the negotiating table in 2013 and agreed to the interim agreement because it was ready to do so since it had sufficiently built up its nuclear program by that time. I believe concessions offered by the Obama administration to convince Iran to negotiate, especially the 2011 Kerry letter, played a more significant role to initiate the nuclear talks than pressure from sanctions. Although increased American and EU sanctions may have played a role in convincing Iran to come to the negotiating table earlier than it may have otherwise, I believe that given how little the Iranian government gave up in the JCPOA talks, Tehran's negotiating strategy was to have sanctions lifted without giving up its nuclear program.

7. Kerry's Huge 2011 Concessions Paved Way to the Obamabomb Deal

We came to the [secret] negotiations [with the U.S.] after Kerry wrote a letter and sent it to us via Oman, stating that America officially recognizes Iran's rights regarding the [nuclear fuel] enrichment cycle.

Sheikh Al-Islam, an advisor to Iranian Parliament Speaker Ali Larijani,
Tasnim news agency, July 7, 2015

To convince Iran to agree to negotiations on a long-term agreement on its nuclear program, the Obama administration began a strategy in 2009 of conciliatory statements by the president, secret letters from President Obama to Supreme Leader Khamenei, and inducements such as the release of Iranians held in American and British prisons and easing visa rules for Iranian students who wanted to attend U.S universities. In November 2010, in another bid to win favor with Iran's ruling mullahs, the Obama administration sanctioned a Pakistan-based militant group known as Jundullah which had attacked Shiite mosques and military bases in eastern Iran, killing hundreds.

Although I believe Iran delayed agreeing to talks on a final nuclear agreement until after it completed a massive increase to its nuclear infrastructure, there were three other major obstacles that prevented negotiations from moving forward: Iran's insistence that it had the right under the NPT to enrich uranium, its refusal to give up its uranium enrichment centrifuges and its insistence that the IAEA's PMD "file" be closed.

The Obama administration reportedly cleared these obstacles through a 2011 letter to Iranian leaders that requested negotiations on Iran's nuclear program, recognized Iran's right to enrich uranium on its own soil, recognized Iran as a nuclear power and offered to lift sanctions within six months.

The Middle East Media Research Institute (MEMRI), a Washington, DC-based policy institute which monitors, analyzes and translates Middle East press, discussed this letter in an August 10, 2015 report[59] According MEMRI, this letter, which Iranian officials disclosed in statements they made in June and July 2015, reportedly was sent by John Kerry when he was Chairman of the Senate Foreign Relations Committee. The MEMRI report says Iranian Vice President and top negotiator Ali Akbar Salehi claims Kerry had been named by President Obama "to handle the nuclear contacts with Iran."

Although it is unclear whether Kerry had a formal mandate from President Obama to conduct secret talks with Iran, the president was aware of them and Kerry coordinated his talking points through National Security Advisor Thomas Donilon with whom Kerry had a close relationship.[60] According to Mark Landler in "Alter Egos," Clinton and some at the NSC thought Kerry was freelancing and might offer proposals to Iran that they could not accept. One of these, according to Landler, was an offer by Kerry to recognize Iran's right to enrich uranium, a claim that Kerry denies. Landler wrote that Kerry pushed the back channel with Oman the hardest while he was in the Senate and was frustrated that the NSC and State Department were slow to embrace it.[61] Clinton takes credit for the back channel to Iran in her memoirs and does not mention her reported reluctance to use it.

According to the MEMRI report, Iranian Supreme Leader Ali Khamenei said in a June 23, 2015 speech that the Obama administration initiated the nuclear talks with Iran during Ahmadinejad's term in office based on U.S. recognition of a nuclear Iran. Khamenei reportedly said the United States informed him through Omani Sultan Qaboos, "We want to solve the nuclear issue and lift sanctions within six months, while recognizing Iran as a nuclear power."

The MEMRI report quotes a statement to the Tasnim news agency on July 7, 2015 by Hossein Sheikh Al-Islam, an advisor to Iranian Parliament Speaker Ali Larijani, who said Kerry sent a letter to Tehran recognizing Iran's enrichment rights. According to Al-Islam "We came to the [secret] negotiations [with the U.S.] after Kerry wrote a letter and sent it to us via Oman, stating that America officially recognizes Iran's rights regarding the [nuclear fuel] enrichment cycle."

According to the MEMRI report, Iranian Vice President Ali Akbar Salehi and head of Iran's Atomic Energy Organization said in an interview with the daily *Iran* that he responded to Kerry's letter a month or two later through Oman:

> I am not sure how serious the Americans are, but I will give you a note. Tell them that these are our demands. Deliver it on your next visit to Oman.' I wrote down four clear issues, one of which was official recognition of rights to

56

[uranium] enrichment. I figured that if the Americans were sincere in their offer, then they must agree to these four demands. Mr. Suri gave this short letter to the mediator, and stressed that these were Iran's demands. [He added that] if the Americans wished to solve this issue, they were welcome to, otherwise dealing with White House proposals would be useless and unwarranted..."All the demands in the letter were related to the nuclear challenge. These were issues we have always come against, such as closing the nuclear dossier [in the Security Council], official recognition of [Iran's] right to enrich [uranium], and resolving the issue of Iran's actions under the PMD [Possible Military Dimensions].

According to Saleh, "After receiving the letter, the Americans said: 'We are certainly willing and able to easily solve the issues Iran has brought up.'"

If these exchanges occurred, they were the turning point for the Obamabomb deal since this is when the United States capitulated to Iran's nuclear program by agreeing to allow Iran to keep its uranium enrichment program and to drop the PMD issue.

These letters and exchanges have not been confirmed. Neither the United States nor Iran have released copies of any secret letters sent by either nation to the other. However, the MEMRI report tracks with how the JCPOA came about. These alleged diplomatic exchanges in 2011 were followed by a series of P5+1 talks in 2012, including a meeting in Baghdad in May 2012 during which the United States offered a major concession to allow Iran to continue to enrich uranium as part of a nuclear agreement. Moreover, the four issues listed in Vice President Salehi's letter were all dealt with in accordance with Iran's wishes in the JCPOA.

The MEMRI report also is important because it debunks the false narrative circulated by the Obama administration that the JCPOA was the result of two years of tough negotiations made possible by the election of the supposedly moderate Iranian President Hassan Rouhani in June 2013. The truth is the nuclear agreement was probably locked in by 2012 due to U.S. concessions conveyed by Kerry in 2011 to Khamenei.

In a September 2015 Politico article, Indira A.R. Lakshmanan attributed the first step toward negotiating the JCPOA to a July 2012 meeting in Oman between Obama NSC aide Puneet Talwar and senior Secretary Clinton aide Jake Sullivan with an Iranian delegation.[62] This meeting, organized by the government of Oman, reportedly was the first face-to-face meeting between U.S. and Iranian officials and resulted in more secret U.S.-Iran meetings that led to the November 2015 interim nuclear agreement in which the parties agreed to begin negotiations on a final nuclear agreement. As stated earlier, Mark Landler makes a similar claim about the Talwar/Sullivan meeting in "Alter Egos." Hillary Clinton confirms some of this in her memoirs but also claims that she conducted the first meeting with Sultan Qaboos in January 2011.[63]

While these meetings may have been significant, I believe the letters Kerry exchanged with Iranian officials in were more important and actually cleared the obstacles for the Obama administration to move forward with the Obamabomb deal. I also believe the U.S. offer allowing Iran to continue to enrich uranium at the Baghdad P5+1 meeting in May 2012 followed up on Kerry's 2011 letter and also was more significant than the July 2015 Talwar/Sullivan meeting with Iranian officials.

I believe it is very likely that John Kerry engineered the Obamabomb deal with the huge U.S. concessions he conveyed to Iran in 2011 and by making more huge concessions four years later when he headed the Iran nuclear negotiations as Secretary of State.

8. Negotiations Begin; An Interim Agreement Is Reached

For years the international community has demanded that Iran cease all uranium enrichment. Now, for the first time, the international community has formally consented that Iran continue its enrichment of uranium.

Israeli Prime Minister Benjamin Netanyahu
November 25, 2015

Due to the major concessions conveyed to Iran by John Kerry in 2011, diplomatic talks with Iran intensified in 2012 with a series of P5+1 meetings, the first in Istanbul in April 2012. Other P5+1 meetings were held in 2012 and 2013 in Baghdad, Moscow, Istanbul and Almaty. In addition to P5+1 meetings, there were bilateral meetings between EU and Iranian officials and secret U.S.-Iran talks. These diplomatic efforts resulted in the Joint Plan of Action (JPA), an interim agreement to start talks on a final agreement to resolve international concerns about Iran's nuclear program.

Formalizing the U.S. Concession on Uranium Enrichment

The Obama administration took its first public step to resolve the uranium enrichment issue by proposing during P5+1 talks held in Baghdad on May 25, 2012 that Iran would be permitted to continue to enrich uranium to the reactor grade level (3 to 5% U-235) as part of a final agreement on its nuclear program if it agreed to cease enriching uranium to the 20% level. In exchange for agreeing to halt enriching uranium to this level, the U.S. proposed providing Iran with 20% enriched uranium reactor fuel for Iran's Tehran Research Reactor, nonmilitary aircraft components and commercial forms of nuclear assistance. Although Iran rejected this proposal, it became the basis of the JPA and the July 2015 JCPOA.

Obama officials tried to sidestep controversy over this concession by claiming reactor-grade uranium was not that dangerous and that this concession had been proposed to convince Iran give up the production and storage of 20% enriched uranium which they claimed was more dangerous. Their argument was that 20% uranium was more of a threat since it was much closer mathematically to reactor grade uranium which is about 90% U-235.

This argument is false because it ignore a peculiarity of uranium enrichment known as "nonlinearity." *The New York Times* discussed this concept in a March 8, 2010 article:

> It is also illustrating one of the peculiarities of uranium enrichment, a version of the rich getting richer, really fast. The tricky process accelerates as it moves ahead. "The higher the concentration, the easier it gets," said Houston G. Wood III, a professor of mechanical and aerospace engineering at the University of Virginia who specializes in nuclear enrichment. The process is, as scientists like to say, nonlinear.[64]

Because of the nonlinearity phenomenon, most of the work to enrich to weapons-grade occurs when enriching from unenriched uranium to the reactor-grade level; a process that may take Iran five to seven months. 2013 estimates by the American Enterprise Institute,[65] the Institute for Science and International Security[66] and the Nonproliferation Policy Education Center[67] on how long it would take Iran to make enough weapons-grade uranium for one nuclear bomb using its stockpile of reactor-grade uranium (in the form of UF6) ranged from four to six weeks. Figure 5 is a 2014 Center for Security Policy chart illustrating the time for Iran to enrich uranium to weapons-grade using the 9,000 centrifuges it was using to enrich at that time.

Figure 5: Estimated Time for Iran to Enrich Uranium to Weapons-Grade[68]

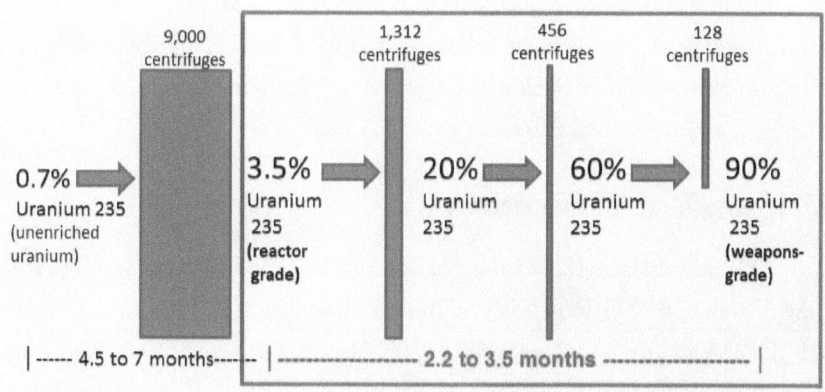

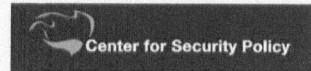

Number of centrifuges needed to enrich to weapons-grade

Obama Administration Politicized Intelligence on an Iranian Nuclear Breakout

Although the above organizations and others concluded in 2013 that nuclear "breakout – when Iran could produce enough weapons-grade enriched uranium for a nuclear bomb – was three months or less, the Obama administration maintained at the time that breakout was a year or more away. However, as the conclusion of the nuclear talks approached, the administration changed its estimate to breakout being two to three months away.[69] Kerry hinted at the shorter estimate in April 2014. An intelligence estimate containing this figure was declassified on April 1, 2015.

Bloomberg writer Eli Lake said in an April 21, 2016 article that the Obama administration had long known Iran's breakout was two to three months but kept this secret to prevent any urgency that might cause Congress to implement new sanctions against Iran. Arguing for a longer breakout also helped the administration counter Israeli Prime Minister Netanyahu's shorter timeline and his efforts to derail the nuclear talks. Lake suggested that the Obama administration revealed the shorter breakout estimate as a key selling point for the JCPOA.

For experts like me who closely follow the Iranian nuclear program, the short timeline to an Iranian nuclear bomb was one of the worst kept secrets in Washington and a prime example of the Obama administration misrepresenting the facts to advance its radical plan to strike a nuclear deal with Iran. This also represented an unethical politicization of intelligence to mislead Congress and the American people which further undermined the administration's credibility.

Politicizing Uranium Enrichment

Obama officials ignored the nonlinearity issue and claimed Iran's agreement in the November 2013 Joint Plan of Action interim agreement and the November 2015 JCPOA to give up its stockpile of 20% enriched uranium to cease enriching to this level was a significant diplomatic victory since Iran had agreed to give up its supposedly more dangerous 20% enriched uranium. Secretary Kerry said this about the enrichment provisions in the JPA in a November 24, 2013 press conference:

> Iran has agreed to suspend all enrichment of uranium above 5 percent. Iran has agreed to dilute or convert its entire stockpile of 20 percent enriched uranium. So let me make clear what that means. That means that whereas Iran today has about 200 kilograms of 20 percent enriched uranium, they could readily be enriched towards a nuclear weapon. In six months, Iran will have zero – zero. Iran will not increase its stockpile of 3.5 percent lower-enriched uranium over the next six months, and it will not construct additional enrichment facilities.

Obama officials worked hard to encourage the news media to spread the fiction that 20% enriched uranium was significantly more dangerous than reactor grade. This claim was repeated by compliant reporters and facilitated by arms control experts with organizations like the Arms Control Association and the Ploughshares Fund who knew better but went along with this deception.

Obama officials also tried to misrepresent the significance of the enrichment concession by making it appear that they were handed the problem of Iran's centrifuges by the Bush administration and not mention the huge increase in this program that took place from 2009-2013. For example, according to *The Dartmouth*, Wendy Sherman said in a Dartmouth University lecture in October 2015:

> In 2003, Iran possessed 164 centrifuges, Sherman said, but by the time the United States began successful negotiations, Iran already had 19,000 centrifuges, 10,000 of which were operational. According to Sherman, the

United States was left with two possibilities for stopping the Iranians – peaceful negotiations or military action. [70]

Sherman said destroying facilities would simply render their program inactive until they could rebuild it again.

> You can't get rid of knowledge. You can get rid of facilities, but you can't get rid of knowledge.

Former Democratic Senator Joseph has a different view. I asked him at a June 1, 2015 Capitol Hill briefing whether he thought a meaningful nuclear agreement with Iran was possible if Iran is allowed to continue to enrich uranium. His answer was:

> Quite simply and clearly no, I don't. I mean, I thought the original purpose of these negotiations was to stop the Iranian nuclear enrichment program, in return for the sequential elimination of all the economic sanctions, which is quite significant for Iran and quite significant when you think about it, that it has unfortunately nothing to do with its terrible human rights record, with its expansionism in the region, with its support of terrorism. To let that enrichment go on, to me just shows that, as Ayatollah Khamenei said himself last fall, the Americans obviously want this agreement much more than we do [and] that's never where you want to be in a negotiation."[71]

Senator Lieberman's comments also reflected promises made by Barack Obama when he was campaigning for president in March 2007 to an AIPAC meeting in Chicago that "the world must work to stop Iran's uranium enrichment program" and comments he made in a 2012 presidential debate with Mitt Romney that "Our goal is to get Iran to recognize it needs to give up its nuclear program and abide by the U.N. resolutions that have been in place. . . . But the deal we'll accept is — they end their nuclear program. It's very straightforward."

It is important to understand the absurdity of a related argument by the Obama administration that because Iran had constructed so many centrifuges, it was unreasonable to ask it to give them up or stop enrichment. There are two major flaws in this argument.

First, Iran constructed these centrifuges in defiance of UN Security Council resolutions and American policies. By giving in to Iran's demands that it be allowed to keep these centrifuges and continue enriching, the United States and its European allies sent a dangerous message to rogue states worldwide that they can defy Security Council resolutions and the policies of the United States with impunity.

Second, this argument ignores the reason that Iran had such a huge number of centrifuges is because it dramatically increased it during the Obama presidency, probably to gain leverage in negotiations on its nuclear program.

Misrepresenting when Iran built its centrifuges and the "you can't get rid of knowledge" were more deceptive arguments by the White House to sell the nuclear talks and the nuclear deal. This was a rationalization to justify the administration's backing away from its previous call for Iran to halt enrichment and to portray this position as an obstacle to a nuclear deal created by the Bush administration even though halting all Iranian uranium enrichment had long been called for by America's European allies. This also was a dishonest argument since asking Iran to halt enrichment was not a burdensome request because Iran could acquire enriched uranium reactor fuel easily and much more cheaply by purchasing it on the global market rather than producing it itself.

The Joint Plan of Action

P5+1 talks on the Iran nuclear question in 2012 and 2013 resulted in an interim agreement setting the stage for the negotiation of a long-term final deal on Iran's nuclear program. This agreement, announced in Geneva on November 24, 2013, was called the Joint Plan of Action (JPA).

In addition to clearing the way for negotiations on a final nuclear agreement, the JPA was a short-term plan to freeze parts of Iran's nuclear program during these talks in exchange for an agreement by Western states for partial sanctions relief and a pledge to not place further economic sanctions on Iran.

Under the Joint Plan of Action, Iran agreed to:

- Cease enriching uranium over the 5% level.

- Uranium enriched to the 5% U-235 during this period would be converted to uranium oxide.

- Convert half of its 20% enriched uranium stockpile to uranium oxide. The rest was to be diluted to 5% U-235.

- Not make further advances at the Natanz enrichment plant, the Fordow enrichment plant, or the Arak heavy-water reactor.

- Not open new uranium enrichment sites.

- Not pursue a reprocessing facility.

- Allowing enhanced monitoring of its nuclear facilities by the IAEA and provide the IAEA with additional information on the Arak heavy-water reactor.

In return, the EU and the United States agreed to take these steps:

- Pause efforts to sanction Iranian oil sales.

- Suspend sanctions on Iranian petrochemical exports, gold and precious metals. The U.S. and the EU did this on January 20, 2014.

- Suspend U.S. sanctions on Iran's auto industry.

- Permit the sale of spare parts and aircraft repairs and associated services to Iran's civilian aviation firms.

- Not implement new UN Security Council or EU nuclear-related sanctions.

- The United States was to refrain from imposing new nuclear-related sanctions.

- Create a new financial channel to facilitate humanitarian trade for Iran's domestic needs using Iranian oil revenues held abroad.

- Increase the EU authorization thresholds for transactions for non-sanctioned trade to an agreed amount.

The JPA was intended to be a six-month agreement that could be extended with the consent of all parties and was supposed to reach a comprehensive agreement no more than one year after it was adopted. It was extended twice – in July 2014 and November 2014 – until a final agreement was announced in July 2015.

The White House portrayed the JPA as the first step toward a long-term nuclear agreement with Iran. A White House fact sheet on the JPA said "the P5+1 will provide limited, temporary, targeted, and reversible relief to Iran" in exchange for it meeting its commitments in the JPA. This fact sheet also said the following on how a final agreement would require Iran to comply with all UN Security Council resolutions and answer outstanding PMD issues:

> The set of understandings also includes an acknowledgment by Iran that it must address all United Nations Security Council resolutions – which Iran has long claimed are illegal – as well as past and present issues with Iran's nuclear program that have been identified by the International Atomic Energy Agency (IAEA). This would include resolution of questions concerning the possible military dimension of Iran's nuclear program, including Iran's activities at

Parchin. As part of a comprehensive solution, Iran must also come into full compliance with its obligations under the Non-Proliferation Treaty (NPT) and its obligations to the IAEA. With respect to the comprehensive solution, nothing is agreed until everything is agreed. Put simply, this first step expires in six months, and does not represent an acceptable end state to the United States or our P5+1 partners.[72]

I initially took a cautious view towards the JPA. In a *National Review Online* blog posted shortly after the announcement of the agreement, I said this deal was not as bad as it could be but still was bad.[73] While I was troubled by the agreement at the time – especially by language that allowed Iran to continue to enrich uranium – I saw a glimmer of hope because of statements made by Secretary of State John Kerry and in language in the White House fact sheet that Iran would be required to resolve PMD issues and come into compliance with its nuclear treaty obligations and UN Security Council resolutions. I also was pleased to hear Secretary Kerry say that concerning a final agreement, "nothing is agreed to until everything is agreed to."

Unfortunately, all of the elements in the JPA that gave me hope were dropped in the July 2015 JCPOA.

The JPA was heavily criticized in Washington. Senators Bob Casey (D-Pennsylvania), Susan Collins (R-Maine), Susan Collins (R-Maine) and John McCain (R-Arizona) rejected the agreement and sent a letter to President Obama not to accept terms that would allow Iran to continue enriching nuclear materials for any reason.

As noted in Chapter 6, bipartisan opposition to the JPA resulted in the 2013 Kirk-Schumer-Menendez bill which rejected major concessions made by the Obama administration to negotiate the JPA and called for it to be revised to require Iran to halt all uranium enrichment, comply with all UN Security Council resolutions, resolve all outstanding PMD questions agree to robust IAEA verification and monitoring of its nuclear sites, and dismantle its nuclear infrastructure, including enrichment and reprocessing facilities. The Senate narrowly failed to approve this bill when it only received 59 votes – one short of a filibuster-proof majority. The White House probably succeeded in fending off this legislation with its call to Congress to "give diplomacy a chance."

Ambassador John Bolton said about the JPA: "This is not, as the Obama administration leaked before the deal became public, a "compromise" on Iran's claimed "right" to enrichment. This is abject surrender by the United States."

Saudi Arabia reportedly was upset about the JPA. Saudi Prince Turki al-Faisal, brother to Saudi Foreign Minister Saud al-Faisal and an unofficial spokesman for the royal family and King Abdullah, said in December 2013 that the Saudis and other Gulf states were stunned by secret U.S.-Iran talks held earlier in the year that set the stage for the JPA.

Prince Turki said Saudi Arabia felt blindsided by the JPA and that it did not go far enough to prevent Iran from developing nuclear weapons. Turki declared at the World Policy Conference in Monaco on December 15, 2013: "What was surprising was that the talks that were going forward were kept from us. How can you build trust when you keep secrets from what are supposed to be your closest allies?"[74]

The JPA also exacerbated Saudi differences with the United States sparked by what Riyadh saw as weak U.S. leadership on several Middle East security issues such as Libya, Egypt, and Syria. As a result, there were press reports in late 2013 that the Saudis were giving consideration to acquiring their own nuclear deterrent, possibly by buying nuclear weapons from Pakistan because of their concerns about the direction of the nuclear talks with Iran and a perception that they could not rely on the United States to protect its security interests.[75]

The Obama administration rejected criticism of the JPA, claiming that the only alternative to it and the nuclear negotiations it set up was war. Obama officials also circulated a false narrative that the JPA took advantage of an opportunity due to a supposedly new moderate Iranian government headed by President Rouhani. While some in the news media took a "let's see" attitude and stressed it was only a first step and a six month agreement, many were strongly supportive and repeated the Obama administration's arguments in defense of the deal.

Conflict With Iran Over the JPA

Hours after the JPA was announced, significant disagreements surfaced between American and Iranian officials on major aspects of the agreement. The major difference concerned Iran's so-called "right" to enrich uranium. Although Iran had long insisted that a final nuclear agreement must recognize this right, the JPA only said that "a final agreement will involve a mutually defined enrichment program."

Iran said this meant the U.S. and its allies recognized an Iranian right to enrich uranium. Foreign Minister Mohammad Javad Zarif said that "in the present agreement, it has been emphasized at two different points that there will be no solution without [the existence of] a nuclear enrichment program inside Iran."

The United States disagreed. Secretary of State John Kerry said "The first step, let me be clear, does not say that Iran has a right to enrich uranium." Kerry also said, "There is no inherent right to enrich" and "We do not recognize a right to enrich."

Russia agreed with Iran. Russian Foreign Minister Lavrov said after the Geneva deal that that the world recognizes Iran's right to peaceful nuclear energy, including the right to enrichment.

In his book "Alter Egos," *New York Times* reporter Mark Landler cited several unnamed officials who claim Kerry told the Iranians in 2011 through the Omanis that the United States would acknowledge Iran's right to enrich at the start of nuclear talks.[76] While this tracked with Kerry's 2009 statement to the *Financial Times* that Iran had a right to enrich under the NPT, Kerry denied making this offer. Landler also wrote that Kerry may have indirectly indicated to Iran that the United States would recognize its right to uranium enrichment:

> It is possible Kerry never uttered the words "right to enrich" and still left the Iranians with that impression. His negotiating style, on public display three years later in the final phase of the talks, was to create a sense of possibility, a win-win atmosphere. He rarely, if ever, played the bad cop. Ismaily [an Omani businessman and emissary of Omani Sultan Qaboos bin Said] may also have embellished Kerry's words. It was generally accepted inside the White House that any comprehensive deal would involve granting Iran some enrichment. In some ways Kerry and his enthusiastic Omani go-between were merely cutting to the chase.[77]

I believe Kerry at least implicitly indicated to Iran that the United States would publicly acknowledge its right to enrich uranium during secret talks in 2011 which led Iranian officials to repeatedly complain beginning in 2013 that they had been conceded this right by the U.S. I have no doubt that Obama officials decided not to publicly concede Iran's right to enrich uranium for political reasons – they believed this was too controversial a concession that would be used against them by opponents of the president's Iran policy. I would not be surprised after President Obama leaves office if he and John Kerry state in their memoirs that they believe Iran has the right to enrich uranium under the NPT.

Iranian Cheating on JPA Delays Nuclear Talks

Talks on a final agreement were supposed to begin in late December 2013 but were delayed for several weeks because Iran cheated on the JPA shortly after it was signed by developing and installing centrifuges with more advanced designs. Iranian officials claimed development and installation of advanced centrifuges was permitted under language in the JPA text allowing nuclear research and development. Western states disagreed, pointing out that the development and installation of new centrifuges was barred by a footnote in the text.

Western states resolved this issue in early 2014 with a compromise allowing Iran to construct new centrifuges with more advanced designs provided it did not insert them with UF6 for testing. However, the Institute for Science and International Security (ISIS) noted in a November 20, 2014 report that a November 7, 2014 IAEA report indicated that Iran violated this agreement by testing an advanced IR-5 centrifuge with UF6.[78] Obama officials dismissed this incident by claiming it was a mistake on Iran's part and that quickly stopped.[79] The Arms Control Association made a similar incredulous claim that it saw no violation because "no enriched uranium is being withdrawn from the machine."

The authors of the ISIS report disagreed, writing that:

> The JPA is intended to freeze Iran's existing centrifuge program and prevent further advances while negotiations toward a comprehensive agreement are underway. The feeding of the IR-5 centrifuge is an apparent violation of that commitment to freeze centrifuge R&D activities at the Natanz pilot plant. [80]

The strong support that the November 2013 Kirk-Schumer-Menendez bill received reflected widespread mistrust of President Obama's nuclear diplomacy with Iran and a belief that the JPA was a blueprint for a terrible final nuclear agreement. The July 2015 JCPOA agreement confirmed these concerns. However, I doubt that any member of Congress who voted for this bill imagined how bad or how controversial the final nuclear agreement with Iran would be.

9. The Kabuki Theater Talks to Reach the Obamabomb Deal

Secretary of State John Kerry meets with Iranian Foreign Minister Mohammad Javad Zarif during nuclear talks in Vienna, Austria, July 1, 2015. (U.S. State Department photo.)

According to a September 25, 2015 *Politico* article by Indira A.R. Lakshmanan, President Obama's diplomats who negotiated the nuclear agreement with Iran were so impressed with their performance that they joked about which Hollywood stars would play the top U.S. negotiators if a movie was made about their efforts. They mused that Ted Danson should play Secretary of State John Kerry and Meryl Streep should play Wendy Sherman, the head negotiator. [81]

Lakshmanan's article was indicative of the fantasy world of the president's foreign policy team and his negotiators at the nuclear talks. They were oblivious to the serious consequences of the huge concessions they were making to reach a final nuclear agreement with Tehran. And like most State Department arms control careerists, they measured success on whether they reached an agreement, not on whether they reached a *good* agreement.

Lakshmanan slavishly praised Kerry and Sherman for supposedly achieving the nearly impossible task of convincing Iran to agree to the July 2015 nuclear deal. Her article mentions all night meetings, over 69 trips across the Atlantic by American negotiators, and a supposed willingness by U.S. diplomats to walk away from the talks. When Iran suddenly toughened its demands towards the end of the negotiations in May 2015, Lakshmanan reported that Kerry told his Iranian counterpart "if you can't do this deal, go back to Tehran."

I do not dispute that the 19-month talks under the JPA to negotiate the JCPOA was arduous for President Obama's diplomats and for Obama administration officials in Washington. But contrary to numerous claims by Obama officials of their heroic diplomatic efforts to convince Iran to agree to a nuclear deal, these talks amounted to America negotiating the terms of its capitulation to Iran's nuclear weapons program.

It also is worth noting that despite claims by Obama diplomats of their success in getting Iran to agree to a formula to reduce the threat from its nuclear program, what was agreed to in the end was little different than what Iran had offered to John Kerry in 2011.

These were negotiations in which Iran was always in the driver's seat because it knew of the Obama administration's desperation to negotiate a legacy nuclear agreement for the president.

U.S. Surrender on Uranium Enrichment Worsens

The main Obama administration capitulation to Iran to get a nuclear agreement was on uranium enrichment. Iran stood firm on its "right" to enrich through the nuclear talks and was offered more and more generous offers by the United States on how large its enrichment program could be in a final agreement.

For example, the *New York Times* reported in November 2014 that the Obama administration proposed limiting Iran to 1,500 operational first-generation IR-1 uranium centrifuges and banning the use of more advanced centrifuges. The article said negotiators also were exploring allowing Iran to keep as many as 4,500 first-generation centrifuges if it agreed to send much of its reactor-grade uranium to Russia "or take other offsetting steps."[82]

According to the Times article, Iran had at the time about 10,000 operational centrifuges and another 9,000 that were nonoperational. Obama administration officials claimed the purpose of these proposals was to keep Iran at least a year away from being able to construct a nuclear weapon which would give the United States and its allies time to respond if Iran decided to move ahead and begin making a bomb.

I explained in Chapter 8 that the Obama administration politicized intelligence estimates on when Iran could produce enough weapons-grade enriched uranium for a nuclear bomb. The administration knew from U.S. intelligence agencies that Iran was two to three months away from producing enough fuel for a nuclear weapon when the JPA was announced in November 2013 but falsely said it was over a year away to discourage Congress from passing new sanctions. A year later, Obama officials said Iran was two to three months away to justify their nuclear deal to keep Iran a year away from a bomb.

U.S. offers to allow Iran to continue to enrich came after Iranian Supreme Leader Ayatollah Ali Khamenei said in July 2014 that Iran would need 190,000 centrifuges. His diplomats had previously been pushing for 50,000. While both figures were unrealistic, they represented Iran's aggressive negotiating tactics.

The *New York Times* reported in February 2015 that the United States raised the number of centrifuges that Iran could keep to 6,500 IR-1 centrifuges if they were re-designed to produce less enriched uranium.[83]

The final number announced in the JCPOA was 6,104 operational IR-1s of which Iran would be allowed to enrich with 5,060 for ten years at the Natanz facility. Uranium could be enriched up to 3.67% U-235. Enriched UF6 over 300 kg would be swapped on the international market for an equivalent amount of natural uranium. Iran would not destroy the rest of its centrifuges; they would be disassembled and put in storage. About two-thirds of Iran's advanced centrifuges at Fordow and all advanced centrifuges at Natanz would be put in storage. Iran also would be allowed to continue limited R&D of advanced centrifuge designs.

Robert Einhorn, who served as a State Department Special Advisor for Nonproliferation and Arms Control during the Obama administration and was a member of the U.S. delegation to the nuclear talks, said in a January 2015 article how U.S concessions on uranium enrichment grew and grew throughout the negotiations:

> The United States has made substantial concessions on the enrichment issue, first moving from a ban on enrichment to allowing a small enrichment program and later from a small number of centrifuges to a significantly higher number. It also agreed that once the agreement expires, Iran would be free to proceed with its enrichment program in a manner and pace of its own choosing.[84]

Obama officials portrayed the JCPOA's provisions on uranium enrichment as a major diplomatic achievement that reduced the threat from Iran's nuclear program by keeping it at least one year away from a nuclear weapon for ten years by reducing Iran's enriched uranium stockpile by 98% and cutting its centrifuges by two-thirds. However, many experts challenged the logic of an agreement to restrict Iran's nuclear program that allowed Tehran to continue to enrich uranium. Olli Heinonen, a senior fellow at Harvard University's Belfer Center for Science and International Affairs and a former deputy director general for safeguards at the International Atomic Energy Agency, told *Business Insider* in February 2015 that "there's no technical reason" for Iran to possess 5,000 centrifuges.[85]

The *Business Insider* article cited three possible reasons why Iran would keep enriching uranium after a nuclear deal: (1) securing its enriched uranium stocks for civilian reactors, (2) maintaining its mastery of the nuclear fuel cycle, and (3) remaining on the threshold of a nuclear weapons capability (or actually obtaining it) so as to further project its power throughout the region. The article noted that only the last reason requires the number of centrifuges Iran was asking for and what U.S. negotiators were reportedly willing to give, believed at the time to be about 5,000.

Other experts raised similar concerns about the wisdom of allowing Iran to enrich uranium while a nuclear agreement was in effect. Former CIA deputy director Michael Morell told Charlie Rose in February 2015, "If you are going to have a nuclear weapons program, 5,000 [centrifuges] is pretty much the number you need."[86] Israeli prime minister Benjamin Netanyahu made a similar statement in September 2014 when he told MSNBC's Andrea Mitchell in an October 2014 interview that Iran's centrifuges "are only good for one thing: to make bomb-grade material."

Washington Free Beacon writer Adam Kredo wrote in a June 30, 2015 article that Pakistan secured nuclear weapons with only 3,000 centrifuges and cited these concerns by Chris Griffin, Executive Director of the Foreign Policy Initiative, on allowing Iran to enrich as part of a final nuclear agreement:

> Iran is poised to walk away from Vienna with more centrifuges than North Korea has ever been known to possess and a U.S.-endorsed R&D program to improve their efficiency. For talks that began with U.S. officials insisting that Iran dismantle its enrichment capability, that outcome will mark a resounding collapse.[87]

Iran's Strategy in the Nuclear Talks

The Obama administration's concessions to Iran on uranium enrichment and other issues resulted from its inability and/or unwillingness to counter Iran's strategy of refusing to yield on its "red lines" for a nuclear deal while also pushing for more concessions. These red lines included Iran's insistence that it had the right under the NPT to enrich uranium, its refusal to give up its uranium enrichment centrifuges and its insistence that the IAEA's PMD "file" be closed. These and other Iranian red lines were depicted in the below graphic tweeted by the Iranian government on October 12, 2014

Figure 6: Iranian government Twitter post on its "red lines" in the nuclear talks

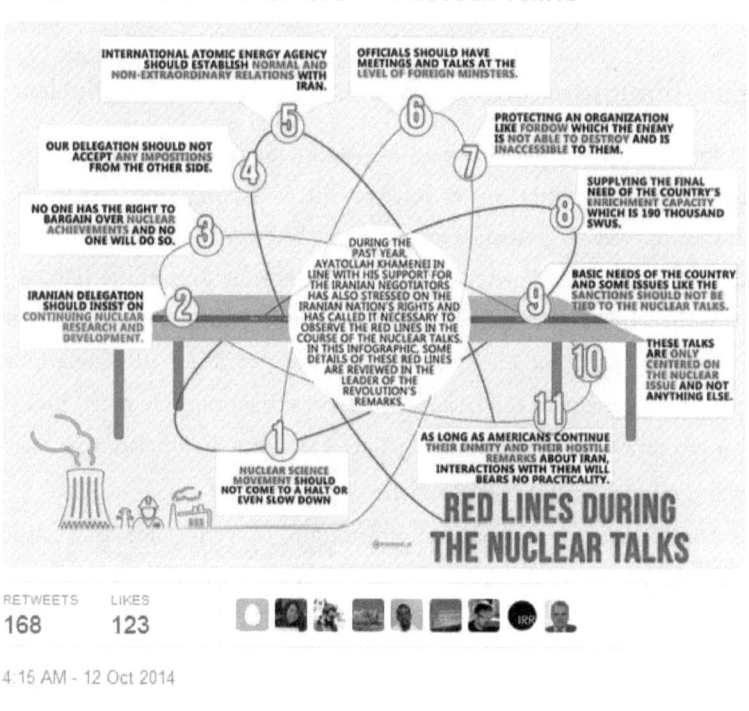

It is remarkable how the JCPOA reflects the above Iranian red lines. These included restricting the talks to the nuclear issue. For this reason, there was no link to Iran's sponsorship of terrorism and its missile program was excluded from the nuclear deal.

Iran also insisted on continuing nuclear R&D. As a result, it will develop advanced uranium centrifuges while the JCPOA is in effect.

Iran demanded normal relations with the International Atomic Energy Agency. This seemed to occur in January 2016 and probably resulted in a secret agreement between the IAEA and Iran to significantly cut the amount of detail in IAEA reports on Iran's nuclear program.

Iran also demanded to retain its Fordow enrichment facility even though Western states previously had called for it to be dismantled. Although Iran agreed to put two-thirds of Fordow's centrifuges into storage and cease uranium enrichment at this facility, it remains intact. One-third of Fordow's centrifuges will operate while the JCPOA is in effect to enrich materials other than uranium for use as medical isotopes.

Obama Administration Acts as "Iran's Lawyer" in the Nuclear Talks

Lee Smith, a senior editor at the Weekly Standard and a senior fellow at the Hudson Institute, wrote in a July 6, 2016 *Tablet* article that the Obama administration was so desperate to get a nuclear agreement with Iran that it had effectively become Iran's lawyer to argue away its violations of the JPA. In addition to dismissing Iran's advanced centrifuge testing, Smith noted that Iran tried to acquire nuclear parts for illicit nuclear activities while the JPA was in effect and refused to cooperate with the IAEA's PMD investigation. He noted that since these issues were excluded from the JPA, State Department officials could declare that Iran was not in technical violation of the JPA.[88]

Smith said the Obama administration lawyering for Iran also included changing the rules on the JPA so Iranian violations would not be violations. Smith wrote:

> The Iranians also violated the JPA by busting through the 1 million barrels per day monthly limit that the agreement puts on their energy exports. The State Department used to rationalize this violation by predicting that in the subsequent month Iran's exports would drop, thereby balancing out the average of their monthly exports. But as it became clear that the monthly exports were

not ever going to balance out, the administration argued that Iran wasn't really cheating because the JPA has a loophole for condensates.

Under the JPA, Iran was supposed to convert all newly produced LEU hexafluoride into uranium dioxide, but a recent IAEA report shows that Iran has converted only 9 percent of it. As a report from the Institute for Science and International Security explains, "When it became clear that Iran could not meet its commitment to convert the LEU into uranium dioxide, the United States revised its criteria for Iran meeting its obligations," and an administration official reasoned that this was okay because the uranium had been transformed into another form of the oxide.[89]

Smith also accused the Obama administration of politicizing and withholding intelligence on Iran's compliance with the JPA, noting that although the Iran, North Korea and Syria Nonproliferation Act requires the State Department to file reports every six months on efforts by these three countries to acquire WMDs and ballistic missiles, as of July 2016, there had not been a report since December. 2014 and this report covered violations from 2011. Smith quoted a General Accountability Office report that said that the Obama administration's foot-dragging on these reports was motivated by "a variety of political concerns, such as international negotiations and relations with countries involved in transfers." Smith wrote that the Obama administration also refused to turn over a Pentagon report showing that Iran was continuing to develop ballistic missile technology to avoid upsetting Iran and the nuclear talks.

Smith claimed in his article that the White House, according to some former officials, put so much political pressure on CIA analysts that they were in an "impossible position regarding analysis of Iran's nuclear program."

A presentation on the Iran deal at a conference for CIA retirees that I attended at CIA headquarters in August 2015 confirmed for me Smith's claim that Agency analysts had been pressured to distort their analysis to support the Obama administration's nuclear diplomacy with Iran. At this conference, a senior CIA WMD analyst gave a presentation about the nuclear deal with Iran that sounded like a sales presentation written by the White House. It had no mention of the many controversial aspects of the agreement that were being debated in Congress and repeated some of the misrepresentations of nuclear science on uranium enrichment and plutonium production that had been put out by the National Security Council to sell the nuclear deal to reporters. Several former agency officers who worked in the arms control field who I spoke with after this presentation were quite upset that this senior agency officer would present such a biased briefing that suggested CIA was promoting the Obama administration's Iran policy instead of providing objective and nonpolitical analysis.

Smith also alleged in his article that the United States and other Western powers were withholding intelligence on Iranian sanctions violations from a UN sanctions committee. Smith wrote that a UN panel suggested that Western governments made "a political decision... to refrain from reporting to avoid a possible negative impact on ongoing negotiations." This included intelligence on North Korea's shipping ballistic missile technology to Iran which Smith claims was briefed to President Obama but kept secret from the United Nations.

Washington Free Beacon reporter Bill Gertz said in an April 15, 2015 article that North Korea sent more than two shipments of missile parts to Iran between September 2014 and April 2015. Gertz said the Obama administration suppressed intelligence on these transfers which appeared to violate United Nations sanctions on both countries.[90]

Even more troubling was a claim by Amir Hossein Motaghi, an Iranian journalist and top media aide to Iranian President Hassan Rouhani who defected and sought political asylum in Switzerland in March 2015. According to Motaghi, U.S. diplomats at the Iran nuclear talks "are mainly there to speak on Iran's behalf with other members of the P5+1 countries and convince them of a deal." Motaghi said he defected because he no longer saw any point in his profession in a country whose government told him what to write.[91]

Motaghi's claim about U.S. delegates speaking on Iran's behalf at the nuclear talks and pressuring other nations – probably mainly the UK, Germany and France – tracks with other information that the negotiations were led and pre-cooked by the United States. His claim also debunked a frequent defense by Obama officials and their supporters that the Iran talks and the JCPOA represented a true multilateral exercise and were not essentially negotiations between Washington and Tehran.

Motaghi confirmed that the JCPOA really is the Obamabomb deal.

I believe the above reports are strong evidence of Iranian cheating that disprove claims made by Obama officials when the JCPOA was announced that Iran fully cooperated with the JPA during the 2014-2015 talks. I also believe there is compelling evidence that the Obama administration did everything possible to cover-up and explain away reports of Iranian cheating during these talks.

The Nuclear Talks, Iraq, Syria and ISIS

Although the nuclear talks supposedly were limited to the Iran nuclear program and no other issue, they also included, possibly only on the sidelines, discussions of the United States partnering with Iran to defeat ISIS in Iraq and Syria. Although Obama officials portrayed these offers as attempts by the United States to change Iran's behavior and convince it to agree to a nuclear agreement, I believe it is more likely Iran used the prospect of partnering with the United States to fight ISIS as another way to pressure U.S. negotiators to agree to a nuclear agreement on Tehran's terms.

Discussions by U.S. negotiators with their Iranian counterparts on this issue were consistent with the radical policies of President Obama who, as explained earlier, gave many indications that he wanted Iran to play a more prominent role in the Middle East. I believe his assumption was that if this happened, Iran would become a more responsible regional player.

According to the *Wall Street Journal*, in October 2014 President Obama sent a secret message to Iranian Supreme Leader Khamenei on how the United States and Iran might work together fighting ISIS in Iraq and Syria if a nuclear agreement could be reached. This letter was extraordinary since it reportedly said that U.S. military operations in Syria and Iraq are not aimed at weakening Iran or its allies, including the Assad regime in Syria. This gave a green light to Iran to expand its role in Iraq and Syria and probably further angered America's allies about Obama's Middle East policy.

Iranian officials probably regarded these offers by the United States and President Obama's letter as an incredible windfall that would allow them to advance their goals of increasing their nation's power and influence in the region with the blessing, if not the assistance of, the United States. I believe Iran's savvy chief negotiator, Foreign Minister Zarif, carefully encouraged discussions of this issue with the U.S. delegation. As a result, it probably became an Iranian inducement to the United States to agree to a nuclear deal on Iran's terms.

This diversion during the nuclear talks had other consequences. By highlighting the weakness and indecisiveness of the Obama Administration's policy toward Iraq and Syria, these discussions, combined with a raft of Obama policy failures in the Middle East, probably encouraged Iran and Russia to significantly increase their presence in Syria in 2015. This propped up the Assad government to such an extent that there is no longer a reasonable prospect of removing him from power. The Obama administration's talks with Iran about partnering against ISIS hurt America's credibility with its regional allies and probably will benefit efforts by Russia to expand its influence in the region, possibly by establishing a new Russia-Iraq-Syria-Iran regional axis.

Last Minute Backtracking By Tehran

Negotiators announced on April 2, 2015 that they had agreed to a framework for a nuclear deal, with Iran agreeing to limit its nuclear stockpile and enrichment capacity and the United States and European Union agreeing to lift nuclear-related sanctions. However, some issues remained unresolved. As the talks approached their conclusion, Iran threw a wrench into the works by backing away from some of the commitments it had made.

One major obstacle concerned Iran's ballistic missile program. The exclusion of ballistic missiles from the nuclear deal would contradict earlier Obama administration claims on what a final nuclear agreement would cover. It also would be controversial because ballistic missiles are considered by most arms control experts as one of three legs of a nuclear weapons program. (These legs are nuclear fuel production, creating a nuclear warhead and a nuclear weapons delivery system, which for all nuclear weapons states is ballistic missiles.) It is worth noting that Iran is the only nation in history that does not have a nuclear-weapons program but has developed missiles with ranges of 2,000 kilometers or more.

Iran's missile program is a grave concern for other reasons. Iran has the largest and most diverse ballistic missile arsenal in the Middle East. Tehran has launched rockets that it claims are space-launch vehicles but most Western experts believe were actually launches to develop ICBMs to carry nuclear warheads as far as the United States and Europe. In March 2005, the *Wall Street Journal* reported that the United States had intelligence indicting indicating Iran planned to adapt a Shahab-3 medium-range missile (estimated range: 900 to 1,200 miles) to deliver a "black box" that U.S. experts believe was almost certainly a nuclear warhead.[92] (This information was part of the "Laptop Documents" discussed in Chapter 5.)

It was reported in early June 2015 that due to demands by Iran, the Obama administration agreed to keep discussions of ballistic missiles out of the nuclear talks and a final nuclear agreement. Administration officials insisted, however, that they would press Iran on this issue outside of the nuclear agreement.[93]

But this was not the end of this issue. In the final two weeks before the announcement of the JCPOA, Iran insisted that all U.N. sanctions on arms and ballistic missile related trade with Iran be lifted as part of a final deal. Russia and China reportedly supported this demand.

There also were last minute differences on when sanctions would be lifted (Iran wanted them lifted immediately, the U.S. said gradually); whether Iran could continue nuclear research and development while a final deal was in effect; IAEA access to military sites, and resolving PMD questions. These issues were resolved in Iran's favor.

On June 11, 2015 the Middle East Media Research Institute (MEMRI) released a report on last minute concessions offered by the Obama administration to break a deadlock on access to military sites and the PMD issue.[94]

With the clock ticking down on a June 30 deadline for a nuclear agreement, these 11th hour demands became a political problem for President Obama who said in April 2015 that Iran had agreed to "the most robust and intrusive inspections and transparency regime ever negotiated for any nuclear program in history." Deputy National Security Adviser Ben Rhodes said the nuclear agreement would allow "anytime, anywhere inspections of any and every Iranian facility."[95] (Rhodes in July 2015 disputed he ever promised "anytime, anywhere" inspections.[96] Wendy Sherman dismissed this concept in July 2015 as "a rhetorical flourish."[97])

Several U.S. organizations, including the Center for Security Policy, the American Israel Public Affairs Committee, the Jewish Institute for National Security Affairs and the bipartisan Iran Task Force made anytime, anyplace inspections and resolving PMD questions red lines for a nuclear agreement with Iran. French Foreign Minister Laurent Fabius said in May 2015 that France would not sign off on a nuclear deal if Tehran ruled out inspections of military sites.

According to the MEMRI report, the Obama administration proposed the following to resolve the deadlock over inspections of Iranian military facilities, undeclared nuclear sites and past nuclear weapons-related work:

- The United States proposed to close the IAEA's PMD dossier and forego actual IAEA inspections of suspect Iranian nuclear facilities.

- Instead, the IAEA would conduct token inspections of a handful of nuclear sites – including two military sites – and question several senior Iranian military officials.

- Inspections of Iranian nuclear sites after the token inspections would be limited to declared facilities.

- Undeclared and suspect nuclear weapons sites will be monitored through intelligence means.

MEMRI sourced its report to statements cited in the Iranian press by Iranian Deputy Foreign Minister/head nuclear negotiator Abbas Araghchi and Hamid Baidinejad, another Iranian nuclear negotiator. Arachchi reportedly said the Iranian negotiating team agreed to the proposed U.S concession but it was subsequently rejected by Supreme Leader Khamenei and triggered harsh criticism of Iranian officials in the so-called pragmatic camp.

Baidinejad claimed the Iranian negotiating team rejected the proposed U.S. concession but agreed to an American request to present it to Khamenei anyway who rejected it outright.

MEMRI said CIA Director John Brennan reportedly was secretly dispatched to Israel in early June to convince Israeli officials (and EU officials via Israel) that remote intelligence monitoring – probably by satellite – of Iranian PMD-related sites was sufficient to address PMD issues and actual physical inspections of these sites therefore could be waived.

These proposed U.S. concessions were worrisome since they would have allowed Iran to shield military and undeclared sites from IAEA inspectors. Obviously, if Iran was engaged in nuclear weapons work, it would not be conducted at declared sites. Moreover, given the poor track record of U.S. intelligence agencies monitoring and discovering covert nuclear facilities in Iran and North Korea, the idea that intelligence was an adequate replacement for inspections of military and suspect nuclear sites is absurd.

Obama officials did not confirm the MEMRI report but there were press reports of other U.S. efforts to resolve these last-minute issues. Congress learned in late July that the Obama administration resolved these issues through secret side deals between the IAEA and Iran. Although the Iranian government reportedly rejected the U.S. offer described in the MEMRI report, I discuss in Chapter 15 that these issues were instead addressed in secret side deals between the IAEA and Iran that Obama officials claimed they had not read.

Weeks before the JCPOA was announced, there was confusion over whether the PMD issue would be included in the nuclear agreement after Secretary Kerry made a statement during a June 16, 2015 State Department press conference that seemed to dismiss this issue in an exchange with Michael Gordon of the *New York Times*.

> QUESTION: Sir, I'm Michael Gordon, *New York Times*. You mentioned that possible military dimensions, which is the term of art for suspected nuclear design work and testing of nuclear components, has to be addressed as part of a prospective Iran agreement. Do these concerns need to be fully resolved before sanctions are eased or released or removed or suspended on Iran as part of that agreement? Is that a core principle or is that also negotiable? Thank you.
>
> SECRETARY KERRY: Michael, the possible military dimensions, frankly, gets distorted a little bit in some of the discussion, in that we're not fixated on Iran specifically accounting for what they did at one point in time or another. We know what they did. We have no doubt. We have absolute knowledge with respect to the certain military activities they were engaged in.
>
> What we're concerned about is going forward. It's critical to us to know that going forward, those activities have been stopped, and that we can account for that in a legitimate way. That clearly is one of the requirements in our judgment for what has to be achieved in order to have a legitimate agreement. And in order to have an agreement to trigger any kind of material significant sanctions relief, we would have to have those answers.[98]

Kerry's comment about the U.S. having "absolute knowledge" of Iran's nuclear weapons-related activities seemed to confirm the MEMRI report's claim that CIA Director Brennan had been dispatched to convince Israeli and EU officials that remote U.S. intelligence monitoring of PMD-related sites was sufficient and inspections of these sites could be waived. In her *Washington Post* blog "Right Turn," Jennifer Rubin described former CIA Director Michael Hayden's rejection of Kerry's "absolute knowledge" claim:

> Former CIA chief Michael Hayden says Kerry's newest position is indefensible. "I'd like to see the DNI or any intelligence office repeat that word for me. They won't. What he is saying is that we don't care how far they've gotten with weaponization. We're betting the farm on our ability to limit the production of fissile material." Now, if they want to make that bet, they can, but the administration should level with us and not insist revelations of PMDs are unimportant. Instead, Hayden says, "He's pretending we have perfect knowledge about something that was an incredibly tough intelligence target while I was director and I see nothing that has made it any easier.[99]

After sharp criticism of his PMD statement to the *New York Times* reporter, Kerry appeared to backtrack a few days later. Reuters reported on June 25, 2015 that

Kerry called Iranian Foreign Minister Zarif to tell him that Tehran must answer questions about whether its past atomic research was arms-related if it waned a nuclear deal.[100] The Reuters report quoted an unnamed Western source who said Kerry told Zarif the PMD issue must be resolved in the negotiations. However, Reuters also cited two other unnamed Western officials who "were not persuaded by the State Department denial."

The final weeks of the Iran talks were very tense. Iran's last-minute demands angered U.S. negotiators and reportedly led to shouting matches between American and Iranian representatives. Secretary of State Kerry said on several occasions that the United States was prepared to walk away from the talks if Iran did not compromise. President Obama said that the United States would not wait forever for a nuclear agreement. Iranian Foreign Minister Zarif said his nation would not back away from its demands and was in no hurry to strike an agreement. These differences created a sense of drama before the JCPOA was announced on July 14, 2015 and caused several self-imposed U.S. deadlines for a deal to be extended.

Despite this supposed drama, Iran knew there was no chance the United States would walk away from the nuclear talks and used the Obama administration's desperation for an agreement to extract additional concessions in the final weeks before the nuclear agreement was announced. This followed a pattern in all of the nuclear talks held between 2012 and 2015 of Iran refusing to yield on its key demands and exploiting U.S. weakness to dictate a nuclear agreement on its terms.

10. The Obamabomb Deal is Reached

President Barack Obama announces the Joint Comprehensive Plan of Action, July 14, 2015, with Vice President Joe Biden in the background.

The culmination of President Obama's efforts to reach a legacy nuclear agreement with Iran was finally reached with the announcement of the Joint Comprehensive Plan of Action (JCPOA) on July 14, 2016. The agreement was announced in triumphant speeches by American, Iranian, European and IAEA officials.

In the first of these speeches, European Union foreign policy chief Federica Mogherini said "today is an historic day" and "we are creating the conditions for building trust." She added that under the agreement, Iran "under no circumstance" will obtain or build nuclear weapons.

In a White House press conference, President Obama said about the JCPOA:

> Today, after two years of negotiations, the United States, together with our international partners, has achieved something that decades of animosity have not: a comprehensive long term deal with Iran that will prevent it from obtaining a nuclear weapon. This deal demonstrates that American diplomacy can bring about real and meaningful change – change that makes our country and the world safer and more secure.

This deal meets every single one of the bottom lines that we established when we achieved a framework earlier this spring. Every pathway to a nuclear weapon is cut off. And the inspection and transparency regime necessary to verify that objective will be put in place. Because of this deal, Iran will not produce the highly enriched uranium and weapons-grade plutonium that form the raw materials necessary for a nuclear bomb.

Secretary of State John Kerry added in a similar speech:

Iran's total stockpile of enriched uranium – which today is equivalent to almost 12,000 kilograms of UF6 – will be capped at just 300 kilograms for the next 15 years – an essential component of expanding our breakout time. Two-thirds of Iran's centrifuges will be removed from nuclear facilities along with the infrastructure that supports them. And once they're removed, the centrifuges will be – and the infrastructure, by the way – will be locked away and under around-the-clock monitoring by the International Atomic Energy Agency.

. . . So when this deal is implemented, the two uranium paths Iran has towards fissile material for a weapon will be closed off.

. . . But this agreement is not only about what happens to Iran's declared facilities. The deal we have reached also gives us the greatest assurance that we have had that Iran will not pursue a weapon covertly.

Figure 7: Timeline of the JCPOA

July 14, 2016, Finalization Day	Announcement of agreement.
July 20, 2015	UN Security Council Resolution 2231 passes endorsing agreement.
August 15, 2015	Iran to answer IAEA's PMD questions.
October 19, 2016 Adoption Day	Deal officially comes into force. Iran begins implementing its commitments. Other parties prepare to lift sanctions on Implementation Day. Iran to answer IAEA's PMD follow-up questions.
December 15, 2015	IAEA to vote on final assessment of PMD issues. It votes to close the file on this matter.
January 18, 2016 Implementation Day	After IAEA declared Iran met its commitments to roll back part of its nuclear program, most U.S., EU and UN sanctions are lifted. Iran gets $150 billion in sanctions relief.
October 2020	UN Conventional arms sanctions lifted. (Could be earlier)
October 2023 Transition Day	UN missile sanctions lifted. Iran to ratify Additional Protocol. EU lifts remaining sanctions. U.S. lifts remaining non-terrorism-related sanctions. (Could be earlier)
October 2025 Termination Day	UN Security Council no longer seized of Iran nuclear issue. Restrictions on Iranian uranium enrichment are lifted. (Some requirements expire later. Limits on enrichment to 3.67% U-235 and enrichment at the Fordow facility extend to 2030.)

Key Provisions of the JCPOA

Uranium Enrichment: Iran Keeps Enriching With 5,060 Centrifuges

Iran will continue enriching uranium with 5,060 centrifuges under the JCPOA and will conduct limited R&D on advanced centrifuges. The heavily-fortified Fordow enrichment facility will remain open and will enrich materials other than uranium with one-third of its centrifuges. Unused centrifuges will be disassembled and put in storage. Iran agreed to send all of its enriched uranium except for 300 kg out of the country in exchange for an equivalent amount of uranium ore.

- Iran will reduce the number of its uranium enrichment centrifuges from about 19,000 installed as of July 2015 to 6,104 installed under the deal, with only 5,060 of these enriching uranium for 10 years. All 6,104 centrifuges will be IR-1 first-generation centrifuges. Most advanced centrifuges will be put in storage. Iran can expand uranium enrichment after 10 years, remove centrifuges from storage and resume enrichment with them.

- Iran will not use its IR-2, IR-4, IR-5, IR-6, or IR-8 advanced centrifuge models to produce enriched uranium for ten years.

- Iran will engage in limited research and development with advanced centrifuges. For ten years, enrichment and enrichment research and development will be limited to ensure a breakout timeline of at least one year. After eight and a half years. Iran may begin testing up to 30 of its most advanced centrifuges.

- Iran agreed to not enrich uranium over 3.67% U-235 for 15 years.

- Iran has agreed to reduce its current stockpile of about 10,000 kg of low-enriched uranium (LEU) to 300 kg of 3.67 percent LEU for 15 years. However, enriched uranium in fabricated fuel assemblies "from Russia or other sources for use in Iran's nuclear reactors will not be counted" against this limit. The words "other sources" have not been explained.

- IAEA inspections of Iran's uranium supply chain will last for 25 years.

- All excess centrifuges and enrichment infrastructure will be placed in IAEA monitored storage and will be used only as replacements for operating centrifuges and equipment.

- Iran agreed not to build new facilities for the purpose of enriching uranium for 15 years.

- The heavily-fortified Fordow enrichment facility will remain open. Iran agreed to convert this facility to a nuclear, physics and technology research center. Iran was allowed to keep 1,044 of its 2,710 centrifuges at Fordow. Removed centrifuges were placed in storage; remaining centrifuges will enrich materials other than uranium for use as medical isotopes. Iran agreed not to enrich uranium or conduct research and development associated with uranium enrichment at Fordow for 15 years.

These provisions contradict President Obama's promises to the American people about what must be in a nuclear agreement with Iran since they leave Iran with a large uranium enrichment infrastructure. For example, Mr. Obama said when campaigning for president in 2007, "the world must work to stop Iran's uranium-enrichment program." In December 2013, Obama said at a speech the Brookings Institution: "They don't need to have an underground, fortified facility like Fordow in order to have a peaceful nuclear program."[101]

Iran will operate 5,060 centrifuges for the first 10 years of the JCPOA and can expand enrichment with more centrifuges after 10 years without giving a reason – it simply needs to provide notification to the IAEA. None of Iran's enrichment technology will be destroyed or removed from the country.

Advanced centrifuges pose a significant nuclear proliferation threat since their improved efficiency will allow Iran to establish more efficient, covert enrichment facilities that will be hard to detect since they employ substantially fewer centrifuge machines. By allowing Iran to enrich uranium and continue centrifuge R&D, the JCPOA enables Iran to shorten the timeline to produce nuclear weapons fuel by increasing its expertise in centrifuge enrichment.

President Obama conceded that Iran's uranium enrichment program could allow Iran's nuclear weapons program to make major gains while the JCPOA in is effect when he told NPR in April 2015 that Iran's breakout time to a nuclear weapon "would have shrunk almost down to zero" in "year 13, 14, 15" of the nuclear agreement.[102]

Figure 8: July 2015 White House graphic promoting the JCPOA

THE U.S. JUST SECURED A DEAL THAT ACHIEVES WHAT WE ASKED FOR:
PREVENTING IRAN FROM OBTAINING A NUCLEAR WEAPON

✓ Increase the time it would take Iran to acquire enough material for 1 bomb from 2-3 months to at least 1 year

✓ Reduce Iran's stockpiles of enriched uranium

✓ Reduce the number of Iran's installed centrifuges by two-thirds

✓ Prevent Iran from producing weapons-grade plutonium

✓ Track Iran's nuclear activities with robust transparency and inspections

WH.GOV/IRAN-DEAL   #IranDeal

Inspections and Transparency

The JCPOA, according to Obama officials, has the most comprehensive and intrusive verification regime ever negotiated for an arms control agreement that will ensure every avenue to an Iranian nuclear weapon is blocked and the international community will have ample warning if Iran decides to engage in covert nuclear weapons work. A close examination of the verification provisions of the JCPOA raises questions as to whether the IAEA will really have the access it needs to ensure Iran's nuclear program remains peaceful.

- The IAEA will have regular access to all of Iran's declared nuclear facilities, including Iran's enrichment facility at Natanz and its former enrichment facility at Fordow.

- IAEA inspectors will have access to the declared supply chain that supports Iran's nuclear program. The Obama administration claims transparency and inspections mechanisms will closely monitor materials and/or components to prevent diversion to a secret nuclear program. Little is known, however, about undeclared nuclear equipment and possible secret stockpiles of parts and supplies for this equipment. Undeclared manufacturing workshops could use undeclared nuclear equipment and supplies to conduct secret nuclear weapons R&D while the JCPOA is in force.

- IAEA inspectors will have access to uranium mines and continuous surveillance at uranium mills, where Iran produces uranium yellowcake, for 25 years.

- IAEA inspectors will conduct surveillance of Iran's centrifuge rotors and bellows production and storage facilities for 20 years. Iran's centrifuge manufacturing base will be frozen and under IAEA surveillance.

- All centrifuges and enrichment infrastructure removed from Fordow and Natanz will be placed under continuous monitoring by the IAEA.

- A dedicated procurement channel for Iran's nuclear program is being established to monitor and approve the supply, sale, and transfer to Iran of certain nuclear-related and dual use materials and technology. However, in an April 21, 2016 memo, the Institute for Science and International Security raised concerns about the Procurement Channel, contending that the Fordow enrichment facility and the modernization of the Arak heavy-water reactor have been exempted from this channel.[103] The Institute report also said Russia appears to have been playing a disruptive role concerning the Procurement Channel that is not being effectively countered.

- Iran agreed to implement the Additional Protocol of the IAEA on a voluntary basis which in theory will give the IAEA greater access to Iranian nuclear sites. Iran will not seek formal ratification of this agreement for eight years. As discussed in the last chapter, Iran made a similar provisional agreement to abide by the Additional Protocol in in the Tehran declaration of 2003, a commitment it broke in 2006.

- Iran agreed to implement Modified Code 3.1 of its IAEA Safeguards agreement requiring early notification to the IAEA of construction of new nuclear facilities. Iran agreed to implement Code 3.1 in 2003 but backed out of this agreement in 2007.

- A procedure was created to give the IAEA access to investigate suspicious nuclear sites. Under this process, a 24-day clock starts when the IAEA requests access to a suspect nuclear site. Iran must respond within 14 days. If it does not, a commission formed by the JCPOA has seven days to approve a plan for IAEA access to the site. Iran then has three days to comply. After this point, the Security Council can "snap back" sanctions within two months if Iran fails to grant the IAEA access.

- The Iranian parliament made the JCPOA's verification provisions weaker in October 2015 when it ratified an amended version of the deal containing new language on dismantling Israel's nuclear weapons program, requiring that sanctions under the agreement be cancelled and not suspended, forbidding IAEA inspections of military installations, and barring IAEA interviews of Iranian military officers and scientists. Iran's unwillingness to allow IAEA inspectors inspect military sites was demonstrated when it insisted on severe restrictions on PMD inspection of the Parchin military base which included only permitting Iranians to inspect the site.

- JCPOA language requiring the sharing of intelligence to justify IAEA inspections of suspect Iranian nuclear sites is problematic for two reasons. First, it may create situations where the United States will need to broadly share sensitive intelligence with IAEA officials, P5+1 members and Iran to justify an inspection request. This likely would put U.S. intelligence sources and methods at risk and enable Iran to develop ways to evade detection by American intelligence agencies. Second, providing intelligence reports in support of requests to inspect suspect Iranian nuclear sites likely will lead to extended arguments since Iran and other P-5+1 nations will dispute it for political reasons or because the intelligence is less than definitive, which is often the case.

Many critics believe the JCPOA's procedures for IAEA access to undeclared Iranian nuclear sites will give Iran ample time to hide weapons-related nuclear activities. David Albright, President of the Institute for Science and International Security, said in August 2, 2015 testimony to the Senate Foreign Relations Committee that Iran has extensive experience in hiding nuclear activities and could disguise many small scale nuclear and nuclear-weapon related efforts including high explosive testing related to nuclear weapons, a small centrifuge manufacturing plant or a small centrifuge plant that uses advanced centrifuges.[104]

Former IAEA Inspection Olli Heinonen expressed a similar view, noting in Senate testimony he gave in July 2015 that concealment efforts taken by Iran in 2003 to hide nuclear activities left no traces to be detected through environmental sampling.[105] Based on his belief that Iran will take every precaution to hide possible nuclear weapons-related work from IAEA inspectors, Heinenon concluded in his testimony that "a 24 day adjudicated timeline reduces detection probabilities exactly where the system is weakest: detecting undeclared facilities and materials." Other experts, including Iran sanctions expert Mark Dubowitz, assesses that it will take over two months to "snapback" sanctions because of the time required for adjudication by the JCPOA's Joint Commission and consideration by the UN Security Council.[106]

Bottom line: the JCPOA's inspection regime is very weak and mostly applies to declared facilities and supply chains. Although there is a convoluted mechanism for the IAEA to access undeclared suspect nuclear sites, it is doubtful this procedure will ever be used because Iran has threatened to withdraw from the agreement if it is sanctioned for noncompliance. Iranian officials have placed military facilities off-limits to IAEA inspectors but Western states and the IAEA have not commented on this decision or taken action to reverse it.

Figure 9: July 2015 White House graphic promoting the JCPOA

THE IRAN NUCLEAR DEAL **WILL CUT OFF ALL OF IRAN'S POTENTIAL PATHWAYS TO A BOMB:**

HIGHLY ENRICHED URANIUM AT NATANZ FACILITY — BLOCKED

HIGHLY ENRICHED URANIUM AT FORDOW FACILITY — BLOCKED

WEAPONS-GRADE PLUTONIUM — BLOCKED

COVERT ATTEMPTS TO PRODUCE FISSILE MATERIAL — BLOCKED

WH.GOV/IRAN-DEAL   #IranDeal

The Arak Heavy Water Reactor and Plutonium Production

Obama officials claim the JCPOA closes off Iran's capability to pursue a nuclear weapon through the production of plutonium from the Arak heavy-water reactor. A close examination of the details of JCPOA provisions on this issue suggests these claims are exaggerated and partially false. Although this reactor was disabled per the JCPOA, after it is rebuilt using a new design, Iran will be able to easily reverse the steps taken to limit its production of plutonium.

- Iran agreed to redesign and rebuild its heavy-water research reactor in the city of Arak based on a design agreed to by the P5+1. As part of this agreement, the core of this reactor, which was under construction, was removed and filled with concrete. An Obama administration's fact sheet on the JCPOA says this redesign will ensure the Arak reactor will not produce weapons-grade plutonium. This is misleading since it still will be possible to extract plutonium from the Arak reactor's spent fuel rods after the redesign.

- China and Iran reportedly signed a deal in January 2016 for China to redesign the Arak reactor based on a plan approved by JCPOA parties in

November 2015.[107] Beijing pushed for this deal after the JCPOA was announced and has called for the reactor's construction to be accelerated.

- Iran agreed not to accumulate heavy-water in excess of the needs of the modified Arak reactor, and will sell any remaining heavy water on the international market for 15 years. Iran also agreed not to build any additional heavy water reactors for 15 years. After Iran could not find a buyer for its heavy-water, the Obama administration sparked controversy in April 2016 when it announced that the United States would buy Iran's excess heavy-water. This is discussed in Chapter 20.

- According to the Arms Control Association (ACA), to reduce the plutonium output of the Arak reactor, its power will be cut in half to 20 megawatts and will be fueled with uranium enriched to 3.67% U-235 rather than using natural uranium fuel, the usual fuel for heavy-water reactors.[108] (Due to a peculiarity of nuclear physics, fueling a heavy-water reactor with enriched uranium instead of natural uranium results in it producing substantially less useable plutonium in the reactor's spent fuel rods.) Under these conditions, the ACA claims this reactor will produce about one kg of plutonium per year in its spent fuel rods. (The ACA believes the Arak reactor would produce seven kg per year if not modified which it says is more than enough for one nuclear weapon. The Obama administration claims the unmodified Arak reactor would produce 1-2 nuclear weapons-worth of plutonium per year.) With the modifications, according to the ACA, Iran would have to run the Arak reactor for four years to produce enough plutonium for one nuclear bomb.

- Iran has committed not to build a separation facility for 15 years and never to reprocess spent fuel to extract plutonium, commitments the ACA regards as further safeguards preventing Iran from pursuing the plutonium route to a nuclear weapon. However, Iran's commitment not to build a facility to reprocess plutonium after 15 years is not binding under the JCPOA.

There are drawbacks to this redesign plan that Obama officials have not disclosed. This redesign scheme is the more dangerous of two plans discussed during the nuclear talks and was opposed by the United States and its European allies because it can be easily reversed to make the Arak reactor capable of producing significant amounts of plutonium. Because heavy-water reactors are such a serious proliferation threat, Western states originally called on Iran to support a different redesign to convert this reactor into a light-water reactor, a design which is considered proliferation resistant since it is more difficult to use to produce plutonium. After Iran refused to do this, it was decided to instead cut the power of the Arak reactor and fuel it with enriched uranium. The ACA report concedes that Iran could reconvert this reactor to run on unenriched uranium fuel – a process ACA believes would take about 18 months – and use it to produce enough plutonium for a nuclear weapon every two years. The ACA also believes Iran could produce enough plutonium for a nuclear weapon in about two years by "misusing" this reactor by "short cycling the fuel."

The ACA dismisses the threat from the above scenarios because it believes the IAEA would quickly detect changes in the reactor's operation. Frank von Hippel, a physicist and former science adviser to the White House who helped develop the redesign plan for the Arak reactor, is a strong supporter of the JCPOA and believes that by agreeing to redesign the Arak reactor, Iran decided to abandon the plutonium route to a nuclear weapon.[109]

Bottom Line: the JCPOA temporarily blocks the plutonium route to a nuclear weapon for Iran. But it will also give Iran valuable expertise in operating and constructing this type of nuclear reactor. The Obama administration's claims that this reactor will not produce weapons-grade plutonium are misleading: like the unmodified design, the new design will also leave plutonium in the reactor's spent fuel rods that can be reprocessed into nuclear weapons fuel. This reactor will still pose a significant proliferation risk because modifications can be easily reversed or defeated to produce enough plutonium for a nuclear weapon every two years.

Sanctions Relief

Sanctions relief to Iran under the JCPOA represents a compromise between Tehran's demand that sanctions be lifted immediately when the nuclear deal was approved and the position of the United States and its European allies that sanctions relief be granted gradually based on Iranian compliance. Under this compromise, most U.S. and EU economic sanctions worth about $150 billion were lifted on "Implementation Day," a date reached when the IAEA certified that Iran met certain commitments to comply with the JCPOA. Implementation Day occurred on January 16, 2016. Nuclear-related Security Council sanctions also were lifted on Implementation Day. The JCPOA includes schedules of Iranian individuals and entities from which sanctions are to be lifted. The lists attracted controversy because some of these individuals and entities listed have been designated by the United States and the European Union as terrorists or terrorist organizations.

- All past UN Security Council resolutions on the Iran nuclear issue were lifted simultaneously under the JCPOA on Implementation Day when the IAEA certified that Iran met certain commitments on centrifuges, its enriched-uranium stockpile, the Arak heavy-water reactor and other issues. Most U.S. and EU financial sanctions also were lifted on this day.

- The U.S. and the EU contend that sanctions against Iran have been suspended, not terminated and, if at any time Iran fails to fulfill its commitments, EU, U.S. and UN sanctions will snap back into place. However, there is considerable doubt this will ever happen since the JCPOA notes Iran's position that sanctions have been terminated not suspended and its intention to walk away from the nuclear agreement if any sanctions are imposed or re-imposed. Since this means attempting to snapback sanctions would kill the nuclear deal, it is very unlikely the Obama administration would ever attempt this.

- The JCPOA stipulates that parties to the agreement should only initiate a snapback for "significant non-performance" by another party. This is another win for Iran since it will be difficult to define "significant" Iranian non-performance and there will be a temptation to avoid sanctioning Iran by declaring any Iranian violations as insignificant or accidental. I noted in Chapter 9 that Hudson Institute Senior Fellow Lee Smith accused the Obama administration of being "Iran's lawyer" for its repeated efforts to do this concerning Iranian violations of the JPA in 2014 and 2015.

- UN Security Council resolutions suspended by the JCPOA dealing with transfers of sensitive technologies and activities were to be replaced by a new UN Security Council resolution which endorsed the JCPOA and urged its full implementation. This resolution, UN Security Council Resolution 2231, was approved on July 20, 2015. The Obama administration did not disclose when the JCPOA was announced that the new Security Council resolution's language on missile and conventional arms transfers – which was activated when Iran met the Implementation Day requirements in January 2016 – is considerably weaker than the language in the UN resolutions it replaced and is considered by Iran and Russia to be nonbinding.

- U.S. sanctions on Iran for terrorism, human rights abuses, and ballistic missiles were to remain in place under the JCPOA. However, the Obama administration supported the JCPOA even though under the agreement the EU, in January 2016, lifted sanctions against the Central Bank of Iran and granted it access to the SWIFT system, an international financial messaging service used by banks to facilitate global payment transactions. Iran sanctions expert Mark Dubowitz said in testimony to Congress in July 2015 that regaining access to SWIFT is "the real prize for Iran in the JCPOA sanctions relief package" because SWIFT is the electronic bloodstream of the global financial system.[110]

- The nuclear deal bars the U.S. from implementing "any policy specifically intended to directly and adversely affect the normalization of trade and economic relations with Iran" Under this language, there is no exemption for imposing new U.S. sanctions on Iran for missile tests, terrorism or human rights violations.

- The JCPOA commits the United States to lift state-level and local sanctions on Iran. I discuss in Chapter 20 Obama administration efforts to convince state governments to lift their Iran sanctions and strong resistance to this effort by many state governors.

- Under Security Council 2231 (but not the JCPOA), UN ballistic missile sanctions will be lifted in eight years and UN sanctions on conventional arms transfers will be lifted in five years unless the IAEA makes a "Broader Conclusion" determination that Iran's nuclear program is peaceful. A separate set of U.S. and EU sanctions – some of which are against terrorist organizations and individuals – also will be lifted in eight years or when the IAEA certifies Iran has reached the Broader Conclusion.

- The Broader Conclusion is an IAEA determination that all of a country's nuclear material remains in peaceful activities if the Agency finds that (1) "No indication of the diversion of declared nuclear material from peaceful nuclear activities" and (2) "No indication of undeclared nuclear material or activities." Although broader conclusion determinations usually take several years, there is reason to believe this determination for Iran will be made much faster. The first requirement was certified by the IAEA in 2014. The second requirement is likely to be met fairly quickly since the IAEA Board of Governors voted in December 2015 to close the IAEA's PMD file. As a result, former Iraq arms inspector David Kay has said he believes this determination could be reached as soon as 2016.[111]

- The rules for Iran to reach the Broader Conclusion appeared to have been eased because it will not be required to fully implement and ratify an additional protocol agreement to its IAEA Safeguards Agreement to receive benefits from the JCPOA. The Additional Protocol is an initiative begun by the IAEA in 1993 to strengthen IAEA Safeguards Agreements after secret nuclear weapons programs in Iraq and North Korea exposed weaknesses in these agreements. Former IAEA Chief Inspector Olli Heinonen pointed out in congressional testimony in July 2015 that although the IAEA normally would not declare the Broader Conclusion until after a state implemented and ratified the Additional Protocol, this is not the case for Iran under the JCPOA. Heinonen expressed concern about this arrangement in his testimony when he said: "This is not a matter to easily dismiss as we need to be mindful of potential complications down the road should Iran seek to leverage, pull back, or dilute some of its obligations at some point in time under its 'provisional' status."[112] I agree with Heinonen and note that Iran made a similar provisional agreement to abide by the Additional Protocol in in the Tehran Declaration of 2003 (an agreement negotiated with the EU-3 on the Iranian nuclear program) but broke this commitment in 2006.

Although Iran did not get its way in having sanctions lifted immediately upon the announcement of the nuclear deal, it scored a big win in having all U.S. and EU nuclear sanctions lifted within six months of the agreement's announcement as well as most Security Council sanctions lifted in response to meeting reversible commitments to roll back parts of its nuclear program. As a result, most of the sanctions infrastructure put in place against Iran since 2003, including many non-nuclear sanctions, has been dismantled. It is likely that little of it, especially EU and UN sanctions, can be re-imposed even in the event of gross Iranian violations of the nuclear agreement.

Obama officials cannot credibly claim the new Iran sanctions regime represents a diplomatic victory because key elements of this regime – provisions giving the IAEA access to suspect military sites and the so-called snapback sanctions provisions – lack credibility because the Obama administration will never risk using them and are reserved for instances that represent "significant non-performance," a high standard that will be very difficult to prove. There also are question as to whether UN sanctions on conventional arms and ballistic missiles, even though they have been weakened, could be lifted much sooner than Obama administration officials have claimed.

There are no restrictions on how Iran can spend the funds it receives in sanctions relief – these funds can be spent on Iran's nuclear program, missiles, conventional arms, funding insurgencies, and supporting Syria's Assad regime. Secretary Kerry admitted that Iran will probably spend sanctions relief on terrorism when he told CNBC on January 21, 2016, "I think that some of it will end up in the hands of the IRGC or other entities, some of which are labeled terrorists."[113]

When UN conventional arms sanctions against Iran are lifted in five years or less, there will be no restrictions on Iranian purchases of tanks, armored combat vehicles artillery systems, combat aircraft, attack helicopters, warships, missiles. However, Iran has and continues to violate UN conventional arms sanctions and has made recent arms purchases from Russia and probably other states. This includes a February 2016 report that Iran planned to purchase Sukhoi-30 fighter jets from Russia.[114] Secretary Kerry avoided commenting on this sale at a February 25, 2016 House Foreign Affairs Committee hearing other than saying the administration was "very concerned" and "we'll stay in touch with you."[115] There have been reports that Iran wants to spend $8 billion on Russian weapons in 2016, including Russian tanks which would violate UN arms sanctions.

Bottom Line: The huge value of sanctions lifted in January 2016, which reportedly are worth $150 billion, and the fact that it will be impossible to re-impose most sanctions to their prior level against Iran represent a significant Iranian victory. There were signs in the spring of 2016 that Iran was trying to widen this victory by extracting more concessions from the United States by pressuring the Obama administration to grant it access to the U.S. financial system and dollarized transactions. This is discussed in Chapter 20.

JCPOA Lifts Sanctions from Iranian Terrorists

One of the most controversial aspects of the JCPOA concerns the lifting of sanctions against Iranian terrorist individuals and organizations. These organizations include the Revolutionary Guard (IRGC) Air Force, the IRGC Air Force Al-Ghadir Missile Command, and the IRGC Qods Force, which manages Iranian terrorism worldwide. Sanctions also will be lifted against several individual Iranians designated as terrorists by the United States such as:

- **IRGC commander Qassem Soleimani**, who provided weapons responsible for killing hundreds of U.S. troops during the war in Iraq, plotted to kill the Saudi ambassador to the United States at a Washington, DC restaurant, is now working to sustain Syria's Assad regime and oversees Iran's global terror operations. When the nuclear deal was announced, Secretary Kerry denied Soleimani was on the list of individuals to be relived of sanctions, telling ABC reporter Jonathan Karl: "No he is not, he is not listed there.

That's another Soleimani."[116] Iranian Foreign Minister Zarif agreed and claimed Soleimani had been confused with someone with a similar name.

- **Ahmad Vahidi, a former defense minister and IRGC commander.** Vahidi participated in the 1994 bombing attack on the Jewish community center in Buenos Aires which killed 85 people. Argentina and Interpol have issued arrest warrants against Vahidi for his role in the 1994 bombing. The United States sanctioned Vahidi in 2010 for his ties to Iran's nuclear program.

- **Mohammad Reza Naqdi, an IRGC general.** Naqdi was sanctioned by the United States in 2011 for "serious human rights abuses" related to his "violent response" to the protests that broke out in Iran after the fraudulent June 2009 presidential election. Naqdi has said "erasing Israel off the map" is "nonnegotiable."

- **Mostafa Mohammad Najjar, a former interior minister, defense minister, and IRGC commander.** The United States sanctioned Najjar in 2010 for "sustained and severe violation of human rights in Iran since the June 2009 disputed presidential election."

Iranian and Western officials insisted when the JCPOA was announced in July 2015 that the nuclear deal only concerned Iran's nuclear program and nothing else. Over the next few months, U.S. officials explained this is why the agreement did not address Iran's missile program, the release of U.S. citizens being held illegally by Iran, and any requirement that Iran cease hostile and belligerent behavior such as sponsoring terrorism, meddling in regional disputes and threatening Israel. The JCPOA's provisions lifting sanctions against terrorists contradict the Obama administration's claims that the agreement was solely limited to Iran's nuclear program.

The Iranian terrorists listed above and the names of others listed in annexes to the JCPOA of individuals be relieved of sanctions is one of the most outrageous aspects of the nuclear agreement and a prime example of Iran dictating the terms of this agreement to the United States. Obama officials have been evasive about this issue and have tried to play it down by claiming that although UN and European sanctions against Iranian terrorist entities and persons will be lifted as a result of the nuclear agreement, American sanctions against Iranian terrorists will remain in place. This weak explanation does not absolve Obama officials for going along with an agreement that lifts international sanctions against Iranian terrorists and terrorist organizations, some of whom have the blood of U.S. soldiers on their hands.

The JCPOA and the Possible Military Dimensions of Iran's Nuclear Program

Although Obama officials previously claimed a nuclear deal with Iran would require Iran to come clear on PMD questions, the agreement fell far short of requiring this. Under the JCPOA, Iran was to provide explanations to the IAEA on its PMD questions by August 15, 2015. Iran met this deadline. However, there was no penalty if these answers were incomplete or evasive (which they were.)

Obama officials indicated in November 2015 that the quality of Iran's answers to the IAEA as it conducted a final PMD investigation did not matter – Iran was only required to respond to them. Unnamed senior U.S. officials said during a State Department briefing on October. 17, 2015 ("Adoption Day", a date by which Iran was required to answer the IAEA's follow-up PMD questions) that Iran only had to perform a series of procedural steps to demonstrate its cooperation with the PMD investigation. [117] The unnamed officials said the PMD investigation is not part of the nuclear agreement text and thus has no bearing on whether sanctions against Iran will be lifted. They also said that the quality of the data Iran provided to the IAEA was not important because "the U.S. government has already made its assessment on Iran's past [nuclear] programs." This comment was reminiscent of John Kerry's controversial June 16, 2015 comment to a *New York Times* reporter discussed in Chapter 9 that the United States has "perfect knowledge" about Iran's PMD activities.

The JCPOA acknowledged a separate agreement between the Iran and the IAEA for a short PMD investigation to be wrapped up by December 2015. The JCPOA did not mention secret side deals on the PMD issue that were discovered by Congress in late July 2015 (See Chapter 15) and did not anticipate Iran's noncompliance with the PMD investigation and IAEA findings of nuclear weapons-related activities that continued at least until 2009. (See Chapter 18)

11: Reception of the Obamabomb Deal

This deal does not require Iran to destroy or fully decommission a single uranium enrichment centrifuge. In fact, over half of Iran's currently operating centrifuges will continue to spin at its Natanz facility. The remainder, including more than 5,000 operating centrifuges and nearly 10,000 not yet functioning, will merely be disconnected and transferred to another hall at Natanz, where they could be quickly reinstalled to enrich uranium. And yet we, along with our allies, have agreed to lift the sanctions and allow billions of dollars to flow back into Iran's economy. We lift sanctions, but – even during the first 10 years of the agreement – Iran will be allowed to continue R&D activity on a range of centrifuges – allowing them to improve their effectiveness over the course of the agreement.

Senator Robert Menendez (D-NJ)
Speech at Seton Hall University, August 18, 2015

The Obamabomb Deal was enthusiastically received by the mainstream media and the foreign policy establishment. Most press coverage was very positive, although much of it repeated White House talking points that although the agreement was not perfect, the only alternative was war with Iran. A July 14, 2015 *New York Times* editorial titled, "An Iran Nuclear Deal That Reduces the Chance of War," was typical of this positive media.

> The final deal with Iran announced by the United States and other major world powers does what no amount of political posturing and vague threats of military action had managed to do before. It puts strong, verifiable limits on Iran's ability to develop a nuclear weapon for at least the next 10 to 15 years and is potentially one of the most consequential accords in recent diplomatic history, with the ability not just to keep Iran from obtaining a nuclear weapon but also to reshape Middle East politics. The deal, the product of 20 arduous months of negotiations, would obviously have provided more cause for celebration if Iran had agreed to completely dismantle all of its nuclear facilities. But the chances of that happening were effectively zero, and even if all of Iran's nuclear-related buildings and installations were destroyed, no one can erase the knowledge Iranian scientists have acquired after working on nuclear projects for decades.

Despite strong support for the JCPOA from Obama administration supporters and the mainstream media, the agreement was widely unpopular when it was announced and remains so today. The deal had zero support from congressional Republicans when Congress voted on it in September 2015. It also was opposed by a significant number of congressional Democrats and the American Israel Public Affairs Committee, a powerful and usually bipartisan pro-Israel lobbying group.

Polling showed a majority of the American people strongly opposed the agreement. An August 2015 poll found Americans opposed the deal by a 2-1 margin, with 64% believing President Obama and Secretary Kerry misled the public about the deal.[118] In this poll, 82 percent of U.S. voters–and 74 percent of Democrats–opposed Obama's plan to grant $100 billion in sanctions relief to Iran over the next several months "without approval from Congress." 57% said the deal should be rejected and that it was not too late to re-open negotiations. Only 24% agreed with President Obama and Secretary Kerry who say we have no realistic choice to avoid war.

A September 2015 Pew Research Center poll indicated popular support for the Iran deal had dropped even lower, showing that 49% of Americans disapproved the agreement and only 21% supported it. The Pew poll found that Democratic support for the JCPOA dropped to 42% and Republican support had plunged to 6%.[119]

The agreement attracted harsh bipartisan criticism. Former U.S. Ambassador to the United Nations John Bolton, in an August 5, 2015 *Washington Times* op-ed, raised concerns that the Iran deal would undermine global nuclear nonproliferation.

> First, the negotiations themselves, clearly long headed in the wrong direction, have fueled an already-nascent nuclear-arms race in the Middle East. Saudi Arabia already had contingency plans to buy nuclear weapons directly from Pakistan, or perhaps even for constructive possession. Now, Riyadh has launched its own domestic nuclear programs, for "peaceful purposes," of course. Egypt, Turkey and Jordan have announced similar plans for indigenous nuclear programs and other regional states could follow.

> Moreover, the nuclear proliferation implications extend well beyond the Middle East. Iran's victory in Vienna, which paves its way to nuclear weapons, is also evidence to all other would-be nuclear states. Mr. Obama's concessions to Tehran have effectively shredded the Nuclear Non-Proliferation Treaty, teaching the lesson that, with persistence and a thick skin, almost any country can thwart international counter-proliferation efforts. Sadly, therefore, the odds are high that the number of nuclear weapons states will grow dramatically in the next decades.

> Second, the Iran deal proves yet again that Mr. Obama gives little or no credence to Israel's security concerns, much like the administration's repeatedly failed efforts to force a settlement between Israel and the Palestinians that would endanger Israel's self-defense capabilities. White House rhetoric notwithstanding, Israel is on the verge of being cast adrift by its closest ally.[120]

Senator Chuck Schumer (D-NY), the number two Democrat in the Senate and a strong supporter of President Obama, gave a speech opposing the JCPOA which stressed weaknesses in the agreement's inspection regime.

> In the first ten years of the deal, there are serious weaknesses in the agreement. First, inspections are not "anywhere, anytime"; the 24-day delay before we can inspect is troubling. While inspectors would likely be able to detect radioactive isotopes at a site after 24 days, that delay would enable Iran to escape detection of any illicit building and improving of possible military dimensions (PMD) – the tools that go into building a bomb but don't emit radioactivity.

> Furthermore, even when we detect radioactivity at a site where Iran is illicitly advancing its bomb-making capability, the 24-day delay would hinder our ability to determine precisely what was being done at that site.

> Even more troubling is the fact that the U.S. cannot demand inspections unilaterally. By requiring the majority of the 8-member Joint Commission, and assuming that China, Russia, and Iran will not cooperate, inspections would require the votes of all three European members of the P5+1 as well as the EU representative. It is reasonable to fear that, once the Europeans become entangled in lucrative economic relations with Iran, they may well be inclined not to rock the boat by voting to allow inspections.

> Additionally, the "snapback" provisions in the agreement seem cumbersome and difficult to use. While the U.S. could unilaterally cause snapback of all sanctions, there will be instances where it would be more appropriate to snapback some but not all of the sanctions, because the violation is significant but not severe. A partial snapback of multilateral sanctions could be difficult to obtain, because the U.S. would require the cooperation of other nations. If the U.S. insists on snapback of all the provisions, which it can do unilaterally, and the Europeans, Russians, or Chinese feel that is too severe a punishment, they may not comply.[121]

Senator Robert Menendez (D-NJ) delivered a speech rejecting the JCPOA that faulted the agreement for allowing Iran to continue to enrich uranium.

> This deal does not require Iran to destroy or fully decommission a single uranium enrichment centrifuge. In fact, over half of Iran's currently operating centrifuges will continue to spin at its Natanz facility. The remainder, including more than 5,000 operating centrifuges and nearly 10,000 not yet functioning, will merely be disconnected and transferred to another hall at Natanz, where they could be quickly reinstalled to enrich uranium.

> And yet we, along with our allies, have agreed to lift the sanctions and allow billions of dollars to flow back into Iran's economy. We lift sanctions, but -- even during the first 10 years of the agreement -- Iran will be allowed to continue R&D activity on a range of centrifuges – allowing them to improve their effectiveness over the course of the agreement.

Clearly, the question is: what do we get from this agreement in terms of what we originally sought? We lift sanctions, and -- at year eight – Iran can actually start manufacturing and testing advanced IR-6 and IR-8 centrifuges that enrich up to 15 times the speed of its current models. At year 15, Iran can start enriching uranium beyond 3.67 percent – the level at which we become concerned about fissile material for a bomb. At year 15, Iran will have NO limits on its uranium stockpile.

This deal grants Iran permanent sanctions relief in exchange for only temporary – temporary – limitations on its nuclear program – not a rolling-back, not dismantlement, but temporary limitations. At year ten, the UN Security Council Resolution will disappear along with the dispute resolution mechanism needed to snapback UN sanctions and the 24-day mandatory access provision for suspicious sites in Iran.

The deal enshrines for Iran, and in fact commits the international community to assisting Iran in developing an industrial-scale nuclear power program, complete with industrial scale enrichment. While I understand that this program will be subject to Iran's obligations under the Treaty on the Non-Proliferation of Nuclear Weapons, I think it fails to appreciate Iran's history of deception in its nuclear program and its violations of the NPT.

It will, in the long run, make it much harder to demonstrate that Iran's program is not in fact being used for peaceful purposes because Iran will have legitimate reasons to have advanced centrifuges and a robust enrichment program. We will then have to demonstrate that its intention is dual-use and not justified by its industrial nuclear power program."[122]

House Foreign Affairs Chairman Ed Royce (R-CA) issued a statement raising concerns about the 11th hour U.S. concession to Iran on ballistic missiles to reach this deal and also taking issue with Mr. Obama for questioning the judgement of anyone who criticized the agreement.

The President didn't even try to justify the 11th hour lifting of the restrictions against Iran's intercontinental ballistic program. That's because there is no excuse for this concession, which was counter to the advice of our military and which leaves our homeland threatened.

The President was quick to question the judgment of those criticizing this deal. But the Obama Administration isn't immune to its own misjudgments in this region; hugely underestimating ISIS is one example. And let's not forget, some of the same people who negotiated this deal were involved in the failed agreement with North Korea — an agreement that was hailed at the time with some of the same language President Obama used today. Of course, North Korea now has multiple nuclear weapons.

The President was quick to refer back to the Cold War, but he was wrong to suggest that this agreement could be extended like a U.S.-Soviet arms agreement. When this deal expires, Iran will have an internationally blessed

106

advanced nuclear program able to quickly produce a nuclear weapon. There will be no second deals. Iran will have won.[123]

Royce's Democratic colleague, Congressman Eliot Engel of New York, the top Democrat on the House Foreign Affairs Committee, issued a statement rejecting the JCPOA similar to those by Senators Schumer and Menendez.

> At the outset, I was troubled that Iran was not asked to stop enriching despite the fact that there were several separate UN Security Council resolutions compelling them to do so. I have raised questions and concerns throughout the negotiating phase and review period. The answers I've received simply don't convince me that this deal will keep a nuclear weapon out of Iran's hands, and may in fact strengthen Iran's position as a destabilizing and destructive influence across the Middle East.

> First, I don't believe that this deal gives international inspectors adequate access to undeclared sites. I'm especially troubled by reports about how the Iranian military base at Parchin will be inspected. With these potential roadblocks, IAEA inspectors may be unable to finish their investigation into the potential military dimensions of Iran's nuclear program. While it may not be essential for Iran to provide a full mea culpa of its past activities, the access levels that Iran grants to the IAEA are indeed critical to our understanding of Iran's progress toward a nuclear weapon. If the IAEA is dissatisfied by December 15th, the JCPOA does not clearly provide for a delay of sanctions relief.

> I also view as a dangerous concession the sunset of the international sanctions on advanced conventional weapons and ballistic missiles. I was told that these issues weren't on the table during the talks. So it's unacceptable to me that after a maximum of five and eight years, respectively, the deal lifts these restrictions. Worse, if Iran were to repeat past behavior and violate the arms embargo or restrictions on its ballistic missile program, such an action wouldn't violate the JCPOA and wouldn't be subject to snapback sanctions.[124]

The top Republican and Democrat on the Senate Foreign Relations Committee – Committee Chairman Senator Bob Corker (R-TN) and Ranking Member Senator Ben Cardin (D-MD) – also came out against the JCPOA.

Israeli Prime Minister Benjamin Netanyahu made blistering remarks rejecting the JCPOA, calling it "a stunning historic mistake" and said Iranian President Hassan Rouhani was correct in saying that with the agreement "the international community is removing the sanctions and Iran is keeping its nuclear program." Netanyahu also said "Israel is not bound by this deal with Iran, because Iran continues to seek our destruction."

The Israeli Prime Minister's comments were consistent with his steadfast opposition to the Iran nuclear talks which included an unprecedented speech to a joint session of Congress on March 3, 2015 in which he warned that the deal being negotiated "would all but guarantee Iran gets nuclear weapons" and "paves Iran's path the bomb." The Obama administration opposed Netanyahu's appearance before Congress and refused to grant him a meeting with President Obama. Obama administration officials and over 60 members of Congress boycotted the speech.

The JCPOA and the 2016 Presidential Campaign

President Obama's nuclear diplomacy with Iran became a much debated issue in the 2016 presidential campaign, reflecting divisions in the country over the nuclear deal and fierce opposition by Republicans.

Democratic candidates Bernie Sanders and Hillary Clinton strongly supported the nuclear talks and the JCPOA.

After it was announced in July 2015, Sanders defended the nuclear deal as "a victory for diplomacy over saber-rattling" and said he believes the deal "could keep the United States from being drawn into another never-ending war in the Middle East."

Clinton has taken credit for the JCPOA by saying her efforts to implement sanctions against Iran forced Tehran to the negotiating table. For example, she wrote in her memoirs, "Hard Choices:"

> Through legislation and executive action, the Obama administration and Congress worked together to pile tougher and tougher sanctions, all building on the original Security Council measures put in place in the summer of 2010.[125]

This claim and others made by Clinton that her support of tough sanctions brought Iran to the negotiating table are contradicted by the record described in Chapter 6 of the Obama administration opposing sanctions proposed by Congress and the European Union but later backing them when they were impossible to stop. Clinton does not say in her memoirs that she harbored reservations to White House's opposition to congressional sanctions bills or that she regretted this resistance – she does not mention the Obama administration's resistance to sanctions at all. In my view, Clinton's claims about being a leading advocate of sanctions against Iran while she was Secretary of State are demonstrably false and were invented to improve her image for her run for president.

Clinton also has claimed credit for the nuclear deal because of a meeting she held with the Sultan of Oman in January 2011[126] and the July 2012 Puneet-Talwar meeting with Iranian officials in Oman.[127] Both of these claims are contradicted by the record and other well-documented claims.

The JCPOA was opposed by all of the 2016 Republican presidential candidates, although there were some differences in how they would deal with it if elected.

During a September 16, 2015 Republican presidential primary debate, seven of the 15 GOP candidates – Scott Walker, Ted Cruz, Chris Christie, Mike Huckabee, Marco Rubio, Lindsey Graham and George Pataki – said they would kill the deal. Cruz and Walker said they would tear it up on their first day as president. Rubio and Huckabee also seemed prepared to do this. Two candidates – Carly Fiorina and Rick Santorum – said they would make tough demands to Iran that would effectively kill the deal.

Donald Trump said in this debate that he would try to renegotiate the agreement with demands that would almost certainly kill the agreement. Bobby Jindal wanted Congress to kill the deal. Dr. Ben Carson did not say how he would treat the deal.

Jeb Bush, Rand Paul and John Kasich said they would abide by the nuclear agreement with Iran and try to improve it. Bush and Kasich criticized Cruz's promise to tear up the agreement as "not a strategy" and a simplistic response that would alienate America's European allies. I responded to this criticism in a September 17, 2015 Newsmax op-ed.

> Sorry, Governor Bush. Tearing up the Iran deal on the first day of the next president's term of office would be a strategy and an act of leadership, since it would repudiate a dangerous and illegitimate agreement with an American enemy that was imposed on our country by President Obama – with zero support from congressional Republicans. [128]

As noted in Chapter 13, Donald Trump and Ted Cruz addressed a huge rally against the Iran deal in front of the U.S. Capitol on September 9, 2015 co-sponsored by the Tea Party Patriots, the Zionist Organization of America, and the Center for Security Policy.

Tearing up the nuclear agreement on his first day in office as president became a central theme of Senator Cruz's campaign as he emerged as one of the last remaining GOP presidential candidates. Meanwhile, Donald Trump stuck to his pledge to renegotiate the agreement while expanding his harsh criticism of it. Trump said at an AIPAC convention in Washington on March 21, 2016:

My number one priority is to dismantle the disastrous deal with Iran. ...I have been in business a long time. And let me tell you, this deal is catastrophic for America, for Israel and for the whole of the Middle East. The problem here is fundamental. We have rewarded the world's leading state sponsor of terror with $150 billion and we received absolutely nothing in return.[129]

In a May 2016 radio interview, Trump's son Eric said the nuclear deal was a deciding factor that compelled his father to run for president.[130]

When this book went to print, Donald Trump and Hillary Clinton were the presumptive presidential candidates of their parties. In chapter 21, I provide recommendations on how they should deal with the nuclear agreement as president, including principles to guide an effort by Mr. Trump to renegotiate the JCPOA.

12: Congressional Review of the Obamabomb Deal

Secretary of State John Kerry testifies on the JCPOA to the Senate Foreign Relations Committee, July 23, 2015

Congressional review of the JCPOA sparked enormous controversy. Many members of Congress believed an agreement of this importance constituted a treaty and should have been submitted to Congress as such for Senate ratification. The Obama administration disagreed but initially pledged to consult with Congress on the agreement. For example, Secretary of State Kerry said on April 8, 2014: "Well, of course, we would be obligated to under the law. … What we do will have to pass muster with Congress. We well understand that."[131]

After the JCPOA was announced it was clear the Obama administration had no interest in having the nuclear deal "pass muster" with Congress and instead moved to implement it despite bipartisan opposition in the House and Senate.

After finalizing the Iran nuclear agreement in July 2015, the Obama administration was required to submit it for review by Congress. This review was due to a law passed in April 2015, the Iran Nuclear Agreement Review Act of 2015 (commonly referred to as the Corker-Cardin bill). Under Corker-Cardin, Congress had an opportunity to vote on a resolution of disapproval of the JCPOA after a review. This review period would be 30 days if the nuclear agreement had been reached by July 9, 2015 or 60 days if reached after that date.

The Corker-Cardin bill passed by overwhelming bipartisan majorities (98 1 in the Senate; 400-24 in the House) because of lawmakers' objections to the direction of the nuclear talks and their belief that Congress had been kept in the dark. Most importantly, this law passed because President Obama refused to submit the nuclear deal as a treaty for Senate ratification. Many in Congress also objected that although the Senate would be denied an opportunity to ratify the JCPOA, the agreement required the approval of the Iranian Parliament, the Majlis.

The Constitution is silent on what constitutes a treaty. For this reason, presidents traditionally decide which international agreements are designated as treaties and submitted for Senate ratification. Corker-Cardin was controversial since it created a way for Congress to vote on the JCPOA that was inconsistent with the requirements of the Constitution on treaty ratification: passing a resolution of disapproval by veto-proof and filibuster-proof majorities in both houses. Under this process, instead of needing two-thirds support for Senate ratification, the JCPOA only needed the support of one-third plus one votes in the House or Senate to sustain a presidential veto or 41 votes in the Senate to support a filibuster. Corker-Cardin therefore allowed the JCPOA to survive a congressional review even though majorities in both house of Congress voted to oppose it.

Many opponents of the JCPOA believed the Corker-Cardin process was unconstitutional. One of the most outspoken opponents, former assistant U.S. District attorney Andrew McCarthy, called the idea of a resolution of disapproval of the JCPOA "a constitutional perversity" and an effort by Congress to escape blame for the nuclear agreement by ignoring its responsibilities under the Constitution.[132] McCarthy argued that the Constitution "does not empower the president to make binding agreements with foreign countries all on his own – on the theory that the American people should not take on enforceable international obligations or see their sovereignty compromised absent approval by the elected representatives most directly accountable to them."

Making this situation worse was the Obama administration's explanation on why it refused to submit the JCPOA as a treaty for Senate ratification. Secretary of State Kerry explained this in an exchange during a House Foreign Affairs Committee hearing with Congressman Reid Ribble (R-WI):

CONGRESSMAN REID RIBBLE: "For 228 years, the Constitution allowed treaties to [pass] with the advice and consent of 67 U.S. Senators. Why is this not considered a treaty?"

SECRETARY OF STATE JOHN KERRY: "Well Congressman, I spent quite a few years trying to get a lot of treaties through the United States Senate, and it has become physically impossible. That's why. Because you can't pass a treaty anymore. It has become impossible to schedule, to pass, and I sat there leading the charge on the Disabilities Treaty which fell to basically ideology and politics. So I think that is the reason why."[133]

Kerry's statement was misleading for two reasons. First, the Obama administration has submitted treaties and other international agreements to the Senate for ratification. For example, in December 2010, the Senate ratified the controversial New START arms control treaty with Russia. The UN Arms Trade Treaty signed by the administration 2013 is awaiting Senate ratification. The administration also has submitted the Trans-Pacific Partnership, a trade agreement, for approval by the House and Senate.

Second, the truth about the JCPOA is not that it is no longer possible to win Senate ratification of treaties but that the Obama administration has engaged in a pattern of going around the Senate to implement controversial international agreements that Congress and the American people would not support. This also was the case with the Paris climate change agreement of December 2015 that was deliberately negotiated as an international accord rather than a treaty so it would not require Senate ratification. The climate change agreement will come into force in 2020 and, according to its supporters, is legally binding. Because an international agreement cannot be binding on the United States without Senate ratification, Congress is certain to bring a lawsuit over this agreement if it is not unsigned by future president before 2020.

President Obama has also been heavily criticized for normalizing relations with Cuba and transferring detainees from the Guantanamo Bay detention facility over the objections of Congress.

The administration's refusal to obtain congressional buy-in for important international agreements undermines their legitimacy and has worsened partisan tensions between the White House and Congress, something that Barack Obama pledged to fix during the 2008 presidential campaign when he said he would work to resolve political infighting in Washington as a "post-partisan" president.

During congressional hearings in the summer of 2015, Obama officials were vague on what kind of agreement the JCPOA was other than saying it was not a treaty. However, in a November 19, 2015 letter to Congressman Mike Pompeo (R-KS), the State Department explained that the agreement

> is not a treaty or an executive agreement and is not a signed document. The JCPOA reflects political commitments between Iran, the P5+1 and the European Union.[134]

The letter also implied the JCPOA is not legally binding.

> The success of the JCPOA will depend not on whether it is legally binding or signed but rather on the extensive ratification measures we have put in place as well as Iran's understanding that we have the capacity to re-impose – and ramp up – our sanctions if Iran does not meet its commitments.

This letter to Pompeo further angered opponents of the JCPOA because they rejected the idea of an unorthodox agreement on such a serious global security issue that is not a treaty, is unsigned, and is nonbinding. Opponents of the deal also were angry that this controversial explanation was not provided to Congress before it voted on the JCPOA in September 2015.

Congressional hearings in July 2015 after the announcement of the nuclear agreement were extremely contentious. Senate Foreign Relations Committee Chairman Bob Corker told Secretary Kerry during a hearing, "I believe you've been fleeced. Iran had gone from being "a rogue nation that had a boot on its neck with crippling international sanctions to a country that would reap a windfall from sanctions relief and be allowed to develop an "industrial"-strength nuclear program." Senator Marco Rubio (R-FL.) said "this is a deal whose survival is not guaranteed" beyond President Obama's term in office, which he hoped the next president would reverse.

Secretary Kerry and other Obama officials stood their ground and defended the agreement before Congress. Kerry dismissed demands by Republicans and Democrats who called for the agreement to be renegotiated when he told a Senate Foreign Relations Committee hearing on July 23:

> Let me underscore the alternative to the deal we have reached is not – as I've seen some ads on TV suggesting disingenuously – it isn't a 'better deal,' some sort of unicorn arrangement involving Iran's complete capitulation." That is a fantasy, plain and simple, and our intelligence community will tell you that.

Senator Jim Risch (R-ID) responded to Kerry's comment by saying "Anyone who believes this is a good deal joins the ranks of the most naïve people on earth."

Congressman Scott Perry (R-PA) said Kerry's testimony on the JCPOA to a House Foreign Affairs Committee hearing was "condescending." He told Newsmax:

It was, unfortunately, the normal kind of condescending: 'We're from the State Department. We spent years working on this deal. You just need to get smart and figure out that we have all the answers and vote for this thing.' They've already determined their course of action regardless of what Congress does, and that is very telling.[135]

Tensions over the JCPOA in Congress worsened when the Obama administration submitted the agreement for ratification by the UN Security Council 24 hours after it sent it to Congress for a 60-day review under Corker-Cardin. The Council unanimously approved the agreement on July 20, 2015 by passing Security Council Resolution 2231.

The Obama administration defended the decision to send the nuclear agreement to the Security Council before Congress had reviewed it by noting the deal would not go into effect until 90 days after the Council voted and claimed Congress did not have the right to tell other nations what to do. Secretary Kerry explained this position in a July 19, 2015 interview on ABC's "This Week:"

> JONATHAN KARL: "Why are you going to the U.N. before you're going to the U.S. Congress with this deal?"
>
> KERRY: "Well, we're not. What we did was negotiate with our P5-+1 partners, who are not subject to the Congress, that it cannot be implemented until after Congress has had a chance to vote."
>
> KARL: "But the bottom line is the U.N. is going to vote on this before the Congress is going to vote on this."
>
> KERRY: "Well, they have a right to do that, honestly. It's presumptuous of some people to suspect that France, Russia, China, Germany, Britain ought to do what the congress tells them to do. They have a right to have a vote. But we prevailed on them to delay the implementation of that vote out of respect for our congress so we wouldn't be jamming them."

Republican and some Democratic Congressmen rejected Kerry's argument and condemned the Security Council vote as a violation of Corker-Cardin and an attempt to box in Congress. Deal opponents were particularly concerned the UN vote would signal that the United States was prepared to dismantle sanctions against Iran before Congress had a chance to vote on the accord.

Republican Senator Bob Corker, the Chairman of the Senate Foreign Relations Committee, and the committee's top Democrat, Senator Ben Cardin, sent a joint letter to President Obama urging him to postpone the Security Council vote until after Congress reviewed and voted on the nuclear agreement. In an unusual move, Congressman Steny Hoyer (D-MD), the second highest ranking Democrat in the U.S. House, sent his own letter to the White House urging that the Security Council not act on the JCPOA until after Congress reviewed the agreement.

The Obama administration's flagrant disregard of congressional oversight of the nuclear agreement was par for the course for its dishonest and secretive efforts to implement the Obamabomb deal. While the administration agreed to let the Security Council and the Iranian Parliament vote on this agreement, it refused to permit a serious vote in Congress. Although this allowed the administration to ram through the nuclear agreement over the objections of House and Senate majorities, it undermined the deal's legitimacy in the United States, intensified opposition and significantly worsened White House relations with Congress. This is unfortunate because an agreement this important needed bipartisan congressional support so the world would know it represented a serious and lasting commitment supported by the American people rather than a partisan maneuver unilaterally initiated by a president that one of his successors will quickly terminate.

13. Opponents Battle to Kill the Obamabomb Deal

It's been apparent for some time that the Obama administration will say anything to implement its disastrous nuclear deal with Iran. For example, the president has claimed it closes all "pathways to an Iranian nuclear weapon." As Democratic Sen. Chuck Schumer has noted, that's not so. Team Obama asserts we know about everything that Iran's secretive program has done in closed sites. As former Clinton Director of Central Intelligence James Woolsey has written, that's not true. The president insists his deal is the only way to avoid war with Iran. Democratic Sen. Bob Menendez disagrees. Now, administration spokesmen are signaling that the deal will provide useful targeting information for a future attack on Iran's nuclear program, instead of making it effectively impossible. Is there really a Democrat – or anybody else – who buys that fraud?

Center for Security Policy President Frank Gaffney
Washington Times, August 25, 2016

Opponents of the Iran nuclear deal fought hard during the summer of 2015 to affect the outcome of congressional votes on the agreement scheduled to be held in September. They knew they had an uphill fight since the deal could survive congressional review with just one-third plus one support in either house of Congress.

The agreement was fiercely opposed by Jewish groups, evangelical Christians, conservative groups and a significant number of Democrats. The American Israel Public Affairs Committee surprised many observers by coming out against the deal and lobbying for its defeat. (See figure 10)

Deal opponents worked to kill the agreement with media appearances, op-eds, and staging rallies across United States. Millions were spent on television and print advertising by deal opponents to convince Congress to reject the nuclear deal. High-profile letters against the nuclear agreement were signed by 840 U.S. rabbis, over 200 U.S. generals and admirals, and 56 leading US nuclear weapons, arms control and intelligence experts. Large rallies against the Obamabomb Deal were held in Times Square on July 23 and in front of the US capitol on September 9. The capitol rally, held the week Congress returned from recess and organized by Tea Party Patriots, the Zionist Organization of America, and the Center for Security

Policy, received a huge amount of publicity and it was addressed by Republican presidential candidates Donald Trump and Senator Ted Cruz. (See Figure 11)

Opponents of the Iran deal concentrated on uncommitted Democrats. This effort scored some significant victories by convincing several senior Democrats who ordinarily provide automatic support to Obama's foreign policy initiatives to oppose the nuclear agreement, including Senator Chuck Schumer, Senator Ben Cardin, and Congressman Steve Israel. Congressional offices reported a flood of phone calls against the Iran deal.

Efforts by opponents of the Iran deal had a significant effect on popular support for the agreement, reducing it to 21% when Congress voted on the accord in September. However, although they succeeded in peeling off a significant number of Democrats, including five members of the Senate, the Obama administration succeeded in convincing just enough Democratic lawmakers to support the agreement to prevent the president from going through the humiliation of having to veto a resolution of disapproval.

Figure 10: Fact Sheet Against the JCPOA issued by the American Israel Public Affairs Committee (AIPAC)

NEGOTIATIONS with IRAN

MYTHS AND FACTS

Below is a series of myths and facts regarding the proposed nuclear agreement with Iran.

MYTH The choice is this deal or war.
FACT The opposite is true. This deal increases the prospects of war. It immediately gives Iran up to $150 billion, which will bolster Iran's support of terrorism and regional conflicts, requiring a vigorous armed response from neighbors. In the long run, an emboldened and strengthened Iran will seek regional hegemony—dramatically increasing the chances for broader conflict.

MYTH Iran won't get a nuclear weapon.
FACT This deal does not block Iran's path to a bomb (see Analysis: An Unacceptable Deal). Instead, the deal legitimizes Iran's nuclear program and allows it to legally reach a nuclear weapons capability with a breakout time measured in only days.

MYTH The whole world backs this deal.
FACT The negotiations with Iran involved the United States and five other countries—none of Iran's neighbors were involved. Many countries in the Middle East, including Israel, Saudi Arabia, and other Persian Gulf countries, are deeply concerned about the impact this deal will have on Iran's ability to fund terrorism and promote instability.

MYTH With no deal, Iran is free from scrutiny.
FACT As a party to the Nuclear Non Proliferation Treaty (NPT), Iran is forbidden from developing nuclear weapons and must undergo regular IAEA inspections of declared sites. With no deal, Iran is still held to inspections of declared sites and cannot pursue nuclear weapons.

MYTH With no deal, Iran will sprint to a bomb.
FACT If Iran turned on all 19,000 installed centrifuges, breakout time would be about two-to-three months to enrich enough uranium to weapons grade. But first, Iran would have to banish IAEA inspectors and reconfigure its centrifuges to produce highly enriched uranium. Iran knows such a breakout would risk a military strike on its nuclear infrastructure, which would grievously damage a program that took decades and billions of dollars to build.

MYTH With no deal, sanctions will fall apart.
FACT On the first day of the deal's implementation nearly all financial, investment, and energy sanctions lift. With no deal, the United States continues to impact the behavior of partners, and U.S. statutory sanctions on elements of Iran's economy continue. Access to the U.S. economy is crucial to most countries and companies, and those that choose to confront the United States on this issue could lose access.

MYTH "Snapback" will work.
FACT The "snapback" mechanism is problematic. It requires up to 65 days to establish and would only apply for major Iranian violations, meaning there are no consequences spelled out for more minor violations. In addition, "snapback" explicitly exempts all international contracts signed before a violation, significantly reducing its impact on Iran.

MYTH This deal strengthens Iran's moderates.
FACT There is no evidence that this deal will impact Iranian foreign policy, support for terrorism or human rights. Instead, the regime will receive an economic boost of up to $150 billion and renewed oil sales, providing Iran additional resources and legitimacy to pursue its agenda. In fact, the agreement is likely to inspire the regime to expand its extreme behavior as a way to demonstrate its faithfulness to the ethos of the Islamic revolution.

MYTH This deal extends Iran's breakout time.
FACT Given all that is unknown, such estimates about Iranian nuclear capabilities are speculative at best. According to the administration, Iran's purported breakout time extends by months, not years. All meaningful restraints on Iran's nuclear program are removed by year 15, allowing Iran to achieve thereafter a breakout time measured in days.

MYTH Rejection of a deal is unprecedented.
FACT Throughout U.S. history, Congress has rejected agreements negotiated by the executive branch and insisted on substantial changes. Nearly 200 treaties, including 80 multilateral accords, have been modified before they were approved.

July 2015

 AIPAC   www.aipac.org   #BadIranDeal

Top Senator Ted Cruz (R-TX) addresses a September 9, 2015 rally against the Iran deal on the West lawn of the Capitol. Businessman Donald Trump, the next speaker, is in the background,

Center: Center for Security Policy President Frank Gaffney speaks to a huge anti-Iran deal rally in New York City's Times Square on July 22, 2015.

Bottom: the author addresses a rally against the deal in New York City outside the office of New York Senator Kirstin Gillibrand (D-NY), September 1, 2015.

14: The Obamabomb Echo Chamber

We created an echo chamber," he admitted, when I asked him to explain the onslaught of freshly minted experts cheerleading for the deal. "They were saying things that validated what we had given them to say.

Deputy National Security Council Adviser Ben Rhodes
comments to *New York Times* reporter David Samuels
New York Times, May 5, 2015[136]

The Obama administration and its supporters conducted an aggressive campaign to affect the outcome of the September 2015 congressional votes on the Iran nuclear deal. Although some tactics by deal supporters were similar to those of deal opponents, the Obama administration's overall effort was very different since it was a massive campaign of deception and intimidation.

Since the Obama administration knew it could never convince a majority of the American people or a majority of Congress to back this deal in light of the significant compromises they made to negotiate the agreement, it concentrated on holding on to enough Democratic votes to support a filibuster or sustain a presidential veto.

New York Times reporter David Samuels revealed in a May 5, 2016 profile of National Security Council advisor Ben Rhodes how the White House conducted a campaign to manipulate the news media by generating false narratives to promote the Iran deal which it distributed to know-nothing reporters. [137] Rhodes told Samuels this campaign was facilitated by making use of "legions of arms control experts [who] began popping up at think tanks and on social media" and who became "sources for hundreds of clueless reporters." According to Rhodes, "we created an echo chamber. They were saying things and validated what we had given them to say. . . . We had test drives to know who was going to be able to carry our message effectively, and how to use outside groups like Ploughshares, the Iran Project and whomever else."[138]

According to Samuels, Tanya Somanader, the NSC "director of digital response," singled out several persons and entities the White House used as part of this echo chamber.

For those in need of more traditional-seeming forms of validation, handpicked Beltway insiders like Jeffrey Goldberg of The Atlantic and Laura Rozen of Al-Monitor helped retail the administration's narrative. "Laura Rozen was my RSS feed, Somanader offered. "She would just find everything and retweet it. . . .

The true influence and huge funding behind the echo chamber was learned after the publication of Samuels' article. According to Bloomberg reporter Eli Lake, the Ploughshares Fund, a non-profit liberal arms control group, began a well-funded effort in 2011 to promote a nuclear agreement by portraying skeptics of Obama's nuclear diplomacy with Iran as pro-war, playing down the dangers of the Iranian nuclear program and giving millions to organizations, experts and journalists to who supported a nuclear agreement with Iran.[139] One of the Ploughshares Fund's major donors is liberal American philanthropist George Soros' Open Society Institute.

Hudson Institute Senior Fellow Lee Smith discussed the recipients of the Ploughshares funds in a May 24, 2016 *Weekly Standard* article.

> It's now been reported that funds were also distributed to an Iranian former nuclear negotiator teaching at Princeton; research organizations and think-tanks, like the Brookings Institution, the Atlantic Council, and the Arms Control Association; to a range of communitarian interest groups, lobbies and faith based organizations like J Street, the National Iranian American Council, and Friends Committee on National Legislation, which calls itself a "Quaker Lobby in the Public Interest"; even to an email listserv, Gulf 2000, that disseminated Iran deal talking points, as well as conspiracy theories, to policymakers, analysts, and journalists, including Iran deal advocates like Al-Monitor journalist Laura Rozen and Ploughshares President Joe Cirincione. Organizations paid to promote a nuclear deal with Iran included the Arms Control Association, the National Security Network, the National Iranian American Council, the Federation of American Scientists, and the Atlantic Council. Experts and journalists who received Ploughshares money include Laura Rozen.

These payments raise serious questions about the objectivity of arms control experts who went on the air in the summer of 2015 to promote the Iran agreement. Experts paid by Ploughshares such as Cirincione and Rozen made frequent media appearances portraying themselves as objective observers without disclosing that they were receiving cash payments from a liberal group working to defend the nuclear agreement with Iran.

Typical of his harsh criticism of anyone who opposed the nuclear deal, Cirincione bashed Senator Ben Cardin for his opposition in a September 4, 2015 Twitter post:

Deeply disappointed my @SenatorCardin caved to the neocon, pro-war camp. Weak statement excusing his vote against the historic Iran Accord.

I want to point out that the Institute for Science and International Security, a Washington, DC arms control think tank that was very critical of the Bush administration's Iran policy, stopped working with Ploughshares and its allied pro-Iran deal organizations and experts because of their knee-jerk support for the Obama administration's nuclear diplomacy with Iran and failure to offer constructive criticism or address ways to address shortcomings in the nuclear agreement.

In December 2014 memo, the Institute accused Ploughshares and its allies of "group think" and "a willingness to uncritically and unwaveringly support the interim deal and defensively react to any compliance questions. [140]

The Institute for Science and International Security has used Twitter on several occasions to scold Ploughshares and its allies for acting as Obama administration stooges to promote a nuclear deal with Iran. On May 7, 2016, it posted the below Tweet in response to David Samuels' reporting that Ben Rhodes manipulated Ploughshares and Al-Monitor journalist Laura Rozen as parts of the Obama administration's echo chamber to sell the nuclear deal.

Inst for Science
@TheGoodISiS

⚙ Following

We tried to warn Rozen, ACA, P-shares that official(s) overselling nuclear deal to them, should be more critical bit.ly/24AG36J

RETWEETS: 28 LIKES: 21

9:54 AM · 7 May 2016

Of even more concern were reports that the Ploughshares Fund gave $100,000 to National Public Radio (NPR) to promote the Iran deal. According to a May 20, 2016 Associated Press report:

> Ploughshares has funded NPR's coverage of national security since 2005, the radio network said. Ploughshares reports show at least $700,000 in funding over that time. All grant descriptions since 2010 specifically mention Iran. [141]

According to the AP report, Ploughshares President Cirincione made several appearances on NPR to discuss the JCPOA on at least two occasions. Ploughshares funding of NPR was mentioned during one these interviews; the other it was not.

On the other hand, Congressman Mike Pompeo (R-KS), an opponent of the Iran nuclear deal, said he repeatedly asked NPR to be interviewed about the Iran deal last year but was refused. Pompeo noted that Rep. Adam Schiff (D-CA) regularly appeared on NPR to promote the JCPOA. NPR at first said it had no record of Pompeo's requests but later said it canceled a scheduled August 2015 interview with Pompeo because it had too many other interviews booked.

An NPR ombudsman said in a May 31, 2016 article that although she did not believe NPR's coverage of the Iran deal was skewed by the Ploughshares funding, NPR should consider avoiding such grants in the future because it creates a perception problem.[142]

On June 1, 2016, Congressman Pompeo called for an independent investigation into the relationship between the Ploughshares Fund and NPR. In his letter, Pompeo objected that the NPR ombudsman's investigation into this matter was conducted in a matter of days without contacting his office or outside experts, raising serious questions about the integrity of the process.[143] Pompeo said in a May 27 statement:

> This NPR whitewash report does not (a) explain why NPR chose to allow Ploughshares its microphone without acknowledging Ploughshares' major role in funding NPR's Iran reporting, (b) explain why NPR denied me, and others that shared my view, an opportunity to present a balancing viewpoint on that treacherous deal, or (c) remotely address the underlying ethical issues connected to NPR's taxpayer financing and its willingness to serve the interests of one political party on the single most important foreign policy legacy of that party's president[144]

There are many indications that the Obama administration's campaign to defend the JCPOA was both desperate and ugly. Senator Jim Webb came out against the Iran deal on August 9, 2015 in spite and – and possibly because of – the administration's efforts to smear opponents of the deal. Senator Webb said in a speech announcing his opposition to the JCPOA:

> "I think it's a bad deal and I've said so for several weeks now. I think we need to put country ahead of party."

"It troubles me when I see all this debate about whether this is disloyalty to the president or the Democratic Party, particularly with what Chuck Schumer has gone [through]."

During an August 5 speech at American University, the president portrayed American opponents of the Iran nuclear agreement as partisan Republicans in common cause with death-to-America chanting Iranian hardliners. These comments went too far for former Ambassador Nicolas Burns, a former State Department official who supported the JCPOA. Burns told MSNBC after the president's speech:

> I don't think it's a fair comparison. I have great respect for the president but frankly I think that speech — the tone of it was ill-advised because what's really happening here as Congress prepares to vote just after Labor Day is really a battle within the Democratic Party.
>
> To suggest that the opponents of the deal are all in effect Iraq War supporters or warmongers, to suggest if the deal is disapproved than war is inevitable – I don't think the facts support those contentions.

The Tablet, a daily online Jewish magazine, ran an editorial on August 7 titled "Crossing a Line to Sell a Deal" that accused the president of using code anti-Semitic language to criticize Jewish Americans for opposing the Iran deal and to blame them if the deal was rejected by Congress. Some liberal pro-Obama groups like MoveOn.org went further and questioned the loyalty to this country of Jewish members of Congress who opposed the deal like Senator Chuck Schumer.

Elliot Abrams decried this bigotry in an August 10 article in *The Weekly Standard*:

> The basic idea is simple: to oppose the president's Iran deal means you want war with Iran, you're an Israeli agent, you are in the pay of Jewish donors, and you are abandoning the best interests of the United States. So Dan Pfeiffer, senior political adviser to Obama until this winter, tweeted that Senator Charles Schumer – who announced his opposition to the Iran deal last week – should not be Democratic leader in the Senate because he "wants war with Iran."

Did the Obama Administration Use the NSA to Spy on Congressional Opponents of the Iran deal?

According to a December 29, 2015 *Wall Street Journal* article by Adam Entous and Danny Yadron, NSA provided the White House with intercepted Israeli communications with the details of private discussions between Israeli Prime

Minister Benjamin Netanyahu and U.S. lawmakers and American Jewish groups on the Iran nuclear deal during the summer of 2016.[145]

The Journal article explained that President Obama decided to stop NSA collection against leaders of U.S allies due to the backlash caused by a disclosure by NSA technician Edward Snowden that NSA had eavesdropped on German Chancellor Angela Merkel's cell phone and also monitored the communications of the heads of state of other close U.S. allies.

However, Obama did not halt NSA spying against Netanyahu. This is not a surprise given the president's chilly relations with the Israeli leader and Israel's aggressive spying against the United States. It's also not a surprise that the Obama administration sought intelligence on Netanyahu's efforts to undermine the nuclear deal. But it was stunning to learn that NSA sent the White House intelligence on private discussions by U.S. Congressmen on a major policy dispute between the White House and Congress.

According to the Journal article, to avoid a paper trail that they wanted NSA reporting on Netanyahu's interactions with Congress, Obama officials decided to let NSA decide how much of this intelligence to provide and what to withhold. The article cited an unnamed U.S. official who explained, "We didn't say, 'Do it.' We didn't say, 'Don't do it.'"

There were complaints when this story was published about the Obama administration spying on Israel. This did not concern me since nations spy on each other all the time. It's no secret that Israel spies on the United States.

I am concerned that NSA appeared to provide intelligence on the conversations of members of Congress to the White House and that White House officials did not immediately tell NSA to stop collecting and disseminating this information. The Journal article reported that a 2011 NSA directive requires direct communications between foreign intelligence targets and members of Congress be destroyed but gives the NSA director the authority to waive this requirement if he determines the communications contain "significant foreign intelligence." This information on discussions by members of Congress and American Jewish organizations about the Iran deal was not significant foreign intelligence – it was domestic intelligence to help defend a presidential policy initiative in Congress.

Congressman Ron DeSantis (R-FL), a member of the House Intelligence Committee, sent a letter to President Obama on January 4, 2016 requesting clarification of this story.[146] DeSantis also co-signed a letter on this issue to NSA

Director Mike Rogers with Reps. Jason Chaffetz, Mark Meadows and Cynthia Lummis.[147] I have been informed that congressional Republicans decided to drop this issue in late January 2016 because no evidence could be found of wrongdoing and NSA officials insisted that any collection of discussions between members of Congress and Prime Minister Netanyahu had been inadvertent. If this was the case, it means the *Wall Street Journal* article was wrong. I believe this article probably was correct but congressional Republicans were unable to confirm it.

White House Retaliated Against Journalists Who Didn't Play Ball on the Iran Nuclear Talks

Wall Street Journal journalist Jay Solomon wrote in his 2016 book "The Iran Wars" that Obama officials played hardball with journalists who wrote negative stories on the Iran deal. Solomon claims he was kicked off Secretary Kerry's plane in the spring on 2015 because of questions he had asked of sources about French opposition to the nuclear deal and whether President Obama "had browbeaten the French leader for insubordination."[148]

According to Solomon, other journalists were also punished by the administration for not sticking to its line on the nuclear talks. David Sanger of the *New York Times*, according to Solomon, was subjected to a State-White House "Twitter assault" for writing that Iran may not have the technical capabilities to dispose of its nuclear stockpile as required by the nuclear deal.

Solomon says Associated Press reporter George Jahn was attacked even more harshly by White House supporters. Jahn, according to Solomon, was accused of being an "Israeli asset" who had "no journalistic ethics" for reporting on a leaked IAEA document which they claimed was a forgery on the details of a secret side deal between Iran and the IAEA that allowed Iran to inspect itself. (I discuss this incident in the next chapter.) The points in the document Jahn reported later proved to be accurate. I know from following this issue at the time that the "White House supporters" Solomon referred to were Joseph Cirincione, Laura Rozen and other members of the White House Iran deal echo chamber.

Censorship of Fox News Reporter's Questions on Iran Nuclear Talks

In early May 2015, the Fox News Channel discovered that eight minutes of video of Fox reporter James Rosen questioning State Department spokeswoman Jen

Psaki on December 2, 2013 about the Iran nuclear talks had been deleted from the department's website and its YouTube channel. Rosen's questions concerned a denial by the State Department earlier that year about secret talks between Iran and the United States. In her answer to Rosen's question, Psaki seemed to confirm her predecessor had lied about this issue when she said: "There are times where diplomacy needs privacy. This is a good example of that"

This eight-minute exchange between Rosen and Psaki had been replaced by a brief white flash. State officials initially said this was due to a technical glitch.

On June 1, 2016, State officials reported that the deletion of this video footage was not a glitch and had been removed deliberately. State officials said they could not determine who ordered it removed or the reason for its removal. The current State Department spokesman, John Kirby, ordered the video be restored and said new rules would be created to prevent this from happening again. Kirby told reporters: "Deliberately removing a portion of the video was not and is not in keeping with the State Department's commitment to transparency and public accountability."

Senator Tom Cotton reacted to this incident by saying "this whole outrageous episode demonstrates how the Iran deal has been sold to Americans through a parade of misleading "narratives" and outright falsehoods." Cotton also asked the administration to identify the official who ordered the Rosen footage be deleted.

On June 3, 2016, Congressman Ed Royce, the Chairman of the House Foreign Affairs Committee, sent a letter to the State Department Inspector General to request an investigation into the deliberate omission of portions of a State Department press briefing video on the Iran nuclear talks.[149] Royce said in his letter:

> In tampering with this video, the Bureau of Public Affairs has undermined its mission to 'communicate timely and accurate information with the goal of furthering U.S. foreign policy.' This is all the more troubling given that the video in question dealt with hugely consequential nuclear negotiations with the Islamic Republic of Iran.

The State Department Inspector General announced on June 9, 2016 that he would investigate this incident.

The censorship of Rosen's questions about the Iran deal was no accident. It represented the desperate, win-at-any-cost strategy by the Obama administration to get a legacy nuclear agreement with Iran. Given the other tactics used by the White House and its supporters to promote and defend the Iran nuclear agreement, including the press echo chamber, false narratives created to sell the agreement, payments to NPR, anti-Semitic attacks on deal opponents, the fact that the administration censored video footage of unwelcome questions by the news media is not a surprise.

15. Congress Discovers Secret Obamabomb Side Deals

Congressman Mike Pompeo (R-KS) (left) and Senator Tom Cotton discuss on the Fox News Channel secret side deals to the JCPOA they discovered during a July 17, 2015 meeting with IAEA officials.

Partisan tensions over the JCPOA rose after Congress learned there were secret side deals to the agreement between Iran and the IAEA that the Obama administration did not share with Congress. Republicans claimed this violated a provision of Corker-Cardin requiring the Obama administration to provide to Congress for its review of the nuclear agreement "any additional materials related thereto, including annexes, appendices, codicils, side agreements, implementing materials, documents, and guidance, technical or other understandings, and any related agreements, whether entered into or implemented prior to the agreement or to be entered into or implemented in the future."

Senator Tom Cotton (R-AR) and Congressman Mike Pompeo (R-KS) discovered the side deals during a July 17, 2015 meeting with International Atomic Energy Agency officials in Vienna. They were told of two secret agreements between the IAEA and Iran that would not be shared with other nations, with Congress, or the U.S. public. One concerned inspection of the Parchin military base, where Iran reportedly has conducted explosive testing related to nuclear warhead development. The other concerned how the IAEA and Iran will resolve PMD issues.

Senator Cotton and Congressman Pompeo said in a statement that they believed the side deals violated Corker-Cardin's requirements that the administration provide all documents related to the JCPOA to Congress for its review of the agreement.

Congressman Pompeo said in a July 21, 2016 press release about the side deals:

> This agreement is the worst of backroom deals. In addition to allowing Iran to keep its nuclear program, missile program, American hostages, and terrorist network, the Obama administration has failed to make public separate side deals that have been struck for the 'inspection' of one of the most important nuclear sites—the Parchin military complex. Not only does this violate the Iran Nuclear Agreement Review Act, it is asking Congress to agree to a deal that it cannot review.[150]

Senator Cotton made similar comments.

> In failing to secure the disclosure of these secret side deals, the Obama administration is asking Congress and the American people to trust, but not verify. What we cannot do is trust the terror-sponsoring, anti-American, outlaw regime that governs Iran and that has been deceiving the world on its nuclear weapons work for years. Congress's evaluation of this deal must be based on hard facts and full information. That we are only now discovering that parts of this dangerous agreement are being kept secret begs the question of what other elements may also be secret and entirely free from public scrutiny.[151]

Outrage in Congress over the side deals exploded the following week when it was learned that under one of the deals, Iranians would collect samples of nuclear weapons-related activity for the IAEA at the Parchin military base and other locations. Senator James Risch (R-ID) criticized this arrangement as Iran inspecting itself and little different than an NFL football player mailing in his own urine samples as part of a drug test.

The Obama administration's responses to congressional questioning about the side deals fed the controversy. Obama officials refused to call these agreements "secret side deals," instead referring to them as routine and "confidential and bilateral arrangement reached between IAEA officials and Tehran." In fact, these secret agreements were not routine – all previous Iran-IAEA agreements on the investigation of PMD issues were public documents and posted on the IAEA website.

Obama officials claimed they had not seen these agreements but had been briefed on them by the IAEA. Further angering deal opponents, the Obama administration classified their briefings to Congress on the side deals and refused to discuss their details in open committee hearings. JCPOA opponents argued this was an abuse of classification rules to hide the details of the side deals from the American people.

On August 19, 2015, George Jahn, a respected reporter who covers the IAEA in Vienna for the Associated Press, published an article on the details of the Parchin side deal.[152] His story was based on a written transcript he made of one of the side deal documents that he was permitted to read, presumably by an IAEA official. According to Jahn's article:

- Iran will provide photos and videos of sites linked to alleged nuclear-weapons work while, in the words of the document, "taking into account military concerns." Jahn wrote that this suggested Iran will not give the IAEA photos or video information from areas Tehran says are off-limits because they have military significance.

- At Parchin, Iranian inspectors will inspect seven sites within a building where alleged nuclear-related experiments took place. No collection will be done outside this building, although Iran will collect samples for the IAEA at locations other than Parchin.

- Iran will use its own equipment to collect samples for the IAEA. According to the side deal document, this equipment will be consistent with technical specifications provided by the IAEA, and that the IAEA "will ensure the technical authenticity of Iran's inspections." Jahn added that the document did not explain how the IAEA would make these certifications.

Jahn's article provided the details of what could only be described as a preposterous and unserious plan to investigate past and ongoing Iranian nuclear-weapons-related activities. A fair and objective arms-control investigation tries to uncover evidence that a host country is trying to hide by collecting samples from unexpected locations using equipment of the investigators' choosing. This process was carefully scripted so that Iran controlled what would be collected to ensure that no evidence would be found indicating covert nuclear or other WMD activities. As a former CIA arms control analyst, I was stunned at this arrangement which violated the normal practice of giving arms control inspectors the freedom to roam around a facility and collect samples where ever they choose.

Jahn's story did significant damage to the Obama administration's already beleaguered efforts to sell the nuclear deal. As a result, Iran deal supporters tried to discredit Jahn's story by claiming it was based on a forgery because the document Jahn read contained some terms and formulations that IAEA and Iranian officials allegedly would not use. For example, Iran was referred to as "the Islamic state of Iran" instead of the correct term, "the Islamic Republic." The document Jahn read also had some language that was inconsistent with the typical prose used by IAEA personnel in official documents.

The argument that Jahn, a veteran journalist, had been fooled by a forgery was difficult to support, especially after the Associated Press backed him. The AP said Jahn was told by two anonymous officials that the document he was shown was a draft and "does not differ from the final, confidential agreement between the IAEA and Iran." So how does one explain the anomalies in the document shown to Jahn?

My view, which I explained in an August 21, 2015 National Review article, is that errors and non-IAEA prose in the transcribed AP document indicated a first draft written by a party other than Iran or the IAEA to resolve the Parchin issue.[153] I believe this indicated the side deal documents were drafted by the United States and handed to the IAEA to finalize after U.S. diplomats were unable to resolve inspections of the Parchin military base and other PMD issues. These documents could have been first drafts written by a political appointee at the State Department or an NSC staffer. I drew this conclusion because the IAEA-Iran side deal was too convenient and too much of a coincidence in light of last-minute statements by U.S. officials reversing their position on the urgency that Iran resolve PMD issues before a nuclear deal was reached.

In my opinion, the secret side deals discovered by Senator Cotton and Congressman Pompeo were a ploy by Kerry to break the deadlock over the PMD issue (discussed in Chapter 9) by handing it to the IAEA. Kerry knew these side deals would be strongly opposed by Congress because they were a way to let Iran off the hook for prior nuclear weapons-related activities. To solve this problem, the side deal texts were made part of a private, IAEA-Iran agreement that Obama officials could claim they were not part of, had not read and could not be shared with Congress.

Although Obama officials and their supporters vigorously disputed the side deal story, it infuriated opponents of the nuclear agreement, especially congressional Republicans, and is a principal reason why every Republican Senator voted for disapproval of the JCPOA and why the Corker-Cardin process to pass a disapproval resolution collapsed in the House. This story also further undermined the deal's legitimacy in the eyes of many Americans.

16. Obamabomb Deal Survives Congressional Review Even Though Most Lawmakers Vote Against It

If Iran is to acquire a nuclear bomb, it will not have my name on it.

Senator Robert Menendez (D-NY)

Congress returned from its August 2015 recess with opposition growing against the JCPOA. Support for the agreement plummeted through the summer and stood at 21% in early September 2015, according to a Pew Research Center poll. [154] Although there was no chance the administration would win majority support in either house of Congress, by early September the White House had enough Democratic votes to prevent a resolution of disapproval from passing.

The secret side deals issue opened a new avenue of attack for opponents of the nuclear agreement and was used by a group of House Republicans to jettison the Corker-Cardin process because they contended President Obama did not comply with its requirements to provide all documents associated with the agreement to Congress, including all side agreements. This group of House Republicans, led by Congressman Peter Roskam (R-Il), forced House Speaker Boehner to drop the resolution of disapproval and instead hold votes on three other resolutions on the Iran deal. These resolutions were:

- To declare that President Obama violated Corker-Cardin by failing to provide the side deals to Congress. This resolution passed 245-186.

- To bar President Obama from lifting sanctions against Iran. This vote passed 247-186.

- A resolution outside of Corker-Cardin to "approve" the Iran deal on which all Republicans (except for one who voted present) voted no. Most Democrats voted yes. This resolution failed by a vote of 162-269. 25 House Democrats voted with Republicans against the Iran agreement.

Congressional Opponents Slam the Nuclear Deal

Some House Republicans said they would follow up these votes with lawsuits against the president for violating Corker Cardin. Such legal action never materialized.

The Senate declined to follow the example of the House and voted on a resolution of disapproval. As expected, Senate Democrats used a filibuster to prevent this resolution from passing. Two Senate votes to end debate and overcome a filibuster (which requires 60 votes) failed 58-42 and 56-42. Four Democratic Senators – Schumer, Cardin, Menendez and Manchin voted with Republicans to disapprove the nuclear agreement.

Senate Majority Leader Mitch McConnell blasted Democrats for using the filibuster tactic, saying that Americans deserved "to know where their elected Senators stand on this important issue." By employing the filibuster, Senate Democrats protected the president from the humiliation of having his legacy foreign policy achievement rejected by Congress and forcing him to use a presidential veto to block a resolution of disapproval.

Many Congressional opponents of the JCPOA made strong statements against the agreement. These included:

- Congressman Alcee Hastings, (D- FL): "In the end, the JCPOA allows Iran to remain a nuclear threshold state while simultaneously reaping the benefits of relief from international sanctions."

- Congressman Brad Sherman (D-CA): "We must force modifications of the agreement, and extensions of its nuclear restrictions, before it gets ugly. My efforts have one purpose: Make it clear that future Presidents and Congresses are not bound by this Agreement—not legally, not morally, not diplomatically."

- Senator Daniel Coats (D-IN): "Rather than negotiate from a position of strength, the P5+ 1 negotiators' desire for a deal led them to negotiate from a position of weakness. The result is an agreement with benefits too small, a duration too short and a cost too high."

- Senator Charles Grassley (R-IA): "We gave practically everything away," the Iowa Republican said Thursday. "Why were we negotiating in the first place?"

- Senator Jerry Moran (R-KS): "I'm convinced more than ever the nuclear agreement negotiated by the Obama administration is damaging to our country's national security and it increases the risk to our allies and friends in the Middle East."

- Congressman Steve Israel, (D-NY): "I'm going to vote against the Iran deal...I tried very hard to get to 'yes.' But at the end of the day, despite some positive elements in the deal, the totality compelled me to oppose it.,"

- Senator Ted Cruz (R-Texas): "If this deal is consummated, it will make the Obama administration the world's leading financier of radical Islamic terrorism."

- Congresswoman Grace Meng (D-NY): "I strongly believe the world could and should have a better deal than that set forth in the Joint Comprehensive Plan of Action, which I will therefore oppose."

Democratic Supporters Believe a Bad Deal is Better Than No Deal

No Republicans in either house voted to support the Obamabomb Deal. Some Democrats who voted in support strongly praised the agreement, including House Minority Leader Nancy Pelosi (D-CA) who called it "a diplomatic masterpiece." However, many Democrats made statements in which they admitted the deal had serious flaws but said they decided to vote for it anyway. These remarks included:

- Senator Richard Blumenthal (D-CT): "While this is not the agreement I would have accepted at the negotiating table, it is better than no deal at all."

- Senator Claire McCaskill (D-MO): "This deal isn't perfect and no one trusts Iran, but it has become clear to me that the world is united behind this agreement with the exception of the government of Israel."

- Senator Joe Donnelly (D-IN): "Despite having questions about Iran's intentions, I am willing to give this agreement the opportunity to succeed."

- Senator Chris Coons (D-DE): "I am a D, and I would like to be able to support this agreement. But I have serious reservations about it."

- Senator Mark Warner (D-VA): "While I believe there are several areas of concern with the agreement, the choice I ultimately had to make was between accepting an imperfect deal, or facing the serious ramifications if Congress rejected a deal that has the support of the rest of the world"

- Congressman Jerold Nadler (D-NY): "While I am concerned that many of the key elements expire in the 10–15 year timeframe, our debate must center on whether the deal is preferable to the available alternatives. The only decision that matters at this moment is whether to support or reject the agreement that is on the table now, not on whether we could or should have gotten a better deal."

- Congressman Scott Peters (D CA): "The JCPOA is not perfect. It doesn't end Iran's support of terrorism or permanently end Iran's civilian nuclear energy program. It does extend the international weapons ban for five years and ballistic missile ban for eight years, but does not make the bans permanent. These issues still need to be addressed. But preventing Iran from a nuclear bomb for at least 15 years is an important achievement, and has been the core objective of the negotiations."

- Congressman John Carney (D-DE): "...this deal is better than no deal at all. The hard truth is, I believe those are our only two choices at this juncture."

- Congressman John Sarbanes (D-MD): "To be clear, supporting this deal does not welcome Iran back into the community of nations. Not even close. At root, the Agreement is a test – a test of Iran's readiness to pursue a different path. If Iran fails that test at any point along the way, I believe the United States will be well-equipped to act."

How the Obama White House Won the Battle in Congress Over the Iran Deal

The Obama administration's aggressive tactics, including its echo chamber to manipulate the news media and mislead the American people intimidating and badmouthing opponents, censoring press coverage and possibly using the NSA to spy on opponents, played a significant role in preventing Congress from passing a resolution of disapproval against the Obamabomb Deal.

There was a lot of political maneuvering behind the scenes. The White House and congressional Democratic leaders reportedly put unprecedented pressure on Democratic congressmen. Many Democrats who were on the fence about the agreement probably received significant inducements to support it from the White House and Democratic leaders. It is very likely that some Democratic members of Congress sold their votes on the Iran deal in exchange for funding for bridges, roads, university buildings and bike paths in their districts and states.

However, I believe more important than all these factors was raw politics. Although many Democratic lawmakers realized the JCPOA is a bad deal that their constituent strongly opposed, they voted for it anyway out of party loyalty. That is, these Democratic members of Congress put politics ahead of national security. As scandalous as this is, I believe it is more important to salute congressional Democrats who stood up to the White House and endured harsh criticism from liberal groups to oppose the Iran deal out of principle because they believed it endangered the national security of the United States. In some cases these Democrats were subjected to anti-Semitic attacks and had their loyalty to this country questioned. These American patriots who opposed the Iran deal are listed in Figure 12.

Figure 12: Democratic Members of Congress Who Voted Against the JCPOA

- Senator Ben Cardin of Maryland
- Senator Joe Manchin of West Virginia
- Senator Robert Menendez of New Jersey
- Senator Chuck Schumer of New York
- Representative Brad Ashford (NE-02)
- Representative Brendan Boyle (PA-13)
- Representative Tony Cárdenas (CA-29)
- Representative Ted Deutch (FL-21)
- Representative Eliot Engel (NY-16)
- Representative Lois Frankel (FL-22)
- Representative Gwen Graham (FL-02)
- Representative Gene Green (TX-29)
- Representative Alcee Hastings (FL-20)
- Representative Steve Israel (NY-03)
- Representative Ted Lieu (CA-33)
- Representative Dan Lipinski (IL-03)
- Representative Nita Lowey (NY-17)
- Representative Carolyn Maloney (NY-12)
- Representative Grace Meng (NY-06)
- Representative Grace Napolitano (CA-32)
- Representative Donald Norcross (NJ-01)
- Representative Collin Peterson (MN-07)
- Representative Kathleen Rice (NY-04)
- Representative David Scott (GA-13)
- Representative Brad Sherman (CA-30)
- Representative Kyrsten Sinema (AZ-09)
- Representative Albio Sires (NJ-08)
- Representative Juan Vargas (CA-51)
- Representative Filemon Vela (TX-34)

Although President Obama and his supporters did victory laps after Congress failed to pass a resolution of disapproval, this was a pyrrhic victory since the Obamabomb Deal was opposed by majorities in the House and Senate and by a large majority of the American people. Moreover, as explained above, key arguments repeated over and over again by the Obama administration on how the nuclear deal would keep America safe, how it would stop Iran from pursuing nuclear weapons, robust verification provision, and other aspects of the agreement were strongly rebutted by members of President Obama's own party, especially Senator Schumer and Menendez and Congressmen Engel, Meng, and Sherman. Opposition to this agreement was not limited to so-called right-wing Republicans. It was forcefully voiced by senior Democrats in the House and Senate.

17. Iranian Behavior Worsens After Congress Votes on Obamabomb Deal

By doing nothing to respond, we run the risk of potentially indicating to the Iranians that we're willing to tolerate non-nuclear activity in a way that could make the Iranians misbehave more than they would otherwise.

Gary Samore, CNN.com
December 17, 2015[155]

After Congress voted on the Iran nuclear deal, Iran's belligerent and destabilizing behavior grew worse through the end of 2015. The Obama administration ignored or explained away this behavior so it would not endanger the nuclear agreement.

Iran Rejects UN Sanctions Barring Ballistic Missile Tests

On October 22, 2015, Iran tested the Emad missile, a long-range missile with a range of about 800 miles. According to Iranian Defense Minister Brigadier General Hossein Dehqan, the Emad is Iran's first long-range missile that can be precision-guided until it reaches its target. This missile appeared designed to strike Israel, located about 650 km from Iran's western border.

Iran conducted a test of a Ghadr-110 medium range ballistic missile on November 21, 2015. The Ghadr-110 has a range of about 1,200 miles and is capable of carrying a nuclear warhead.

A few days later, Iranian TV broadcast pictures of an underground tunnel storing medium and long-range ballistic missiles. While the location was not provided, the broadcast said the facility is one of hundreds of underground missile bases scattered across the country.

On the surface, these developments looked like Iranian noncompliance with the JCPOA since they conflicted with statements by President Obama and Secretary of State John Kerry that the nuclear agreement required Iran to comply with UN missile sanctions which they claimed would remain in place for eight years.

Iranian president Hassan Rouhani said on August 22, 2015 that Iran would not comply with UN Security Council Resolution 2231's provisions on UN missile sanctions. According to the government-controlled Fars News Agency, Rouhani said: "We will purchase weapons from wherever we deem necessary and we are not waiting for anyone's permission; if we deem necessary we will sell our weapons and we will do this without paying attention to any resolution."

However, on October 17, 2015 Iran modified its position when Iranian Foreign Minister Zarif said the JCPOA has nothing to do with missile sanctions because it "made no mention of missiles." While Zarif conceded there are provisions concerning missile sanctions in Resolution 2231 that endorsed the nuclear deal, he claimed Iran's missile tests had nothing to do with this resolution because it only barred missiles capable of carrying nuclear warheads.

Most arms control experts regarded Zarif's claim that Iran's missile are not nuclear capable as ridiculous. Not only is this the only logical purpose for these missiles, Iran is the only country in history to develop missiles with ranges of 2,000 km or more without having a nuclear weapons program. Iran is not building long-range missiles to carry warheads full of dynamite or to fire monkeys into space.

Incredibly, as Andrew McCarthy explained in an October 13, 2015 *National Review Online* article, the Obama administration seemed to support Zarif's argument. McCarthy said White House Spokesman Josh Earnest believes the Iranian missile test was separate from the JCPOA because

> (a) nuclear activities are somehow separate from activities involving ballistic missiles that can deliver nuclear weapons; (b) Security Resolution 2231 that implements the Iran deal is somehow separate from other Security Council resolutions that ban Iran's ballistic missile activities even though Resolution 2231, too, bans Iran's ballistic missile activities; and (c) Iran's pattern of violating international law pertaining to ballistic missiles that can deliver nuclear weapons is somehow irrelevant to the administration's level of confidence that it will adhere to its commitments regarding nuclear weapons development, notwithstanding that it has a history of flouting those commitments, too.[156]

Washington was surprised in late December 2015 when the Wall Street Journal reported on December 30 that the U.S. Treasury Department, in response to the Iranian missiles tests during the fall, notified Congress that it was planning to sanction about a dozen companies and individuals in Iran, the United Arab Emirates and Hong Kong for their suspected role in Iran's missile program.[157] According to the Journal article, the sanctions notification to Congress said: "Iran's ballistic missile program poses a significant threat to regional and global security."

The Treasury Department announcement came less than a week after Iran fired rockets in the Strait of Hormuz on December 26 that came within 1,500 yards of a U.S. aircraft carrier.

These sanctions were abruptly cancelled on December 31 when the Obama administration notified Congress they would be indefinitely delayed due to "evolving diplomatic work." This stunning reversal came after Iranian President Hassan Rouhani ordered his defense minister to speed up the country's missile program in response to reports of new U.S. sanctions over its missile tests. Some in Washington speculated that the Treasury officials who approved this sanction had not cleared it with the NSC and the State Department before notifying Congress.

Deputy National Security Adviser Ben Rhodes defended the decision to call off the new sanctions on Iran by saying "We just have additional work that needs to be done" with Iran and "they [the Iranian government] don't get a say on who we impose sanctions on." Congressional supporters and opponents of President Obama didn't buy Rhodes' explanation and strongly criticized the delay of the new sanctions.

Senator Bob Corker (R-TN) said about the cancellation of these sanctions: "I fear that pressure from our 'partners' – or threats from the Iranian government that it will walk away from the deal or threaten the US in other ways – have caused the administration to rethink imposing sanctions for Iran's violations of the testing ban."

Probably due to congressional pressure, the Treasury Department imposed sanctions on Iran for the missile tests on January 16, 2016 that Iran sanctions expert Mark Dubowitz dismissed as "symbolic and ineffective."

Obama officials may privately argue that the postponement of the December sanctions was so they would not interfere with ongoing diplomacy associated with the JCPOA's "Implementation Day" (January 16, 2016) and the release by Iran of American prisoners on that day. Such an argument is hard to defend since Iran's behavior worsened after Implementation Day – including more missile launches – but were met with no significant U.S. response. Instead, Obama officials were working in the spring of 2016 to grant Iran more concessions. This is discussed in Chapter 20.

Iranian Parliament Alters Nuclear Deal

The Iranian parliament in October 2015 approved its own amended version of the JCPOA that was drastically different, substantially limits Iran's cooperation, and demanded additional concessions. Supreme Leader Khamanei "endorsed" the nuclear deal with a letter to President Rouhani that placed ten conditions on Iran's acceptance of the agreement. According to Yigal Carmen and Ayelet Savyon of the Middle East Media Research Institute:

> The set of conditions laid out by Khamenei creates a situation in which not only does the Iranian side refrain from approving the JCPOA but, with nearly every point, creates a separate obstacle, such that executing the agreement is not possible.[158]

According to Reuters, on October 21, 2015, Khamenei declared that he would accept the JCPOA deal but only conditionally and demanded that the United States and the European Union acknowledge that the future imposition "of any type of sanctions, at any level or under any pretext would be considered by Iran a violation of the deal and release Iran from its obligations.[159] Khamenei also said Iran should delay sending its stockpile of enriched uranium abroad and reconfiguring a heavy water reactor to ensure it cannot make bomb-grade plutonium until the IAEA closed its file on Iranian PMD issues.

According to Amir Taheri, an Iranian-born Western journalist, the Iranian Parliament's bill on the JCPOA contains these provisions:

- The elimination of Israel's nuclear arsenal.

- Forbids the inspection of any military site and interviewing any officers.

- Calls on strengthening Iran's defenses, especially by developing its missile arsenal.

- Sanctions in the deal are canceled not suspended.

The United States and the IAEA have not commented publicly on the Iranian Parliament's alternate version of the JCPOA and how it will affect the IAEA's efforts to inspect Iranian military facilities and undeclared nuclear sites.

Other Hostile and Belligerent Behavior

Iranian behavior grew worse in other ways between September and December 2015. Iran stepped up its destabilizing behavior in the region by sending hundreds of troops and Hezbollah fighters to Syria to prop up the Assad regime. Iran also reportedly increased its support to the Houthi rebels in Yemen. Saudi officials announced on September 30, 2015 that a Saudi-led coalition seized an Iranian fishing boat loaded with weapons en route to these rebels

General John Campbell, the commander of U.S. forces in Afghanistan, said in testimony to the Senate Armed Services Committee October 2, 2015 that Iran was arming the Taliban in Afghanistan.[160]

On September 30, 2015, Bahraini security officials reported they discovered a large bomb-making factory and arrested a number of suspects linked to Iran's Revolutionary Guards.

On October 11, 2015 an Iranian court convicted *Washington Post* reporter Jason Rezaian of espionage. Iran continued to imprison three other innocent Americans: Iranian-American Christian pastor Saeed Abedini, former U.S. Marine Amir Hekmati, and former FBI agent Robert Levinson.

On October 30, 2015, Iran arrested another American, Iranian-American businessman Siamak Namazi, while he was visiting relatives in Tehran. Namazi's arrest was puzzling since he strongly backed the JCPOA and the lifting of sanctions against Iran. Iran also arrested in October 2015 Nizar Zakka, a Lebanese businessman who held a U.S. permanent resident green-card.

A November 4, 2015 *Wall Street Journal* article reported a surge in Iranian cyber attacks and an alleged effort by the Iranian Revolutionary Guard to hack email and social-media accounts of Obama administration officials.[161]

In October 2015, Iranian Qods Force commander Qassem Soleimani reportedly visited Moscow to meet with Russian officials despite a UN travel ban. Soleimani made another visit to Moscow in April 2016. Both trips reportedly were to negotiate the delivery of the Russian S-300 air defense system and to discuss Russian-Iranian support to the Assad regime in Syria.

This surge in belligerent Iranian behavior after Congress voted on the JCPOA greatly concerned critics of the nuclear deal since it disproved claims by President Obama and Secretary Kerry that the deal would lead to better U.S.-Iran relations and promote peace in the Middle East. Deal critics were more concerned, however that Obama officials ignored this behavior so it would not threaten the nuclear agreement.

18. Iran Defies IAEA Investigation of Past Nuclear Weapons Work

However, whether Iran actually has closed down all of its nuclear weapons related activities remains uncertain, given its poor level of cooperation with the IAEA, including the absence of any official admission of its past efforts. Some of its activities may continue in highly secret facilities or be actively retained for later use. When a country lies so often, as Iran has done on the nuclear issues, prudence requires continued pressure to reveal what it did and assessments that must assume the worst about its capabilities.

David Albright, Andrea Stricker, and Serena Kelleher-Vergantini "Analysis of the IAEA's Report on the PMD of Iran's Nuclear Program" Institute for Science and International Security, December 8, 2015.

The most important unresolved issue for the JCPOA the after the September 2015 congressional votes concerned the IAEA investigation of Iran's past nuclear weapons-related work (the possible military dimensions of Iran's nuclear program or PMDs). As explained in chapter 5, resolving PMD issues is important for establishing a meaningful nuclear agreement with Iran for two reasons. First, resolving PMD issues would give the international community confidence that Iran actually ceased all nuclear weapons related activities. Second, PMD-related information is important to establishing a baseline for verification of the nuclear accord since it will help IAEA inspectors understand what types of nuclear activities in which Iran was engaged and where they were conducted.

I explained in chapter 5 the seriousness of the 2011 IAEA PMD report which discussed disturbing information the agency had acquired on covert Iranian nuclear activities, including that Iran was developing a nuclear warhead, a reentry vehicle for a nuclear warhead, and researching how a Shahab missile could be modified to carry a nuclear warhead. A December 2015 IAEA PMD report was even more disturbing.

Opponents of the Iran deal strongly criticized Secretary Kerry in June 2015 when he dismissed the need to resolve PMD issues. Opponents also charged that language in the JCPOA appeared to indicate that Iran would suffer no penalties if it failed to provide honest and forthcoming answers to the IAEA's PMD inquiry and that it was unrealistic for the IAEA to investigate and resolve the remaining PMD questions in only five months.

Kerry seemed to reverse himself on his June 2015 comments on the need for Iran to resolve PMD issues when he said in a July 24, 2015 speech:

> PMD has to be resolved – before they get one ounce of sanctions relief. Now that could take six months, it could take a year. I don't know how long. But the IAEA has to certify that all of that has been done and we have received our one-year breakout before they get a dime.[162]

The State Department backed away from this position in October 2015. An unnamed senior U.S. official said during a State Department briefing on October 17, 2015 that Iran only had to perform a series of procedural steps to demonstrate its cooperation with the IAEA's PMD investigation.[163] The official said that the quality of the data Iran provides to the IAEA was not important because "the U.S. Government has already made its assessment on Iran's past [nuclear] programs." This official also said the PMD investigation is not part of the nuclear agreement text and thus has no bearing on whether sanctions against Iran will be lifted.

This statement confirmed the worst fears of critics of the JCPOA and confirmed the June 11, 2015 Middle East Media Research Institute report cited in Chapter 9: the Obama administration caved on the PMD issue in response to last minute demands by Iran. Meanwhile, Iran continued to insist if the IAEA did not close its file on the PMD issue, it would pull out of the nuclear agreement.

Per the secret IAEA-Iran side deal to the JCPOA, Iranians collected samples at the Parchin military base without IAEA officials present on September 20, 2015. Further muddying the waters, IAEA director general Yukiya Amano made a ceremonial visit to Parchin over the same weekend that Iranians conducted inspections for the IAEA. According to Amano, "We entered a building which the agency had previously only been able to observe using satellite imagery. Inside the building, we saw indications of recent renovation work. There was no equipment in the building." Predictably, supporters of the JCPOA tried to portray Amano's visit to Parchin as an inspection by IAEA officials.

The IAEA issued a statement on October 15 that Iran had provided sufficient cooperation for it to issue a report by a December 15, 2015 deadline with its final assessment on outstanding PMD issues. However, Amano hinted at problems with his upcoming PMD report in a November 26, 2015 speech when he indicated that Iran's failure to fully cooperate with the PMD investigation would prevent him from concluding that all of Iran's nuclear materials were being used for peaceful purposes:

> As my latest report on safeguards implementation in Iran shows, the Agency continues to verify the non-diversion of nuclear material declared by Iran under its Safeguards Agreement. But we are not in a position to provide credible assurance about the absence of undeclared nuclear material and activities in Iran, and therefore to conclude that all nuclear material in Iran is being used for peaceful activities. [164]

Amano also told reporters that his PMD report "won't be black and white" and described it as a jigsaw puzzle for which the IAEA has gathered "pieces."

The IAEA Issues a "Final Report" on PMD Issues

The IAEA issued its report on the possible military dimensions of Iran's nuclear program on December 2, 2015.[165] This report, carried out in response to a "roadmap" agreement reached between Iran and the IAEA in July 2015, was intended to address 12 unresolved PMD issues raised in the November 2011 IAEA PMD "dossier." This report's title, "Final Assessment on Past and Present Outstanding Issues regarding Iran's Nuclear Programme," appeared to reflect Iran's demand that the IAEA must close its Iran PMD "file" for the JCPOA to proceed.

The short time the IAEA was given to investigate and resolve so many complex PMD issues and the refusal by Iran to allow the IAEA to interview Iranian nuclear scientists was criticized by opponents of the JCPOA. Former IAEA Chief Inspector Olli Heinonen questioned the investigation's scope in Senate testimony in July 2015 by noting it was limited to PMD issues raised in the IAEA's November 2011 PMD report.[166] Heinenen said in his testimony that IAEA Director General Amano "has stated on several occasions that there is information that some [Iranian PMD] activities have continued in recent years that may not be identical to those in the 2011 report."

Per the July 2015 roadmap agreement, Iran provided answers to the IAEA's PMD questions by August 15, 2015. The IAEA then met with IAEA officials to discuss its follow-up questions between September 15 and October 15, 2015.

Critics of the nuclear agreement considered the IAEA PMD report to be a bombshell since it indicated Iran had not fully cooperated with the IAEA investigation and provided some answers that were false. The Institute for Science and International Security gave this blistering overview of the IAEA PMD report in an initial assessment it issued on December 2, 2015:

- Despite obfuscation and stonewalling by Iran, the IAEA confirmed that Iran had a coordinated nuclear weapons development program until the end of 2003 and conducted some weapons development activities after 2003.

- Overall, Iran provided little real cooperation. Denials and lack of truthfulness should not be confused with cooperation in the context of the JCPOA, any more than such "cooperation" by a defendant in a criminal investigation would be construed as real cooperation.

- Faced with such outright Iranian efforts to deceive the inspectors, the IAEA broke relatively little new ground.

- The truth of Iran's work on nuclear weapons is probably far more extensive than outlined by the IAEA in this report.

- The IAEA drew conclusions where it was able to. The bottom line is that the IAEA's investigation into the possible military dimensions of Iran's nuclear programs cannot be understood to be concluded, certainly it cannot be closed.[167]

The Obama administration endorsed the PMD report, saying Iran's cooperation was sufficient for the nuclear deal to stand and that it enabled the removal of sanctions from Iran as early as January 2016. Obama officials also said they never expected Iran to admit engaging in nuclear weapons work and stressed that the JCPOA was a forward looking document.[168]

In an article on a government-controlled Iranian news service, Iranian Deputy Foreign Minister Abbas Araghchi was cited as saying the IAEA report closed the IAEA's Iran PMD file:

Therefore, all measures over the past issues have been completely concluded and PMD has been left behind. No phrase denoting Iran's diversion from its commitments regarding NPT is seen in the report, he said, the agency has also verified Iran's nuclear program in its report.

Araqchi claimed the IAEA report endorsed the peaceful nature of Iran's nuclear program and paved the way for closing the file of PMD in Board of Governors.[169]

On December 8, the Institute for Science and International Security provided an even harsher assessment of the IAEA PMD report.

> Iran's answers and explanations for many of the IAEA's concerns were, at best, partial, but overall, obfuscating and stonewalling. Faced with evidence, Iran offered largely civilian or conventional (non-nuclear) military justifications for many of the outstanding issues of concern, denied the activities' relation to nuclear weapons work, or denied the activities or evidence outright. In many cases its answers appeared contrived. In no single case did Iran admit to the central conclusion reached by the IAEA in the report or by the United States and several other governments – that it had a structured nuclear weapons program prior to 2003 and a limited effort afterwards. It did not explain how the activities of concern related to this program. It also did not allow the IAEA to interview key scientists and other people of interest associated with the program. Needed access to sites was either denied or tightly controlled as to preclude adequate inspections.
>
> In a new revelation, the IAEA stated that its evidence of nuclear weapons efforts extended to 2009. On one side, it stated that it had no credible evidence of nuclear weapons-related work after that year, but on the other, the IAEA was also unable to conclude with certainty that the program ended in 2009. Thus, the best that can be said is that the program continued to at least 2009. This revelation refutes the unclassified 2007 U.S. National Intelligence Estimate (NIE) which assessed that Iran's nuclear weapons program was halted in the fall of 2003, and that Iran had not restarted this program as of mid-2007. The IAEA's finding is more in line with the assessments of Britain, France, Germany, and Israel, which stated that nuclear weapons related activities continued after 2003. This IAEA finding also shows that Iranian government claims of a fatwa against nuclear weapons is more for outward show.[170]

Given the Institute's steadfast opposition to the Bush administration's Iran policy, it was significant to see it finally admit that the 2007 Iran NIE had been refuted. I took a similar line in an December 21, 2015 *Town Hall* article titled "James Schlesinger and Alan Dershowitz Were Right About 'Stupid' Iran Intelligence" in which I explained how Schlesinger and Dershowitz were right when they slammed the 2007 NIE.[171]

The Obama administration took a different view. State Department spokesman Mark Toner said after the release of the PMD report that it was "consistent" with the 2007 Iran NIE.[172]

Iran's Nuclear Program May Have Continued After 2009

In a December 2, 2015 *National Review Online* article, I discussed the PMD report's language suggesting that Iran's nuclear weapon research efforts may not have ended in 2009.

> The IAEA's contention that there are no "credible indications" of nuclear-weapons related activities in Iran after 2009 is suspicious since it is possible that the United States stopped providing intelligence to the IAEA on Iran's nuclear weapons work after Barack Obama became president. Congress must press for answers about this and determine whether the IAEA has what it considers "less than credible" indications that Iranian nuclear weapons work continued after 2009. I find it hard to believe that Iran stopped all nuclear weapons related-work the year Mr. Obama assumed the Oval Office.[173]

The Institute report also discussed whether Iran's nuclear weapons program had not been halted in 2009.

> The evidence does not allow a conclusion that Iran's nuclear weapons efforts ended in 2009, but notably the year 2009 coincides with the revelation of and then confirmed re-purposing of the Fordow enrichment facility. In September 2009, the United States, France, and Britain publicly revealed the existence of the then-secret Fordow enrichment facility. IAEA evidence supported the assessment that this enrichment site was part of an on-going secret nuclear weapons effort. The rapid modifications made at the site and its original nature (small, deeply buried, and unable to handle large natural uranium feed cylinders) pointed to a plant designed to make weapon-grade uranium. After the plant was revealed, Iran extensively modified the insides of the plant and declared that the site would produce low enriched uranium under safeguards. The revelation of the advanced construction of a secret centrifuge plant was highly embarrassing to Iran and shifted international opinion significantly against it. As in 2003, faced with the risk of further disclosures, Iran may have decided to close down any remaining nuclear weapons related work.

> However, whether Iran actually has closed down all of its nuclear weapons related activities remains uncertain, given its poor level of cooperation with the IAEA, including the absence of any official admission of its past efforts. Some of its activities may continue in highly secret facilities or be actively retained for later use. When a country lies so often, as Iran has done on the nuclear issues, prudence requires continued pressure to reveal what it did and assessments that must assume the worst about its capabilities.

Former IAEA Chief Inspector Olli Heinonen drew a related conclusion in a December 8, 2015 memo.

> ...for the first time, the IAEA has linked various instances of previously reported clandestine activities into a coherent account of Tehran's nuclear-weapons development process. In other words, the IAEA has noted that Iran's

clandestine nuclear activities represented a parallel nuclear program (from mining to uranium conversion and enrichment) carried out alongside its declared one.[174]

Iran Misled the IAEA About Nuclear Weapons Work at Parchin

Another startling revelation in the IAEA PMD report concerned the Parchin military base where Iran reportedly had engaged in explosive testing related to the development of a nuclear warhead, including installing a large cylinder for hydrodynamic experiments with high explosives. The report referenced satellite imagery showing activities at this site since 2012 to shroud building, removal of five buildings, and "significant ground scraping and landscaping." The IAEA report also mentioned uranium particles that Obama officials later said were probably evidence of a nuclear weapons program.

Despite a controversial secret side deal allowing Iranians to conduct a limited investigation of the Parchin military base, the IAEA concluded that Iran's explanation that a suspect building at Parchin was used for the storage of chemical explosives was not consistent with environmental sampling and satellite imagery. The IAEA also reported that it found two particles of what appeared to be "chemically man-made particles of natural uranium" at the Parchin site although the Agency said this was not enough evidence to conclude the use of nuclear material at the site.

Although Obama officials did not comment on this finding when the IAEA report was released, Wall Street Journal writer Jay Solomon revealed in June 2016 that the Obama administration had concluded these particles likely were tied to Iran's past covert nuclear weapons program.[175]

The report also noted that when IAEA Director General Amano paid a ceremonial visit to a suspect Parchin building in September 2015 there was no sign of the explosive chamber but there were recent signs of "internal refurbishment" of the building.

Many experts have accused Iran of trying to hide evidence of nuclear weapons-related work at Parchin. The IAEA report agreed, saying that "extensive activities" at this site seriously undermined the Agency's ability to conduct effective verification.[176]

The most significant aspect of the IAEA's findings about Parchin was not what the IAEA found, but what it was not allowed to find. The extremely limited investigation of this site using Iranian inspectors and a small number of pre-determined sampling locations was a mockery of arms control verification. One has to wonder what Iran is hiding at Parchin and what independent IAEA inspectors would have found if they had been given the freedom to inspect the Parchin base without restrictions. Given the extraordinary steps Iran has taken to remove possible evidence of nuclear or other WMD-related work from Parchin, there must be some very damning evidence at this site that Tehran is desperate to hide from the international community.

Iran Offered Misleading Information, Non-Answers and Refused to Answer IAEA PMD Questions

Of the 12 issues the IAEA pursued in its PMD investigation, Iran provided limited cooperation to nine but generally provided explanations of non-nuclear military or commercial uses. It refused to reply to three issues: "Nuclear Components for an Explosive Device" [concerning a document on the fabrication of uranium metal hemispheres Iran may have received from the A.Q. Khan Network], "Conducting a Test" [on whether Iran conducted an explosive test with explosive bridgewire detonators], and "Fuzing, Arming, and Firing System" [concerning alleged Iranian efforts to construct what was believed to be a nuclear warhead for a Shahab missile].

The IAEA report said Iran provided some cooperation to resolve the PMD issue "Integration into a Missile Delivery Vehicle" which concerned reports that Iran was engaged in an effort to construct a reentry vehicle for a nuclear warhead. However, this cooperation consisted of Iran showing the IAEA a video of two workshops where this work allegedly took place and inviting the Agency to visit two of the workshops. Iran was not required to explain the reentry vehicle information and the IAEA did not provide details on its visits to the workshops.

Bottom Line: Iran did not fully cooperate with the IAEA's PMD investigation and went through the motions to answer questions with misleading or false responses, non-answers or refusing to answer. Former IAEA Chief Inspector Heinonen also came to this conclusion in a December 8, 2015 memo on the PMD report.

> The JCPOA provided the Islamic Republic with an opportunity to clarify its past nuclear-weapons work, but it refused to come clean. Instead, Tehran yet again failed to fulfill its obligations under Security Council resolutions

demanding it "cooperate fully with the Agency on all outstanding issues, particularly those which gave rise to concerns about the possible military dimensions to Iran's nuclear programme, including by providing access without delay to all sites, equipment, persons and documents requested by the Agency." Without Iran's cooperation and transparency, the file simply cannot be closed.
177

The IAEA Board of Governors Votes to Close the IAEA's Iran PMD File

Ordinarily, an IAEA investigation like the Iran PMD inquiry which uncovered this level of incriminating information and encountered such poor cooperation and deceptive answers would require follow-up investigations and threats of sanctions by other IAEA members if this state continued to refuse to fully cooperate with IAEA investigators. That's not what happened in response to the IAEA's December 2, 2015 Iran PMD report. Instead, in mid-December 2015 the United States proposed a resolution at the IAEA Board of Governors to close the IAEA's Iran PMD file. In a speech to the Board on the resolution, U.S. Ambassador to the IAEA Henry Ensher said the IAEA's report was consistent with previous IAEA assessments regarding Iran's nuclear program and noted that the report found that Iran had pursued "a coordinated program of nuclear weapons-related activities, and that certain activities relevant to nuclear weaponization remained ongoing in Iran until at least 2009." Ensher made no reference to the unanswered questions in the PMD report or Iran's failure to fully cooperate with the investigation.

Ambassador Ensher said in his speech that the U.S. resolution "terminates relevant IAEA Board resolutions and decisions regarding Iran" which meant it was closing the file on prior IAEA resolutions and investigations of previous Iranian weapons related activities.

The 22-member IAEA Board of Governors unanimously passed this resolution to close the IAEA's Iran PMD file on December 15, 2015. This was one a blatant examples of the Obama administration ignoring violations of Iran's international commitments to protect the Obamabomb Deal. This resolution was passed because Iran refused to budge on the PMD issue and insisted that it must be quickly resolved or it threatened to back out of the nuclear agreement. The Board of Governors resolution and Ambassador Ensher's statement suggests that it was intended to permanently close the IAEA's Iran PMD files. It is my hope that a future U.S. president will force the IAEA to reopen its Iran PMD file and require Tehran to provide truthful answers to all PMD questions as part of a new, much tougher nuclear agreement that actually halts all Iranian nuclear activities with weapons applications.

19. Iran's Big Payoff: Implementation Day

Today marks the moment that the Iran nuclear agreement transitions from an ambitious set of promises on paper to measurable action in progress. Today, as a result of the actions taken since last July, the United States, our friends and allies in the Middle East, and the entire world are safer because the threat of the nuclear weapon has been reduced.

Secretary of State John Kerry, January 16, 2016

2016 began with growing anticipation that "Implementation Day" – when most sanctions against Iran would be lifted under the JCPOA and Tehran would receive over $100 billion in sanctions relief – would soon occur. Implementation Day was declared on January 16 by the IAEA when it assessed that Iran had met certain requirements to roll back its nuclear program.

President Obama fed this anticipation in his final State of the Union address on January 12 when he lauded his administration's efforts to negotiate the nuclear deal and again insisted the agreement prevented a war with Iran:

> That's why we built a global coalition, with sanctions and principled diplomacy, to prevent a nuclear-armed Iran. As we speak, Iran has rolled back its nuclear program, shipped out its uranium stockpile, and the world has avoided another war.

Iran Captures and Mistreats American Sailors

Screen shot from Iranian television of U.S. sailors taken prisoner by Iran, January 12, 2016.

The President did not mention in his speech that Iran's belligerent and destabilizing behavior worsened since the announcement of the nuclear deal in July. There was no reference to Iran's ballistic missile tests. Mr. Obama also did not mention the latest Iranian provocation: the seizure by Iran earlier that day of 10 sailors aboard two small Navy ships that drifted into Iranian waters in the Persian Gulf after experiencing mechanical problems.

During the 15 hours the sailors were held, Iran humiliated them, forced an American female sailor to wear a hijab, and released photos of the sailors with their hands up surrounded by armed Iranian soldiers. The sailors also were interrogated, filmed while crying and forced to apologize at gunpoint. One of the sailors was forced to make a video apologizing for wandering into Iranian territory and thanking Iran for "your hospitality and your assistance." Despite the mistreatment and humiliation of the U.S. sailors, Secretary of State John Kerry thanked Iran for treating the sailors well and credited improved U.S.-Iran relations due to the nuclear deal with Iran for the quick resolution of this incident.

I believe Iran seized the U.S. sailors and publicly humiliated them on the day of President Obama's last State of the Union address to send a message to the United States and the world that it had no intention of backing away from its belligerent policies in the Middle East due to the nuclear deal. Obama officials took a different view, claiming that the quick resolution of this incident proved "diplomacy works" and the benefits to U.S. national security gained due to the nuclear agreement. This interpretation was ridiculed by Republicans.

Four months later, Congressman Randy Forbes (R-VA) raised new questions about this incident when he said that the full details on how badly the American sailors were mistreated by Iran will shock the nation but won't be released for at least a year because the Obama administration has classified this information. I wrote in a June 10, 2016 Fox News Opinion op-ed that like most Americans, I am already outraged by what has been publicly released about this incident and posed the question: "What could have happened that the Obama administration does not want us to know?"[178] Although I support Congressman Forbes' legislation, I also called on members of Congress to release the classified report on Iran's mistreatment of American sailors last January.

Senator John Cornyn (R-TX) and Congressman Mike Pompeo (R-KS) introduced legislation on May 26, 2016 to hold Iran accountable for possible violations of the Geneva Convention related to the apprehension and detention of the American sailors in January 2016. The "No Impunity for Iranian Aggression at Sea Act" would require the Obama administration to impose sanctions on those responsible, if violations occurred.[179]

IAEA Declares Implementation Day

On January 16, 2016 the IAEA announced that Iran had satisfied the conditions necessary to lift most international sanctions under the JCPOA. In exchange for reducing its number of operational uranium enrichment centrifuges, sending most of its enriched uranium out of the country, and removing the core of a plutonium-producing heavy-water reactor, Iran received approximately $150 billion in sanctions relief, and the United States agreed to pay $400 million plus $1.3 billion in interest to pay a debt to Iran related to an unfulfilled pre-1979 arms contract.

Also on Implementation Day, U.S. officials announced that Iran would release five Americans it had held prisoner in exchange for the release of seven Iranian criminals held by the United States. 14 others wanted by the United States for illegally transferring military technology to Iran also were removed from an INTERPOL watch list as part of the prisoner exchange.

Implementation Day brought huge economic benefits to Iran. It was able to sell oil again on world markets and reconnect to the world banking system, although U.S. financial sanctions remained in place. On January 28, Airbus announced a $25 billion deal to sell Iran 118 airliners. Boeing announced a similar $25 billion deal on June 21, 2016. The Obama administration granted Boeing and Airbus licenses to proceed with this deal on September 21, 2016.

The White House and Iran deal supporters argued that Iran's compliance with the nuclear deal and its willingness to swap prisoners proved the wisdom of the president's Iran policy. But there are three reasons to believe these developments were actually dangerous wins for Iran.

First, the bar Iran had to meet to get to Implementation Day was very low. Iran was allowed to continue to enrich uranium and develop advanced centrifuges. Iran was continuing to produce heavy-water. Iran signed a deal with China to redesign and rebuild the Arak heavy-water reactor which, as described in Chapter 10, remains a serious nuclear proliferation concern. The IAEA reported that Iran sent most of its enriched uranium stockpile to Russia, but did not say how much was sent or whether it monitored the transfer. The enriched uranium Iran sent to Russia was swapped for an equivalent amount of uranium ore from Kazakhstan which can be converted into enriched uranium in a few months. In January 2016, IAEA began to water down its reports on Iran's nuclear program and stopped reporting how much uranium Iran was enriching every month.

Iran also was granted secret exemptions to meet the Implementation Day requirements that were not revealed to Congress and the American people until September 2016.

Second, Iran's ballistic missiles and the PMD issue had no bearing on Implementation Day. Since missiles were removed from the agreement, Iran's missile tests in the fall of 2015 (and more tests in the spring of 2016) did not violate the nuclear deal. In addition, although Iran did not fully comply with the IAEA's PMD investigation, IAEA members ignored this and voted unanimously on December 15, 2015 to close the Agency's PMD file.

Third, the agreement did not hold Iran accountable for its destabilizing and belligerent behavior, including increased support to Syria's Assad regime, backing the Houthi rebels in Yemen, and threatening Israel and Persian Gulf shipping. Implementation Day also was not affected by the Iranian Parliament's action to pass a revised version of the Iran deal in October 2016 that put Iranian military bases off-limits to IAEA inspectors.

U.S.-Iran Prisoner Swap Frees Five Americans

The exchange of American and Iranian prisoners on Implementation Day raised many serious concerns. The five U.S. citizens released by Iran, several of whom were brutally mistreated while behind bars, were arrested because they were Americans, and thus made good bargaining chips in Iran's efforts to influence U.S. policy. For this reason, many Obama administration critics referred to the U.S. prisoners as hostages. They were released for Iranians and other nationals who had been convicted or accused of violating U.S. laws barring transfers of WMD technology and arms to Iran.

This swap alone was criticized by many experts for setting a dangerous precedent. Criticism of the swap intensified after details emerged of a large cash payment to Iran that appeared to be a ransom payment.

The five Americans released by Iran were *Washington Post* journalist Jason Rezaian (held 18 months), Marine veteran Amir Hekmati (held 4½ years), Christian pastor Saeed Abedini (held 3 ½ years), an Iranian-American man named Nosratollah Khosravi (held 19 months), and Matthew Trevithick (held 41 days), a U.S. student.

Khosravi reportedly was arrested by Iranian authorities after he attempted to send the FBI information on the whereabouts of Robert Levinson, a former FBI agent and U.S. citizen who disappeared in Iran in 2007.[180] Levinson was not released in the prisoner swap. The Iranian government denies knowing anything about Levinson's whereabouts.

Trevithick left Iran on January 16. The other four U.S prisoners were not allowed to leave Iran until a plane carrying $400 million in cash from the United States had landed the next day.

The Americans were freed in exchange for the release of seven Iranians by the United States: Nader Modanlo, Bahram Mechanic, Khosrow Afghahi, Tooraj Faridi, Arash Ghahreman, Nima Golestaneh and Ali Saboonchi.

All of these Iranians had been convicted of violating U.S. laws on transfers of military technology to Iran. Modanlo, an aerospace expert and former NASA contractor, had been found guilty of money laundering and helping facilitate a deal between Iran and Russia to launch a satellite. Golestaneh was convicted of hacking U.S. aerodynamics/defense contractor Arrow Tech Associates to steal software on behalf of Iran.

All of the released Iranians were dual U.S.-Iranian nationals except for Golestaneh, an Iranian national. The six U.S.-Iranian nationals were permitted to remain in the United States if they wished and were expected to do so. Golestaneh's social media accounts in September 2016 indicated he was living in Iran. As a condition of their pardon, all of the released Iranians had to agree not to sue the U.S. government or accept payment for "any book, movie, or other publication or production" about their situations.

Fourteen others accused of similar crimes by the United States were removed from an INTERPOL wanted list as part of the prisoner swap deal: Mohammad Abbas Mohammadi, Kurosh Taherkhani, Sajjad Farhadi, Seyed Ahmad Abtahi, Gholamreza Mahmudi, Hamid Arabnezhad, Ali Mo'attar, Mohammad Ali She'rbaaf, Amin Ravan, Behruz Dowlatzadeh, Said Jamili, Jalal Salami, Matin Sadeghi, Alireza Mo'azami-Gudarzi.

All of the 14 dropped from the INTERPOL list had sole Iranian citizenship except for Sadeghi, a Turkish citizen, and Salami, a dual U.S.-Iranian citizen. These 14 suspects were outside the United States in January 2016 and deemed unlikely to be apprehended by U.S. authorities for violating U.S. laws on transfers of arms and military technology to Iran. All were accused of transferring advanced military technology to Iran except for Dolatzadeh who was wanted for attempting to send thousands of U.S. assault rifles to Iran.

Not all of the Americans being held by Iran were freed. Former FBI agent Robert Levinson (detained in 2007), Iranian-American businessman Siamak Namazi and Nizar Zakka, a Lebanese businessman with permanent green-card (both arrested in November 2015), were not released. Iran may have illegally detained other U.S. citizens whose names have not been released by the U.S. government.

Iran reportedly arrested at least six more Iranian dual citizens from Western countries in 2016 after the prisoner swap who travelled to Iran to visit relatives. These include Reza "Robin" Shahini, a U.S.- Iranian national (arrested in July); Nazak Afshar, a French citizen (arrested in March); Nanzanin Zaghari-Ratcliffe, a

British charity worker (arrested in April) and Homa Hoodfar, a Canadian academic (arrested in June). In addition, Baquer Namazi, an Iranian citizen and father of Siamak Namazi, was arrested in February when he tried to get his son out of prison.

Abdolrasoul Dorri Esfahani, an Iranian-Canadian national who reportedly was part of Iran's nuclear talks negotiating team, was arrested on August 19, 2016 on charges of espionage.

The Ransom Payment Controversy

Critics of the JCPOA have criticized the Obama administration for paying ransom to Iran to free U.S. prisoners because four of them were not allowed to leave Iran until an unmarked plane from Geneva carrying $400 million in bales of euros and Swiss francs had landed. Although Congress was told by the Obama administration on January 17, 2016 that the U.S. agreed to a $1.7 billion settlement with Iran, Obama officials did not give any details about this payment, including that it had been made in cash.

Iranian officials claimed in January 2016 that the $1.7 million was a ransom payment. That also was the view at the time of many Republican members of Congress.

This story became a major scandal on August 3, 2016 when the *Wall Street Journal* reported that the U.S. secretly flew a planeload of $400 million in cash from Geneva to Iran on January 17, 2016.[181] This scandal grew worse over the next two months due to a series of shifting explanations by Obama officials and the surfacing of new details which contradicted these explanations.

Although the release of the five American prisoners was announced on Implementation Day (January 16), four of them – Jason Rezaian, Amir Hekmati, Saeed Abedini, and Nosratollah Khosravi – were not allowed to leave Iran until January 17. Khosravi left Iran by himself. The other three Americans were on a plane that was held at Tehran's Mehrabad Airport until the planeload of cash had landed.

Abedini said in an August 4, 2016 Fox Business Channel interview that he and two other American prisoners were released from an Iranian prison on January 16 and arrived at the Mehrabad Airport around 2 or 3 PM that day. The three Americans spent the night at the airport until another plane arrived. Abedini said their plane was allowed to take off at about 10 AM, January 17. Abedini was told by

Iranian authorities about the delay: "we are waiting for another plane" but was not told what this plane was carrying.[182]

The Obama administration has been adamant that the $400 million paid to Iran was not ransom but payment of a debt the United States owed Iran for a pre-1979 arms purchase. According to Obama officials, the United States was legally obligated to make the $400 million payment plus interest due to a claim Iran had filed against the United States in the Iran-United States Claims Tribunal. This tribunal was set up in The Hague in 1981 to conduct third-party arbitration of financial claims by each country against the other. The Obama administration maintains the $400 million payment was in America's interests because the tribunal would have made a much larger award to Iran if it had ruled on this claim. Iran reportedly was seeking a $10 billion settlement.

Obama officials said the $400 million had to be made in cash because U.S. sanctions laws prevented wire transfers to Iran by the United States and because Iran was unable to receive wire transfers due to international sanctions. These claims later proved to be untrue since wire transfers were possible through third countries. In addition, Andrew McCarthy wrote in *National Review* on August 6, 2016 that the $400 million payment violated U.S. law on financial payments to Iran regardless of whether the payment was wired or paid in cash.[183] According to McCarthy, this payment violated the Treasury Department's Iranian Transactions and Sanctions Regulations (ITSR), the part of the Code of Federal Regulations that implements anti-terrorism sanctions initiated by President Clinton under federal law. McCarthy argued that the $400 million sent to Iran was illegal regardless of how it was paid because under ITSR:

> The exportation, re-exportation, sale, or supply, directly or indirectly, from the United States, or by a United States person, wherever located, of any goods, technology, or services to Iran or the Government of Iran is prohibited.

Obama officials claimed the $1.7 billion payment to Iran was entirely separate from the nuclear talks and was conducted by a different negotiating team in Geneva. However, the administration seemed to backtrack on this claim on August 18 when a State Department spokesman said the $400 million payment had been delayed to use as leverage to assure a plane carrying three freed American prisoners had left Iran.[184]

The idea that there was no relationship between the payment to Iran and the release of the U.S. prisoners also was undermined by an August 3, 2016 *Wall Street*

Journal article which reported that senior Justice Department officials objected to sending the planeload of cash to Iran at the same time Iran released the imprisoned Americans because the payment would look like ransom and the Iranian government would regard it as such.[185] As mentioned earlier, the Justice Department officials were right: Iranian officials did publicly portray the $400 million payment as ransom.

Despite the August 3, 2016 *Wall Street Journal* revelation about the secret planeload of cash, for several weeks Obama officials refused to provide details about this payment to the public or Congress because they claimed they wanted to protect the confidentiality of U.S. agreements with Tehran.

Claudia Rosett, a journalist and national security expert, put enormous pressure on the Obama administration to explain how the $1.3 billion in interest was paid when she revealed in an August 22, 2016 *New York Sun* article that 13 transfers of $99,999,999.99 were made on January 19, 2016 from the Treasury Department to the State Department's "Judgment Fund" – a fund used to pay foreign claims against the United States.[186] These payments totaled $1,299,999,999.87, – 13 cents less than $1.3 billion. Rosett also wrote that a 14th transfer to the Judgment Fund of $10 million also was made on January 19.

Rosett reported that that the Obama administration informed Congress in March 2016 that the $1.3 billion interest payment to Iran was made from the Judgment Fund but gave no details on the logistics of this payment.

Rosett's article fed growing outrage over the alleged ransom payments to Iran and forced the Obama administration to give more details on the $1.3 billion payment to Tehran. The administration finally admitted during classified briefings to congressional staff and members on September 6, 2016 that the $1.3 billion was paid to Iran in two additional planeloads of cash on January 22 and February 5.[187] Although the administration confirmed that the $1.3 billion came from the Judgment Fund, it did not explain the purpose or recipient of the additional $10 million transfer to the Judgment Fund revealed by Rosett.

Claims by Obama officials that the prisoner swap was the result of separate negotiations and were not part of the nuclear talks are hard to take seriously. I believe the truth is that the prisoner exchange was always part of the nuclear talks and the Obama administration created the fiction of unconnected, separate talks to avoid disclosing the controversial aspects of the prisoner exchange to Congress. Moreover, the secrecy of these cash payments probably was to avoid reporting them to Congress as required by the Corker-Cardin Act. (See discussion of Corker-Cardin in Chapter 12.) Under this Act, all JCPOA side deals were required to be reported to Congress for a congressional review before Congress voted on the agreement in September 2015. I therefore believe the ransom payments were another secret JCPOA side deal that Obama officials illegally withheld from Congress.

Given that one of Iran's main goals in the nuclear talks was the lifting of UN and international sanctions, I believe Iranian diplomats insisted throughout the nuclear talks that no U.S. prisoners would be released until this happened. I also believe the Obama administration desperately wanted the U.S. prisoners released on Implementation Day to distract from the $150 billion Iran would receive in sanctions relief. To make this happen, Iran probably demanded the $1.7 billion be paid in cash.

Prisoner Swap Set Dangerous Precedent, Enraged Congress

The prisoner exchange and ransom payment set a dangerous precedent. It was disturbing to see President Obama and Secretary Kerry on January 16, 2016 thanking and praising Iran for releasing innocent American citizens it had imprisoned and tortured instead of clearly stating these Americans should not have been arrested in the first place and the United States will not stand for innocent Americans being held for years and brutally mistreated in foreign prisons. The celebratory comments by Obama and Kerry about the prisoner swap and the fact that the United States exchanged Iranian criminals for innocent Americans could lead other rogue nations and terrorist groups to capture and kidnap more Americans in the future to trade them for concessions from Washington.

Senator Ted Cruz reflected the views of most Republicans when he told Fox News Sunday on January 17, 2016:

> . . . this deal is a problematic deal, and it reflects a pattern we have seen in the Obama administration over and over again of negotiating with terrorists, and making deals and trades that endanger U.S. safety and security.
>
> This deal has a lot of deals in common with the Bowe Bergdahl deal, where in exchange for Bowe Bergdahl – someone now facing court-martial – we released five senior Taliban terrorists.
>
> And this instance, this deal to bring back Americans who were wrongly imprisoned, we release seven terrorists who helped Iran with their nuclear program and we agreed not to prosecute another 14 terrorists for doing the same thing. That's 21 terrorists helping Iran develop nuclear weapons that they intend to use to try to murder us.

And I think it's a very dangerous precedent. The result of this, every bad actor on earth has been told go capture an American. If you want terrorists out of the jail, capture an American and President Obama is in the let's make a deal business. That's a really dangerous precedent."[188]

Conservative pundit Charles Krauthammer disagreed, claiming Republicans were wrong to oppose the prisoner swap.

And in denouncing the swap, they were wrong. True, we should have made the prisoner release a precondition for negotiations. But that preemptive concession was made long ago (among many others, such as granting Iran in advance the right to enrich uranium). The remaining question was getting our prisoners released before we gave away all our leverage upon implementation of the nuclear accord. We did.

Republicans say: We shouldn't negotiate with terror states. But we do and we should. How else do you get hostages back? And yes, of course negotiating encourages further hostage taking. But there is always something to be gained by kidnapping Americans. This swap does not affect that truth one way or the other.

And here, we didn't give away much. The seven released Iranians, none of whom has blood on his hands, were sanctions busters (and a hacker), and sanctions are essentially over now. The slate is clean.[189]

The payment of ransom made the prisoner swap much worse, especially because of how these payments were made. The series of embarrassing leaks about the ransom payments in August and September 2016 made a mockery of the administration's insistence that they had not paid ransom to Iran. Comedian Stephen Colbert joked about the Iran ransom scandal when he said on his program "Late Night" that "a lot of people are saying this sounds like ransom because they know what the word 'ransom' means."[190]

Many Republican Congressmen condemned the Obama administration for paying ransom to a state sponsor of terror. They also raised concerns that Iran demanded cash because it wanted untraceable funds to finance illegal activities such as terrorism, purchasing WMD technology and helping fund North Korea's nuclear weapons program.

Senator Marco Rubio on September 6, 2016 introduced the "No Ransom Act" to prohibit the federal government from paying ransom to Iran and stopping any further payments to Iran from the State Department's Judgment Fund until Iran returns the ransom money it received and pays the American victims of Iranian terrorism what they are owed, a sum estimated to be $53 billion. Rubio's bill was co-sponsored by Republicans Senators Cornyn, Kirk, Ayotte, Barrasso, Capito, Scott,

Burr, Johnson, Fischer, Cotton, Perdue, Collins, Isakson, Risch and Heller. Congressman Mike Pompeo introduced this bill in the House and was joined by many Republican co-sponsors.

Secret Exemptions Granted to Ensure Iran Met Implementation Day Requirements

Already enraged by the Obama administration's concealment of the planeloads of cash secretly flown to Iran, congressional opponents of the JCPOA were further angered in early September 2016 by news that to reach the Implementation Day requirements for sanctions relief, Iran was secretly granted several exemptions.

The exemptions, reported in a September 1, 2016 report by the Institute for Science and International Security, [191] were granted by the JCPOA's "Joint Commission" which is composed of the parties to the agreement: Iran, the United States, the United Kingdom, France, Germany, China and Russia. Some of the exemptions were significant and allowed Iran to not report activities with nuclear weapons-related applications. These exemptions were:

> 1. Allowing Iran to violate a cap of 300 kg for its enriched uranium stockpile under certain circumstances. The Commission gave Iran an exemption for reactor-grade enriched UF6 in the form of low-level and sludge waste. This may have been a minor violation although the report said the amount of this material is unknown.

> 2. Ignoring "lab contaminant" UF6 enriched to 20 percent uranium-235 judged as "unrecoverable." Although this may also be a minor violation, the report says the amount of this material and how it was judged unrecoverable is not known.

> 3. Exemption for large "hot cells." The JCPOA allows Iran to operate or build hot cells (shielded chambers used to handle radioactive substances), but to ensure they are used for peaceful purposes such as producing medical radionuclides, Iran agreed that for 15 years the size of these cells will be limited to no more than six cubic meters. The Commission gave Iran an exemption to operate 22 larger hot cells. According to the Institute report, these larger cells could be secretly misused for plutonium separation experiments. The Institute also raised concerns that the IAEA is not adequately monitoring Iran's hot cells and that Iran is exploiting this exemption to win approval to operate more hot cells with volumes greater than six cubic meters. This is a potentially serious exemption because plutonium separation experiments have only one purpose: developing the capability to produce plutonium nuclear weapons fuel.

It is unclear whether and how the Obama administration informed Congress about the JCPOA's secret exemptions and loopholes described in the Institute's report.

The Institute report says the Obama administration "informed Congress of key Joint Commission decisions on Implementation Day but in a confidential matter." This indicates Congress was not informed before Implementation Day about the exemptions. I also note Implementation Day fell on a Saturday, which means there was no one around in Congress that day to receive notification of the exemptions.

I am concerned that the report's language indicates the Obama administration did not provide full details of the Joint Commission's decisions to Congress and that any information it did provide was not made available to most members – it probably was contained in classified documents sent only to top congressional leaders, the Senate Foreign Relations Committee and the House Foreign Affairs Committees.

James Rosen reported on Fox News Special Report on September 1, 2016 that a congressional source told him senior congressional aides were briefed on the Joint Commission's decisions.[192] However, Rosen also noted that Democratic Senator Robert Menendez (D-NJ), one of the JCPOA's leading critics and a senior member of the Senate Foreign Relations Committee, said he was never briefed on the Commission's decisions or the exemptions.

My guess is that the alleged briefings given to senior congressional staff probably were incomplete and, like most JCPOA documents, mired in incomprehensible technical jargon to confuse the issue of the exemptions. If Senator Menendez did not know about the exemptions, I refuse to believe a clear briefing was provided on them to Congress.

Bottom line: Implementation Day was a rigged game and part of the Obamabomb deal fraud. The JCPOA set the bar so low for Iran that its compliance was assured. In addition, Iran was granted secret exemptions to help it pass over this low bar. As a result, Iran could continue nuclear weapons-related activities like uranium enrichment and test ballistic missiles and still be in compliance with the Implementation Day requirements. The U.S. and the IAEA also chose to ignore other Iranian actions that appeared to violate the nuclear deal such as barring nuclear inspectors from military bases and failing to fully cooperate with the PMD investigation.

The prisoner swap and the ransom payments are integral parts of the fraudulent nuclear deal and are more evidence of the Obama administration's deception to sell the deal and conceal its controversial aspects from Congress. However, I agree with Charles Krauthammer that it is pointless to complain about the prisoner swap since it did free several innocent Americans and our country long ago gave up its leverage to Iran to get the nuclear deal.

20. Iran Presses for More Concessions from the United States After Implementation Day

Instead of insisting on an end to Iran's continuing malign activities (terrorism, human rights violations, and other destabilizing activities in Syria, Iraq, Yemen, Lebanon, and other countries across the Middle East), and using non-nuclear sanctions to deter and punish these activities, the administration is now effectively acting as Iran's trade promotion and business development authority.

> Mark Dubowitz
> Testimony to the Senate Committee on
> Banking, Housing, and Urban Affairs
> May 24, 2016

Critics of the Iran deal grew more concerned in the months following Implementation Day. There were reports of significant Iranian cheating on its JCPOA commitments. Iran's belligerent behavior continued. What appeared to be another secret side deal surfaced. There were efforts by the Obama administration to make new concessions to Iran that violated promises it made to Congress during the summer of 2015. And, as explained in Chapter 19, it was revealed in August and September 2016 that the U.S. secretly sent planeloads of cash to Iran in January 2016 – payments which critics said was ransom to free U.S. prisoners – and voted with other JCPOA parties to secretly grant Iran exemptions so it would receive $150 billion in sanctions relief in January 2016.

Growing Evidence of Iranian Cheating

Despite victory laps by Obama officials celebrating the success of the JCPOA on its one-year anniversary, there were troubling signs at the time that Iran was engaged in significant cheating on the agreement.

In an annual security report issued in June 2016, German intelligence said Iran engaged in clandestine efforts in 2015 to acquire illicit nuclear technology and equipment from German companies at a "quantitatively high level" and that "it is safe to expect that Iran will continue its intensive procurement activities in Germany using clandestine methods to achieve its objectives." [193] *The Jerusalem Post* reported on July 9, 2016 that half of Germany's state governments reported in their 2015 annual intelligence reports clandestine attempts by Tehran to secure nuclear-related goods. *The Jerusalem Post* cited a report by the North Rhine-Westphalia state's domestic intelligence report for 2015 which said there were 141 clandestine Iranian attempts to acquire nuclear and missile technology in 2015 versus 83 in 2013.[194]

According to a July 7, 2016 memo from the Institute for Science and International Security, Iran tried unsuccessfully to covertly purchase tons of high-strength carbon fiber which it uses to make rotors for uranium enrichment centrifuges. Under the JCPOA, Iran is required to seek approval for such purchases from a JCPOA procurement working group. The Institute said the JCPOA group probably would not have approved this sale, since Iran has enough carbon fiber to replace the rotors of centrifuges it is permitted to operate under the agreement.[195]

It is unclear whether Iran tried to acquire these materials for ongoing covert nuclear activities or whether Tehran was trying to stockpile them for a decision by Iranian leaders in the near future to abandon the JCPOA and resume uranium enrichment with no restrictions.

In a separate report, the Institute said many Iranian entities that had been sanctioned for illicit nuclear and missile procurement but were relieved of these sanctions by the JCPOA in January 2016 "are now very active in procuring goods in China." [196]

Secret Agreement to Dumb-Down IAEA Iran Reports

On March 7, 2016, IAEA Director General Amano explained a mystery: why the IAEA's recent reports on Iran's nuclear program had become vague and contained little data. As it turned out, due to the JCPOA, there are now limitations on what the IAEA is allowed to report about Iran's nuclear program.

According to Amano, due to new UN Security Council and IAEA resolutions, the agency will only monitor and verify Iran's compliance with its JCPOA commitments and will no longer provide broad reporting on the Iranian nuclear program. Moreover, not only are the new IAEA reports much narrower in focus, they also omit important data on how Iran is complying with the nuclear deal.

Many experts were concerned at the vagueness of an IAEA report issued on January 16, 2016 which declared Iran had met the JCPOA's Implementation Day requirements. This was an atypical report for the IAEA which the Institute for Science and International Security said provided few details about the steps Iran took to comply with the JCPOA.

For example, the January report lacked information on how much enriched uranium Iran allegedly sent to Russia, whether the IAEA monitored this transfer, and how much enriched uranium Iran may have kept in the country by converting it into uranium dioxide powder, a process that can be quickly reversed.

Experts were even more concerned by a February 26 quarterly IAEA report on Iran – the first report issued after Implementation Day – which left out important data needed to assess Iran's compliance with the JCPOA such as the size of its enriched uranium stockpile, how much uranium Iran is enriching, and details on its centrifuge research and development.

In an analysis for the Foundation for the Defense of Democracies, Olli Heinonen said the February IAEA report provided "surprisingly scant information on key issues." According to Heinonen, "without detailed reporting, the international community cannot be sure that Iran is upholding its commitments under the nuclear deal."[197]

I am one of many critics who have argued that a legitimate nuclear deal with Iran would bar all uranium enrichment and centrifuge development. The fact that the JCPOA permits these activities to continue and also bars the IAEA from releasing public reports on them is disturbing and will prevent the U.S Congress and outside experts from assessing the implications of these dangerous U.S. concessions to Tehran.

Heinonen offered this explanation for the missing data in the recent IAEA reports:

> For years, Tehran has advocated for less-detailed IAEA safeguards reports, citing concerns ranging from confidentiality matters to IAEA inspection authorities under the comprehensive safeguards agreement.[198]

Based on Heinonen's assessment and the way the nuclear negotiations were conducted, I see only one possible explanation for why the IAEA's Iran reports were dumbed down – this was done at Iran's insistence and probably represents another secret side deal that the Obama administration failed to disclose to Congress.

Barbara Slavin, a strong supporter of the Obama administration and the Iran nuclear deal, defended the new IAEA Iran reports in a March 8, 2016 al-Monitor article.[199] In her article, Slavin tried to refute criticism of the IAEA's new reporting style by two arms control experts when she said "Experts acknowledge that the tone as well as the length of the reports has changed as the IAEA has moved from a position of questioning what amounted to a suspected criminal – the agency's attitude toward Iran because undeclared nuclear facilities were discovered in 2002 – to monitoring what amounts to that country's nuclear probation."

Slavin's comment is key to understanding what is going on with the new IAEA reports: the IAEA will no longer investigate alleged "criminal" nuclear activities by Iran because it has been absolved of these activities. The U.S. and other nations voted in December 2015 to close the books on Iran's past nuclear weapons related work. In January, 17 IAEA resolutions on Iran were terminated, many of which were the basis for inspections of its nuclear program. By taking these actions, IAEA members ended the IAEA's mandate for comprehensive inspections of Iran's nuclear program and investigating unresolved issues of past nuclear weapons-related work.

Some European states believed the IAEA's February 2016 report on Iran was too superficial and called for the next report to provide "the necessary information" according to the Associated Press. Although the U.S. initially expressed its satisfaction with the February IAEA report, it reversed itself after press criticism and called on these reports to be "factual, impartial and include the information which the agency considers necessary."

Based on an IAEA quarterly report issued on May 27, 2016, it was clear that the Agency had refused to change its reporting style on Iran's nuclear program. According to a May 31, 2016 report by the Institute for Science and International Security, the May 27 quarterly report "continues to lack technical details about critical implementation issues." The Institute's report added:

> It would greatly increase transparency of the JCPOA's implementation if the IAEA released this missing information. Without this information, an independent determination of whether Iran is complying with the JCPOA is not possible. The lack of information also inevitably leads to questions about the adequacy of the IAEA's JCPOA verification effort. The IAEA strategy, evident in the first two reports, appears to be that it is committed to only report violations in detail. However, this strategy is not credible and undermines confidence that the JCPOA is being verified. It also raises a fundamental question: if the IAEA is unwilling to provide routine and adequate

transparency, can it be trusted to be transparent every time a violation occurs? It is in fact unclear if the IAEA has reported all the violations thus far. It also appears that the IAEA is not reporting information relevant to loopholes in the agreement that Iran is exploiting.[200]

The Institute criticized the IAEA over its third 2016 Iran quarterly report issued on September 8 for excessive secrecy and excluding crucial information the world needed to assess Iran's compliance with the JCPOA. The Institute said in a September 9, 2016 memo about this IAEA report:

> The IAEA reporting continues to lack critical technical details about implementation of the agreement. This lack of information in the IAEA reports combined with the secrecy surrounding the decision-making of the Joint Commission is a serious shortcoming in the implementation of the JCPOA and erodes support for this important deal.[201]

The dumbing down of Iran's IAEA reports is a very troubling development. I believe there is no question this was done at the insistence of Iran. I agree with the Institute's assessment above that the weakness of these reports makes it difficult for the world to have confidence in the IAEA's efforts to verify the nuclear agreement. But I also see a political angle at work here: by agreeing to prevent the IAEA from publicly disclosing the full details of Iran's compliance with the JCPOA, the Obama administration found a way to perpetuate the myth that this is a good agreement and keep Republicans from using reports of Iranian cheating against Democrats in the 2016 presidential and congressional campaigns.

Secret Side Deal to Install Advanced Centrifuges

Associated Press IAEA reporter George Jahn reported on July 18, 2016 a secret agreement allowing Iran to replace the primitive 5,060 P-1 uranium centrifuges it is allowed to operate while the JCPOA is in effect with more advanced designs in January 2027 even though other restrictions on Iranian uranium enrichment remain in place for 15 years.

I believe this is a significant development because it represents another secret JCPOA side deal that the Obama administration illegally withheld from Congress.

This agreement means Iran will be permitted to substantially increase its capability to produce nuclear fuel faster and in larger amounts in only 11 years. Since Iran is permitted to conduct R&D on advanced centrifuges while the JCPOA is in place – and can expand this effort after 8½ years – it likely will be able to quickly construct and install these advanced centrifuges.

179

Jahn reported that although this undisclosed, confidential agreement is "an integral part" of the JCPOA, Iran will not be permitted to accumulate more than 300 kg of low-enriched uranium for 15 years. It is hard to believe Iran will continue to abide by this restriction after it installs more advanced centrifuges in light of recent reports that it is already cheating on the nuclear agreement.

Some media outlets treated Jahn's story as a major revelation. I agree but for different reasons.

I don't regard the fact that Iran can begin enriching under the JCPOA with advanced centrifuges after 10 years as news. I explained in Chapter 10 that there is no limit on the number of uranium centrifuges Iran can operate after 10 years.

It is news that the Obama administration is a party to another secret side deal to the JCPOA that explicitly recognizes Iran's plan to greatly expand its uranium enrichment program. Jahn's revelation also raises questions about whether there are more secret side deals to the JCPOA that have not been made public or the U.S. Congress.

According to Jahn's article, "U.S. officials say members of Congress who expressed interest [in the document] were briefed on its substance." Translation: the administration did not provide this side deal document to Congress or mention it in committee briefings. Instead, the substance of this document was only briefed to members of Congress who asked about this issue. I suspect the administration briefed a handful of congressmen on the contents of this side deal without revealing the side deal's existence. This is the same kind of sleight-of-hand tactics that the Obama administration used in congressional notification secret exemptions granted to Iran on its obligations to reach Implementation Day and receive $150 billion in sanctions relief.

Jahn did not reveal a previously unknown flaw of the JCPOA. He revealed something more disturbing: another instance of the Obama administration deceiving Congress and the American people as part of its effort to ram through President Obama's deeply unpopular legacy nuclear agreement with Iran.

Iran's Sponsorship of Terror and Efforts to Destabilize Middle East Expand

Tehran significantly expanded its military support to Syria's Assad regime since January 2016. Combined with similar support from Russia, this has undermined the effectiveness of cease-fire efforts, strengthened Assad and further complicated efforts to negotiate a peace agreement.

The *Wall Street Journal* reported in April 2015 that because of stepped-up Iranian support to the Assad government, "several thousand Iranians are now fighting in Syria in addition to over 20,000 Shiite fighters from Afghanistan, Lebanon, Iraq and Pakistan who are part of militias reporting directly to the Revolutionary Guards."[202] The Journal article said that Iran increased the number of its own fighters to help the Assad government regain control of Aleppo in northern Syria. The article noted Iranian Foreign Minister Zarif recently claimed Iran's involvement in Syria was overstated and "denied that Iran had either obliged or encouraged Afghan refugees in Iran to fight with for the Assad regime, saying those who went were purely volunteers."

Increased Russian and Iranian military support for the Syrian army over the last six months helped the Assad government take advantage of a weak cease-fire agreement to target Syrian rebels and help government forces retake key rebel towns and cities. This includes Aleppo, an opposition stronghold, where there has been fierce fighting between government, rebel fighters and ISIS this year. Iranian, Hezbollah, and Afghani fighters reportedly suffered significant losses in May 2016 near Aleppo. Although Iran reportedly withdrew half of its Revolutionary Guards from Syria over the last few months, Iranian leaders have given no indication that that they plan to end their military support for Assad.

Iran hosted a conference with Russian and Syrian officials on June 10, 2016 to discuss the Syrian conflict. At the conference, Iranian Defense Minister General Hossein Dehghan said Iran, Russia and Syria were determined to deliver a "decisive" battle against "all terrorist groups" in Syria and added "we agree to a guaranteed ceasefire that doesn't lead to the strengthening of terrorists in this country."

Iran increased its support to other insurgencies and terrorist groups over the last six months. In late May, Iran pledged $70 million to the Palestinian terrorist group Islamic Jihad to conduct "jihad" against the State of Israel.[203]

Iran's continued its support to the Taliban in Afghanistan was highlighted by news that Taliban chief Mullah Mansoor had spent two months in Iran before he was killed by a U.S. drone strike in Afghanistan in May 2016.[204] An Iranian official denied his country had any ties to Mansoor or to the Taliban which he called a terrorist group. Experts believe Iran is supporting the Taliban in Afghanistan both to counter a growing ISIS presence and to help undermine the pro-U.S. Afghan government in Kabul.

Iran increased its support for the Houthi rebels in Yemen between January and June 2016. The U.S. Navy intercepted a ship carrying 1,500 AK-47s automatic rifles, 200 RPG launchers and 21 .50-caliber machine guns from Iran to Yemen on March 28, according to the U.S. Naval Institute News. Two similar ships transporting Iranian weapons to Yemen were intercepted by the Australian and French navies in February and March 2016. The Yemeni government said in early June 2016 that it was losing ground to the Iranian-backed Houthi rebels.[205] In March 2016, Brigadier General Masoud Jazayeri, deputy chief of staff of the Iranian armed forces, said Iran might provide the Houthis with the same type of support it has given to the Assad regime adding that Iran is prepared to send "military advisers" to assist the Houthis.[206]

In a related development, it was reported in June 2016 that the $1.7 billion payment the U.S. government made to Iran was used to help fund a 90% increase in Iran's 2016-2017 military budget.[207] This means U.S. tax dollars are helping subsidize a large Iranian military build-up.

On June 2, 2016, the U.S. State Department listed Iran as the top state-sponsor of terror in its annual report on global terrorism. The report said Iran "remained the foremost state sponsor of terrorism in 2015, providing a range of support, including financial, training, and equipment, to groups around the world." In addition, the report said:

> In 2015, Iran's state sponsorship of terrorism worldwide remained undiminished through the Islamic Revolutionary Guard Corps-Qods Force (IRGC-QF), its Ministry of Intelligence and Security, and Tehran's ally Hezbollah, which remained a significant threat to the stability of Lebanon and the broader region.
>
> Iran and Hezbollah reportedly continued to prepare for attacks against Israeli targets outside the country. In late November, Kenyan security agencies announced that they had arrested two Iranian citizens, allegedly sent by the Iranian IRGC/Quds force to execute a terrorist attack against Israeli targets in Nairobi. In May, Cypriot police arrested a Lebanese-Canadian national, Hussain Abdallah, who later admitted he was working for Hezbollah's External Security Organization. Abdallah possessed about 8.5 tons of chemicals used for manufacturing explosives. Abdallah acknowledged to Cypriot investigators that that the explosive pre-cursors interrogation showed the explosives were supposed to be used against Israeli targets in Cyprus and other places in Europe. Iran has stated publicly that it armed Hezbollah with advanced long-range

Iranian-manufactured missiles, in violation of UN Security Council Resolutions 1701 and 1747.[208]

During a press conference on the new terrorism report, a State Department spokesman added "we're concerned about a wide range of Iranian activities to destabilize the region and that includes, certainly, their support for some of these allied groups, proxy groups that operate in Iraq and in Bahrain and in various parts of the Gulf region." In response to a question about Iranian activity in Central and South America, the spokesman said "I think Iran's presence in the Western Hemisphere and its support for groups that might be engaged in facilitation or operational planning is a continued concern."

Muted U.S. Response to Surge in Iranian Missile Tests

Iran continued ballistic missile tests in 2016, testing medium-range missiles on March 8 and 9 and in late April. Some of the missiles launched in March reportedly had the words written on the sides "Israel must be wiped off the earth." On April 19, Iran conducted a launch of its Simorgh rocket which it claims is a space-launch vehicle. Most arms control experts believe the launch of this rocket was actually a test to develop an ICBM capable of carrying a nuclear warhead against the United States and Europe. The Simorgh test reportedly was only partly successful because it did not reach orbit.[209]

It is worth noting that after North Korea tested a rocket similar to the Simorgh in February 2016, the UN Security Council held an emergency meeting and unanimously passed a statement that said "even if characterized as a satellite launch or space launch vehicle," this launch contributed to North Korea's development of systems to deliver nuclear weapons. The North Korean rocket launch also led to calls for increased missile defense in Japan and South Korea. There was no similar reaction to Iran's Simorgh launch.

It was learned after Iran conducted missile tests in March 2016 that tough language in prior UN Security Council resolutions had been replaced in a July 2015 resolution (Resolution 2231) which endorsed the nuclear agreement with new language that Iran and Russia maintain no longer requires Iran to refrain from conducting ballistic missile tests. The new language replaced prior language when the IAEA certified Iran met the requirements for Implementation Day in January.

Resolution 2231 has a vague provision calling on Iran not to test missiles in an annex to a July 2015 Security Council resolution which endorsed the JCPOA,

Resolution 2231. This provision says: "Iran is called upon not to undertake any activity related to ballistic missiles designed to be capable of delivering nuclear weapons" for eight years or until the IAEA makes a certification that Iran's nuclear program is entirely peaceful, whichever comes first."

Resolution 2231's missile language is much weaker than language in the six Security Council resolutions that it replaced. Russia pointed this out on March 13 by arguing that Iran's recent missile tests do not violate Resolution 2231 because this resolution only "calls" on Iran not to test rather than barring them. Russian Ambassador to the UN Vitaly Churkin explained that "A 'call' is different from a ban so, legally, you cannot violate a call. You can comply with a call or you can ignore the call, but you cannot violate a call."

Iranian Foreign Minister took a similar view in a speech at the Australian National University in which he explained how he hoodwinked Western diplomats in negotiating language in Resolution 2231 that permitted Iran to conduct missile tests:

> It doesn't call upon Iran not to test ballistic missiles, or ballistic missiles capable of delivering nuclear warheads ... it calls upon Iran not to test ballistic missiles that were 'designed' to be capable."
>
> "That word took me about seven months to negotiate, so everybody knew what it meant.[210]

Diplomats cited by Reuters in April seemed to confirm the Iranian and Russian interpretation of Resolution 2231's missile language, saying that this new formulation is not legally binding and cannot be enforced under Chapter 7 of the U.N. Charter, which deals with sanctions and authorization of military force.[211] There was no mention of this in the Obama administration's briefings to Congress before of voted on the JCPOA in September 2015.

The Obama administration appeared to concede this interpretation when it co-signed a joint letter to the UN Secretary General in late March which said Iran's missiles tests were "inconsistent with" and "in defiance of" Resolution 2231 but did not refer to them as a violation. However, the letter also said these missiles were "inherently capable of delivering nuclear weapons."[212]

U.S. Ambassador to the UN Samantha Power took a similar approach on March 14 in responding to Ambassador Churkin's March 13 comments by saying Iran's missile tests "merits a Council response" and faulted Russia for blocking the Security Council from taking action.

Don't be fooled by Powers' statement. It indicated that the Obama administration will only respond to Iranian missile tests in the Security Council with nonbinding Security Council presidential statements which require unanimous support. If the Obama administration was serious about taking action in the Council over Iran's missile tests, it would submit a resolution imposing new sanctions.

Like many in Congress, the *Washington Post* was not reassured by the Obama administration's response to Iran's missiles tests or White House attempts to play them down by insisting the tests were not a violation of the JCPOA. The Post said in an April 6, 2016 editorial:

> Tehran's behavior comes as no surprise to the many observers who predicted the deal would not alter its hostility to the West or its defiance of international norms. Unfortunately, the Obama administration's response has also been much as critics predicted: It has done its best to play down Iran's violations and avoid any conflict out of fear that the regime might walk away from a centerpiece of President Obama's legacy.

> The missile tests are one example of U.S. waffling. The administration has described them as a violation of U.N. Resolution 2231 and responded with mostly symbolic sanctions of several individuals and companies associated with the program. But it has appeared to yield to Russia's contention that Iran did not, technically, breach the resolution because it was only "called upon," not ordered, to stop testing. A letter sent by the United States, Britain, France and Germany to the Security Council last week described the tests as "inconsistent with" the resolution, rather than a violation that would mandate enforcement action.[213]

Perhaps the strongest indictment of Iran's belligerent behavior since the JCPOA was in an April 3, 2016, *Wall Street Journal* op-ed by United Arab Emirates Ambassador to the United States Yousef Al-Otaiba, in which he said:

> Sadly, behind all the talk of change, the Iran we have long known – hostile, expansionist, violent — is alive and well, and as dangerous as ever.

> Iran's destabilizing behavior in the region must stop. Until it does, our hope for a new Iran should not cloud the reality that the old Iran is very much still with us –as dangerous and as disruptive as ever.[214]

Among several bills submitted in Congress in response to Iran's ballistic missiles tests is the Iran Ballistic Missile Sanctions Act of 2016, introduced by Senator Kelly Ayotte in March 2016 with 18 Republican co-sponsors. (This bill actually is an amendment to the National Defense Authorization Act.) According to Senator Ayotte, her bill will impose hard-hitting sanctions on every sector of the Iranian economy supporting Tehran's ballistic missile program.[215] It also will extend the Iran Sanctions Act (which expires at the end of 2016) to December 31, 2031 and imposes broader banking sanctions on Iran.

Tensions Grow in the Persian Gulf

Tensions grew in the Persian Gulf throughout 2016 as Iran harassed and threatened to attack U.S. ships and planes. These incidents concerned U.S. military officials who worried they could result in a military confrontation due to a miscalculation by either side.

Reuters reported that U.S. officials said there were 30 close encounters between U.S. and Iranian vessels in the Gulf through September 2016, over twice as many as in the same period of 2015.[216]

On May 4, Iran threatened to block the Strait of Hormuz. In August 2016, Iranian naval vessels made dangerous maneuvers near U.S. warships, including one episode in which the U.S. ships fired warning shots from a 50-caliber deck gun to prevent a collision. One of the U.S. Navy vessels employed unidentified "devices" to dissuade Iranian ships from harassing it.

Also in May 2016, Iranian ships fired at and aggressively tailed several commercial vessels, including a U.S.-flagged merchant ship.

Reuters quoted Pentagon officials who said a U.S. Navy coastal patrol ship in the central Persian Gulf was forced to changed course on September 4 after an Iranian Revolutionary Guard fast-attack craft came within 100 yards of it. Pentagon officials said this was at least the fourth such incident in less than a month.[217]

On September 10, Iran threatened to shoot down two Navy reconnaissance planes. The planes, a P-8 Poseidon and an EP-3, were flying a reconnaissance mission 13 miles off the coast of Iran, in the Persian Gulf, in the Strait of Hormuz and in the Gulf of Oman. Iran demanded the plane change course or risking being shot down. The U.S. planes ignored the Iranian warning.

U.S. officials defended the flight, noting that the U.S. planes were in international airspace, but also conceded that the flight was in part intended to test Iran's reaction.

Iran Deploys S-300 Anti-Aircraft Missiles to Defend Fordow Enrichment Facility

Iran's state-controlled media announced on August 29, 2016 that Iran deployed an advanced Russian surface-to-air missile defense system, the S-300, to protect its underground Fordow uranium enrichment facility from airstrikes. The S-300 is the most advanced Russian anti-aircraft system that Moscow exports. It has long been understood that Iran sought these missiles to protect its nuclear sites from airstrikes by the United States and Israel.

Iran signed a contract with Russia to buy the S-300s in 2007. This contract caused tension between the two countries because Moscow refused to deliver the missiles. Russia delayed delivery in 2010 after UN sanctions were imposed in response to a major expansion of Iran's nuclear program. Iran sued Russia in 2012 in the Geneva Arbitration Court to force Moscow to deliver the missiles. Russian officials said in response to the lawsuit that they could not deliver the S-300 missiles due to UN sanctions. Iranian officials disputed this, claiming that UN sanctions on Iran exempted weapons intended for defensive purposes, including air defense missiles.

Iran's recent deployment of S-300s to the Fordow facility was possible because Russia agreed to deliver the missiles after an outline of the July 2015 nuclear pact was agreed to in April 2015. Iran announced the first delivery of the missile system in April 2016.

If Iran truly agreed not to enrich uranium at Fordow for 15 years, there obviously was no reason to deploy advanced anti-aircraft missiles at this site in 2016 unless it was planning on violating the JCPOA in the near future.

Fordow was already a difficult target for U.S. and Israeli airstrikes and would probably take multiple strikes by America's largest bunker buster bomb – the 15-ton GBU-57 MOP (massive ordnance penetrator) – to destroy. Only the B-2 stealth bomber and the aging B-52 can carry the MOP.

Stealth U.S. aircraft such as the B-2, F-22 Raptor, and F-35 reportedly can evade the S-300 but they could be vulnerable if Iran deployed enough S-300 systems.

There has been talk of Israel destroying Fordow with bunker buster bombs by repeatedly bombing a single point at this facility. Although Israel does not have the MOP nor a bomber capable of carrying this weapon, it does have the 5-ton GBU-28 bunker buster bomb which can be carried by its F-15E fighters. Unfortunately, the S-300 poses a serious threat to fourth-generation fighters like the F-15.

The Israeli Air force will be able evade S-300 missiles when it receives its first fifth-generation F-35s in December 2016. However, the F-35 cannot carry the GBU-28 bunker buster. Bunker busters for the F-35 are under development but are many years away from deployment.

I believe Iran's deployment of the S-300 anti-aircraft missiles at Fordow is another indication that Iranian leaders are contemplating violating or terminating the JCPOA in the short to medium term by resuming uranium enrichment at Fordow and want to prevent Israel from responding with airstrikes and discourage the United States from doing so.

Tehran "Blackmails" Washington for Access to U.S. Financial System

While Iran continued testing ballistic missiles, boosting its support to the Assad regime and increasing its support to terrorist groups in 2016, it also was pressing the Obama administration for new concessions because Iranian officials contend their nation has been shortchanged by the nuclear agreement. *Washington Free Beacon* reporter Adam Kredo wrote in a May 24, 2016 article that by using the threat to walk away from the president's legacy nuclear deal, Iran reportedly was blackmailing the United States for greater concessions.[218] Kredo quoted experts who testified to a Senate hearing that the Obama administration is becoming "dangerously close to becoming Iran's trade promotion and business development authority."

In March 2016, it was reported that the Obama administration was planning to violate promises it made to Congress in the summer of 2015 that it would not give Iran access to U.S. financial institutions or allow it to enter into financial arrangements with U.S. banks. The Associated Press reported on March 24 "the Obama administration is leaving the door open to new sanctions relief for Iran, including possibly long-forbidden access to the U.S. financial market," specifically granting "Iranian businesses the ability to conduct transactions in dollars within the United States or through offshore banks."[219]

During a March 22, 2015 House Financial Services Committee hearing, Secretary of the Treasury Jack Lew refused to give a direct answer to questions by Congressman Ed Royce (R-CA) on whether he stood by his July 23, 2015 testimony to the Senate Foreign Relations Committee that under the JCPOA "Iranian banks will not be able to clear U.S. dollars through New York, hold correspondent account relationships with U.S. financial institutions, or enter into financing arrangements with U.S. banks" and that "Iran, in other words, will continue to be denied access to the world's largest financial and commercial market."

However, in a May 31, 2015 speech, Lew expressed support for easing restrictions on Iranian access to the U.S. financial system and dollarized transactions because he claimed Iran had lived up to its obligations under the JCPOA and the United States therefore had the responsibility to uphold its end of the deal "in both letter and spirit." Lew also said the U.S. lifted nuclear sanctions against Iran but continues to enforce "sanctions directed at support for terrorism and regional destabilization, and missile and human rights violations."[220]

Kerry made similar comments in an April 5 MSNBC interview.[221] In response to questions on why the U.S. Treasury and the Obama administration was considering helping Iran get access to the U.S. financial system, Kerry replied "Iran deserves the benefits of the agreement they struck."

MSNBC co-host Joe Scarborough then challenged Kerry how the United States could give Iran more sanctions relief after President Obama said it had not followed the spirit of the nuclear agreement by launching ballistic missiles and calling for the destruction of Israel. Scarborough said to Kerry:

> By not living up to the spirit of the agreement, they're sending the wrong signal to the world community, they're sending the wrong signal to businesses. Should they not first take care of the problem that both you and the president have diagnosed and then you all start helping them financially?

Kerry replied:

> We're under an obligation ... if we said we would lift the sanction, we're under an obligation to lift the sanction. ...everybody should be encouraging Iran not to continue its missile activities, not to continue to ship arms, because that will upset and rile the marketplace.

Valiollah Seif, the governor of the Central Bank of Iran traveled to Washington in mid-April 2016 to press for access to the U.S. financial system. Seif told the al-Monitor during the trip that "Iran expects the US government to reinstitute limited access to the US dollar to facilitate Iran's financial transactions with the rest of the world and fully implement the recent nuclear deal.[222]

Experts sharply criticized reports that the Obama administration was considering making new financial concessions to Iran. Former Senator Joseph Lieberman (D-CT) said in a March 28, 2016 press release:

> We are deeply concerned by reports that the Administration is preparing to permit Tehran access to America's financial and commercial markets.
>
> U.S. officials have previously pledged that Iran would not be granted access to the U.S. financial system and the ability to "dollarize" payments.
>
> Lifting this restriction would violate Section 311 of the USA PATRIOT Act, which designates the entire Iranian financial sector as a jurisdiction of primary money laundering concern. It also ignores recent notices of the international anti-money laundering and terror-finance watchdog, the Financial Action Task Force (FATF), which warn of Iran's "failure to address the risk of terrorist financing and the serious threat this poses to the integrity of the international financial system."
>
> This move would also undercut the Administration's actions last week to charge Iranians for engaging in cyber attacks against the U.S. financial sector and critical infrastructure, as well as sanctioning individuals and entities supporting Iran's ballistic missile program and on-going terrorism campaign.
>
> We call on the Administration to continue to deny Iran access to the American financial system and dollar transactions.[223]

Mark Dubowitz and Jonathan Schanzer of the Foundation for the Defense of Democracies raised similar concerns in a March 28, 2016 *Wall Street Journal* editorial, noting that Obama officials told Congress during the summer of 2015 that it would not grant Iran access to U.S. financial markets and would withhold this concession to give the U.S. leverage over Iran after the nuclear deal was done.[224] Dubowitz and Schanzer asked, "Why throw away that leverage for no new concessions?"

Lieberman, Dubowitz and Schanzer focused on the main reason easing sanctions on Iran's access to the U.S. financial system and the dollar is so dangerous: the threat Iran poses to the global financial system and how the easing of these sanctions will allow Iran to gain full access to this system without ending its criminal financial practices. In February 2016, the Financial Action Task Force (FATF), an international standard-setting body for anti-money laundering and terrorist financing rules and regulations, issued a statement on its continuing concerns about this threat:

The FATF remains particularly and exceptionally concerned about Iran's failure to address the risk of terrorist financing and the serious threat this poses to the integrity of the international financial system.[225]

The FATF said it would urge its members to strengthen countermeasures against Iran as of June 2016 if Tehran did not take immediate action to address its concerns.

Due to pressure from Congress and an outcry in the news media, in April 2016, the Obama administration appeared to back away from its plan to grant Iran full access to the dollar and the U.S. financial system. However, there are indications that Obama officials decided to instead create a "backdoor" arrangement allowing Iran to access the U.S. dollar via foreign transactions outside the American financial system. The Wall Street Journal reported on April 1, 2016:

> The Treasury is considering how to issue licenses to offshore dollar clearing houses for specific Iranian financial institutions, an approach that wouldn't require the involvement of American banks, according to the congressional officials. The clearing houses, likely involving select foreign banks, would conduct the dollar transactions instead, shielding the U.S. financial system from any direct contact with Iran, these officials said.[226]

Kerry seemed to confirm that the United States had reached a backdoor agreement with Iran on access to the U.S. financial system in this statement he made after an April 19, 2016 meeting with Iranian Foreign Minister Zarif.

> QUESTION: "Mr. Secretary, did you reach any agreement (inaudible) with the dollar issue and the (inaudible) sanctions issue?"
>
> SECRETARY KERRY: "We agreed to – we're both working at making sure that the JCPOA, the Iran agreement – nuclear agreement – is implemented in exactly the way that it was meant to be and that all the parties to that agreement get the benefits that they are supposed to get out of the agreement. So we worked on a number of key things today, achieved progress on it, and we agreed to meet on Friday. After the signing of the climate change agreement, we will meet again to sort of solidify what we talked about today."[227]

The alleged backdoor arrangement angered many congressional Republicans who claim it still violates the administration's promises not to lift terrorism-related sanctions from Iran. Several U.S Senators, led by Mark Kirk (R-IL) and Marco Rubio (R-FL), have called on Congress to block any additional U.S. financial concessions to Iran. In March 2016, the two senators announced they would seek to block any Treasury Department nominees until the White House agreed to abandon this effort. On April 6, Rubio and Kirk introduced legislation to block foreign banks from to carrying out currency exchanges for Iran that involve U.S. dollars.

House Foreign Affairs Committee Chairman Ed Royce (R-CA) introduced a similar bill on April 19 that will prevent the Obama administration from allowing Iran access to transactions involving the U.S. dollar as long as the Iranian regime continues to engage in illicit activities, including the development of ballistic missiles and terrorism. Royce's bill codifies existing U.S. regulations that prohibit the administration from allowing the U.S. dollar to be used to facilitate trade transactions with Iran and upholds Iran's designation as a primary money laundering concern.[228]

The Obama administration not only has tried to grant Iran access to the U.S. financial system and the U.S. dollar, it has been involved in other activities that resemble acting as "Iran's trade promotion and business development authority."

For example, Kerry said during a May 10, 2016 visit to London, "businesses should not use the United States as an excuse if they don't want to do business, or if they don't see a good business deal ... that's just not fair, that's not accurate." Although Kerry said it was not America's job to convince foreign firms to do business in Iran, he also said it was America's job to "make clear to them what the rules are" and added "Consequently, we must promote the fact that Iran is the safest and most profitable country for investment."

Secretary Kerry met with foreign bank officials in May 2016 to persuade them to do business with Iran. This meeting was in response to concerns raised by some foreign banks about dealing with Iran because of its sponsorship of terror and the possibility that they could be sanctioned by the United States in the future for business ties to Iran.

Former Treasury Under Secretary Stuart Levey, now the chief legal officer with UK bank HSBC, participated in a meeting between Kerry and European banking officials on May 12, 2016. Levey expressed his concern in a *Wall Street Journal* op-ed that Kerry encouraged non-U.S. banks to do business with Iran even though Washington is barring American banks from doing this and "without a U.S. repudiation of its prior statements about the associated financial-crime risks."[229] Levey wrote that he rejected Kerry's call to invest in Iran because "our decisions will be driven by the financial-crime risks and the underlying conduct. For these reasons, HSBC has no intention of doing any new business involving Iran."

U.S. Governors Resist Obama Administration Efforts to Convince Them to Drop Iran Sanctions

After Implementation Day was declared in January 2016, the Obama administration began an effort to convince U.S. states to lift their economic sanctions against Iran to meet a U.S. obligation in the JCPOA to "actively encourage officials at the state or local level to take into account the changes in the U.S. policy … and to refrain from actions inconsistent with this change in policy."[230] According to Brown University's Watson Institute for International and Public Affairs, two-thirds of U.S. states have imposed their own sanctions against Iran.[231] Although many of these sanctions can be waived at the request of the President or lifted under certain conditions such as Iran's removal from the State Department's state-sponsor of terror list, several of these state-sanctioned laws can be lifted only at the discretion of state governments.

In a June 1, 2016 *Washington Post* op-ed on state-level Iran sanctions and the JCPOA, Jo-Anne Hart and Sue Eckert of Brown's Watson Institute said Iran is complaining that sanctions relief has not resulted in the economic benefits it had anticipated and portrayed state-level sanctions as a major obstacle to the JCPOA that are putting the agreement at risk.[232]

The State Department sent letters to U.S. governors in April 2016 urging their states to lift sanctions against Iran because the entities sanctioned by state sanctions are addressed by federal sanctions or lifted by the JCPOA. One of these letters, sent to North Carolina Governor Pat McCrory on April 8, 2016, said the JCPOA is an historic agreement that cuts off all of Iran's pathways to a nuclear weapon and that Iran is complying with this agreement.[233] The letter said the federal government had lifted nuclear-related sanctions but sanctions related to terrorism, human rights abuses, Iran's destabilizing activities in the Middle East and activities related to ballistic missiles remain in place

Many state governors rejected the Obama administration's request to lift state-level sanctions against Iran. In a May 16, 2016 letter to President Obama, Texas Governor Gregg Abbot condemned the administration's request that Texas drop its sanctions against Iran.

> Because the Iran deal is fundamentally flawed and does not permanently dismantle Iran's nuclear capability, Texas will maintain its sanctions against Iran. …Further, because your administration has recklessly and unilaterally

removed critical sanctions, I have called on the Texas legislature to strengthen the Iran sanctions that Texas already has in place.[234]

Abbott sent a letter on May 31, 2016 to other governors calling on them to join Texas and pass or strengthen legislation prohibiting state pension and retirement funds, local governments and all state entities from investing in Iran or entities that do business in Iran, barring local governments.

Fourteen governors joined Abbott in sending a letter to President Obama last September opposing the JCPOA and pledging that they would not lift state-level sanctions against Iran.[235] This letter was signed by the governors of Arizona, Arkansas, Florida, Indiana, Louisiana, Mississippi, New Jersey, North Dakota, Ohio, Oklahoma, South Carolina, North Dakota, Texas, Utah, and Wisconsin.

Given how unpopular the nuclear deal with Iran is with most Americans and outrage by Republicans at the deceptive efforts the Obama administration used to implement this agreement, it is not a surprise that Republican governors and state governments oppose the JCPOA and are keeping sanctions against Iran in place and in some cases strengthening them.

Due to this opposition to the nuclear deal by state governors and lawmakers, the Obama administration (and a Hillary Clinton administration if Clinton wins the 2016 presidential election) probably will eventually seek legal action at the Supreme Court to have state-level sanctions against Iran thrown out. Such a legal challenge may not succeed because the JCPOA is not a treaty, which means it is not binding U.S. law.

U.S. Buys Heavy-Water From Iran/Heavy-Water Loophole

Congressional Republicans criticized an April 22, 2016 announcement by the Obama administration that it would purchase 32 tons of heavy water from Iran as another dangerous American concession to Tehran. Obama administration officials said the United States agreed to the purchase because Iran is required under the JCPOA to sell excess heavy-water but was unable to find a buyer on the commercial market. This heavy-water purchase is problematic because it legitimizes Iran's heavy-water production instead of requiring Tehran to cease this effort and the construction of a heavy-water reactor.

In a September 1, 2016 report, the Institute for Science and International Security reported that the JCPOA's Joint Commission secretly granted Iran an exemption to the JCPOA's heavy-water stockpile cap.[236] According to the report, the Commission agreed to a loophole on a 130-ton cap for Iran's heavy-water stockpile by allowing Tehran to store large amounts of heavy-water in Oman that remain under Iran's control.

House Speaker Paul Ryan (R-WI) said in a statement condemning the U.S. purchase of Iranian heavy-water:

> For Tehran, the nuclear agreement is the gift that keeps on giving. This purchase – part of what appears to be the administration's full-court press to sweeten the deal – will directly subsidize Iran's nuclear program. It's yet another unprecedented concession to the world's leading state-sponsor of terrorism.[237]

The Institute report expressed concern that Iran is producing more heavy-water than it needs and far faster than experts had predicted. The Institute worries that the loophole to store heavy-water in Oman and America's purchase of some of Iran's heavy-water risks legitimizing Iran as a seller of heavy-water on the global market without Tehran demonstrating that it will abide by international nonproliferation norms for the sale and procurement of this substance.

The House on May 26, 2016 adopted an amendment submitted by Congressman Ron DeSantis prohibiting U.S. funds to be used to purchase heavy-water from Iran.[238] The amendment passed 251-168 but is not expected to survive in the Senate due to Democratic opposition and the certainty of a presidential veto.

Redesign of Heavy-Water Reactor Exempted From JCPOA Oversight

Further complicating the risk from Iran's Arak heavy-water plant and heavy-water reactor, there are new concerns about the proliferation risks from the Arak reactor which is being redesigned per the JCPOA so it produces less plutonium. (I explained in Chapter 10 that the Arak reactor will produce enough 1/4 of a weapons-worth of plutonium per year after the redesign versus one to two weapons worth of plutonium under the original design.) These concerns stem from the fact that China is rebuilding the reactor and, according to an April 2016 Institute for Science and International Security report, the reconstruction of this reactor has been exempted from the JCPOA's oversight process to monitor the procurement of nuclear-related technology and materials.[239]

This poses significant proliferation problems. First, exempting the rebuilding of the Arak reactor from the JCPOA's Procurement Working Group means this process will not be available to prevent Iran from exploiting this project to acquire materials and technology to promote a nuclear weapons program. This is especially concerning because the rebuilding of the Arak reactor is being conducted by China. The Institute believes this is a problem because China has been "less vigilant about proliferation-sensitive exports [and] may not be diligent about checking the end use of a Procurement Channel-authorized, dual-use good it has sold to Iran."

Boeing and Airbus's Multi-Billion Dollar Deals with Iran

On June 14, 2016 the *Washington Post* reported Iran was set to unveil the terms of a deal to purchase about 100 commercial passenger planes from Boeing.[240] This deal, according to the Post, will cover deliveries and services over nearly a decade at a cost of $25 billion. Mark Dubowitz told the Post that the sale "would pose "a massive sanctions, money-laundering and corruption risk for Boeing and the banks doing the deal because of ongoing concerns that the American equipment will be used to ferry Revolutionary Guard troops, weapons and money to the Assad government as well as to other terrorist groups."

Boeing announced on June 21, 2016 a tentative agreement with Iran Air to proceed with this deal.

Three members of Congress – Representatives Peter Roskam (R-IL), Bob Dold (R-IL) and Randy Hultgren (R-IL) – sent a letter to Boeing on May 2, 2016 expressing their opposition to the sale and warning "We urge you not to be complicit in the likely conversion of Boeing aircraft to IRGC warplanes."[241] The letter also said "We urge Boeing – in the strongest possible terms – not to do business with Iran until it ends its support for terror."

Congressmen Roskam and Jeb Hensarling (R-TX) said in a July 16, 2016 letter to Boeing:

> "Iran's commercial aviation sector is deeply involved in sponsoring hostile actors. The Islamic Revolutionary Guard Corps systematically uses commercial aircraft to transport troops, weapons, military related parts, rockets, and missiles to hostile actors around the world, including, but not limited to, Hezbollah, Hamas, Islamic Jihad, the Houthi rebels in Yemen, and the Bashar al-Assad regime in Syria. These terrorist groups and rogue regimes have American blood on their hands. Your potential customers do as well."[242]

Boeing has said no agreement with Iran would be finalized without the approval of the U.S. government. Roskam also has called on Airbus to cancel its deal to sell planes to Iran. Many other companies, including General Electric, reportedly are interested in exploring sales to Iran and are closely watching the Boeing and Airbus deals.

Despite strong objections from Congress, the Obama administration granted licenses to Boeing and Airbus to sell airliners to Iran on September 21, 2016. (Airbus required a U.S. license because more than 40 percent of the parts in its planes are made in the United States.) The Treasury Department said in a statement that these licenses "contain strict conditions to ensure that the planes will be used exclusively for commercial passenger use and cannot be resold or transferred."

Several members of Congress expressed grave concerns over the licenses. Congressmen Roskam and Jeb Hensarling (R-TX) said in a letter to the Treasury Department protesting this decision:

> "There is little evidence indicating that Iran Air has indeed stopped transporting weapons, troops and cash to terrorist groups and rogue regimes." [243]

Roskam, Hensarling and other members of Congress pledged to continue to fight to stop the transfer of civilian airliners to Iran.

Extension of the Iran Sanctions Act

Many national security experts are concerned that the Obama administration does not intend to extend the 1996 Iran Sanctions Act which expires on December 31, 2016. This law imposed sanctions on entities that assist Iran in acquiring or developing chemical, biological or nuclear weapons or assist Iran in acquiring or developing advanced conventional weapons. Congress needs to extend this law but congressional Democrats may prevent this from happening due to the opposition of the White House. The Obama administration has not made clear its intentions on the extension of the Iran Sanctions Act. I believe the White House wants this act to expire because it worries its reauthorization would offend Tehran. I also suspect Obama administration officials are counting on the confusion of the 2016 presidential election and a short legislative calendar to give them cover on this issue.

The American Israel Public Affairs Committee (AIPAC) has called on Congress to reauthorize the Iran Sanctions Act, arguing that it does not violate the JCPOA and provides legal underpinnings for Congress to sanction nonnuclear activities such as advanced conventional weapons transfers to Iran and Iran's sponsorship of terrorism. [244]

Conclusion: The Obama Administration is Ignoring Iran's Lawless Behavior to Protect the Obamabomb Deal

The nuclear deal with Iran and the consequences of the Obama administration's nuclear diplomacy with Tehran continued to worsen in the months after Tehran received over $100 billion in sanctions relief. IAEA reports on Iran's nuclear program were dumbed-down. There was an increase in Iran's belligerent and destabilizing behavior, including ballistic missile launches. The Obama administration is seeking to give Iran at least partial access to the US financial system even though it promised Congress last summer not to do so. The administration also bought heavy-water from Iran. Iranian cheating on the JCPOA and the deployment of advanced anti-aircraft missiles near a key nuclear site suggests Iranian leaders could renege on the agreement in the near future after they acquired the concessions and sanctions relief they were looking for.

These developments not only prove that Iran was a clear winner in the nuclear deal but that the Iranian government is using the Obama administration's determination to protect the JCPOA to press for more U.S. concessions to widen this victory.

21. The Future of the Obamabomb Deal and Recommendations

At a May 25, 2016 House Foreign Affairs Committee hearing, Ambassador Stephen Mull, who oversees implementation of the JCPOA, said he was happy to report the nuclear deal with Iran is a great success and that Tehran is fully in compliance. Ambassador Mull's statements are reflective of many similar claims the Obama administration will make in July 2016 to commemorate the one-year anniversary of the Obamabomb Deal.

While Obama officials claim Iran is in full compliance with the JCPOA, this does not mean the agreement is a success because the bar for Iran to meet in this agreement was set so low. Moreover, in light of numerous concessions and exemptions provided to Iran, it is clear this deal was negotiated almost entirely on Iran's terms.

The JCPOA was negotiated and sold to the American people by the Obama administration with unprecedented deception, dishonesty and stealth. The United States made indefensible concessions because of the obsession by Obama officials to strike a legacy nuclear agreement for President Obama. The agreement is much worse than the Obama administration has admitted and at best will leave Iran with an industrial-scale nuclear program in 10-15 years with the blessing of the international community.

In a more dire scenario, which I believe is more likely, Iran will use the provisions of the nuclear agreement to continue to increase its expertise in uranium enrichment and the production of advanced uranium centrifuges to significantly increase its capability to produce greater amounts of weapons-grade nuclear fuel in a much shorter time while the nuclear agreement is in place. Recent reports of Iranian cheating on its JCPOA commitments suggest this could happen sooner than critics of the agreement had predicted. Iran will also gain significant expertise due to the JCPOA in the construction and operation of a plutonium-producing heavy-water reactor.

Verification measures in the nuclear agreement are a fraud. The supposed tough verification measures promised by the Obama administration are limited to Iran's declared nuclear facilities and supply chain. Since Iran has placed military facilities off-limits, the world can have no confidence that this agreement has halted all Iranian nuclear weapons-related activities. In addition, although there is a convoluted process giving the IAEA access to undeclared and suspect nuclear sites, this process is reserved for major breaches of the agreement and is unlikely ever to be used – especially by the Obama administration – because Iran has said it will withdraw from the agreement if sanctions are re-imposed due to its noncompliance.

The international sanctions regime against Iran on nuclear and non-nuclear matters has been eviscerated by the JCPOA. Most of these sanctions will never be re-imposed even in the event of gross violations of the nuclear deal by Iran. By building international financial and business ties since the announcement of the JCPOA, including striking multibillion-dollar deals with Boeing and Airbus, Tehran is creating huge disincentives for the implementation of new economic sanctions. This effort plus language in the JCPOA that discourages imposing new sanctions on Iran may immunize the Iranian economy from any serious sanctions in the future.

The nuclear agreement also will have a profound destabilizing effect on regional and global security. By granting Iran the right to enrich uranium, the United States abandoned a decades-old policy to prevent the proliferation of this dangerous technology. Allowing Iran to operate a heavy-water reactor will also damage global nuclear nonproliferation efforts. As a result, nations in the region and around the world are likely to press for their own uranium enrichment programs and heavy-water reactors. This may lead other states to pursue nuclear weapons and possibly make weapons-grade nuclear fuel more accessible to terrorist groups.

Despite the Obama administration's claims that the nuclear deal reduces the threat from the Iranian nuclear weapons and keeps Iran a year away from the bomb, regional states feel betrayed by this agreement and believe it is a serious threat to their security because it allows Iran to keep virtually all of its nuclear infrastructure that it developed in defiance of UN Security Council resolutions. These states are also concerned that Iran has not been required to answer questions about nuclear weapons related work, including developing a nuclear warhead, outfitting a ballistic missile to carry such a warhead and developing a nuclear warhead reentry vehicle.

Regional states are also concerned that the nuclear deal will bolster Iranian power and influence and make it a regional hegemon. Iran's increasingly brash and threatening behavior since the announcement of the JCPOA in July 2015 – including firing rockets near an American aircraft carrier, briefly taking U.S. sailors prisoner, and firing missiles with the words "Israel must be wiped off the earth" written on the sides, threating U.S. ships in the Persian Gulf and threating to shoot down U.S. Navy planes – suggests Iran sees itself as a powerful regional player unafraid to take on the United States.

Many regional states are angry at the Obama administration for encouraging Iran to expand its influence by co-mingling the nuclear talks with discussions about roles Iran could play in fighting ISIS and stabilizing Iraq. Part of this effort reportedly included a secret October 2014 letter from President Obama to Iranian Supreme Leader Khamenei on how the United States and Iran might work together fighting ISIS in Iraq and Syria if a nuclear agreement was reached. This letter reportedly said U.S. military operations in Syria and Iraq are not aimed at weakening Iran or its allies, including the Assad regime in Syria. This letter gave a green light to Iran to increase its support to the Assad regime and probably emboldened Iran to significantly increase its military presence in Syria after the JCPOA was announced, including sending Revolutionary Guards, Iranian army troops and Hezbollah fighters.

As stated earlier, Iranian officials may have encouraged discussions during the nuclear talks of making Iran a partner to fight ISIS because they knew the Obama administration was looking for ways to address the instability in Syria and Iraq without increasing America's commitment in this fight and sending U.S. ground troops.

The Obama administration's belief that Iran can be a partner for peace in Iraq and Syria is deeply mistaken. Iran's presence in Iraq increases sectarian tensions and drives Sunni support to ISIS and other Sunni terrorist groups. Violence against Iraqi Sunnis after President Obama pulled all U.S. troops from Iraq in 2011 stoked sectarian tensions that led to the rise of ISIS. The more Iran is involved in Iraq, the more these tensions will rise, making the country more unstable. Similarly, Iran's presence in Syria bolsters the Assad regime and its efforts to defeat moderate Syrian rebels backed by the United States.

The weakness and incompetence of the Obama administration's Middle East policies and its reluctance to take decisive action in Syria and Iraq created a power vacuum. The JCPOA is seen by regional states as a manifestation of American weakness. This may be why after the announcement of the nuclear deal, Russia and

Iran took steps to increase their influence in the Middle East at America's expense. Russia, Iran and Syria have been collaborating on the crisis in Syria. Moscow may hope to take advantage of the power vacuum caused by Obama administration policies by creating a Russian-led power axis with Iran, Iraq and Syria. Russia also is strengthening its ties with Egypt.

Russia's intervention in Syria in September 2015, especially airstrikes, coupled with increased Iranian support to the Assad regime appear to have tilted the balance of the Syrian conflict in Assad's favor and may have made it impossible to force him from power as part of a future peace settlement.

The JCPOA has significantly increased Iran's capabilities to engage in destabilizing and belligerent activities. Even Secretary of State Kerry believes Iran will spend sanctions relief funds on terrorism.[245] Iran's 2016-2017 military budget will be increased 90%, probably in large part due to sanctions relief from the JCPOA. Sanctions relief to the Iranian Central Bank and its access to the SWIFT system will allow Iran to continue and expand illicit financial activities, including funding terrorism and insurgencies, money laundering, and financing its WMD and ballistic missile programs.

The Iranian government is not waiting for UN conventional arms sanctions to be lifted in five years per Security Council Resolution 2231 – it is already pursuing multi-billion arms deals with Russia. The Obama administration has done nothing to stop these arms sales.

For these reasons, regional states, especially Israel and Saudi Arabia, probably are taking steps to protect themselves from the Obamabomb deal. There have been press reports that Saudi Arabia may be considering purchasing nuclear weapons from Pakistan. Several regional states, possibly Saudi Arabia, Turkey, Egypt and Jordan, may start their own uranium enrichment efforts. The JCPOA's failure to address Iran's missile program probably will lead to missile proliferation in the region. Israel likely has several attack plans to strike Iranian nuclear sites with airstrikes, drones and missiles. Israel may be discussing these plans with Saudi Arabia.

In September 2016, the Obama administration was forced to admit that Iran's behavior had worsened since the JCPOA was announced and *because of this agreement.* On September 14, 2016 in the wake of an Iranian threat to shoot down U.S. Navy reconnaissance planes in the Persian Gulf, State Department spokesman Mark Toner said in response to a question posed by Fox News reporter James Rosen that Iran's behavior may have worsened because of the nuclear agreement.[246]

I believe the threat from Iran due to the JCPOA will continue to worsen through the end of this year as the Iranian government tries to cash in on the Obama administration's desperation to protect the president's legacy nuclear agreement. This means destabilizing and belligerent behavior by Iran, including ballistic missile tests, threats to Israel, sponsorship of terrorism, support to terrorist groups and insurgencies and threats to shipping in the Persian Gulf are likely to increase.

How Could the Obama Administration Agree to Such a Terrible and Dangerous Agreement?

Given how bad the JCPOA is and strong opposition to this agreement in the United States, one has to ask how the Obama administration could agree to such a deal. Legendary national security expert Richard Perle explained this in a January 19, 2016 Secure Freedom Radio interview with Center for Security Policy President Frank Gaffney.

> Their concept is that the terms of the agreement and the likely consequences if the Iranians choose to do what they are able to do under the agreement don't matter because this agreement is somehow going to magically transform an Iranian regime that regards the United States as the great Satan and engages us through the subvention of terrorism in many places throughout the world. . . . And so for people who hold this view – and I believe the president is among them -- the details of the agreement and the consequences of the agreement are of no significance. They are making an enormous and I think an improvident bet. This bet is that this agreement, which satisfies what the Iranians are looking for, will somehow lead the Iranians to become our friends. In this they are certainly mistaken.[247]

Earlier I discussed the radical and naïve policies of President Obama, his incompetent staff and the deceptive efforts his administration used to ram through an international agreement that a majority of the American people and Congress opposed. But Perle put it best: the details of the nuclear agreement do not matter because the purpose of the Iran deal is to transform Iran into an American ally. Because President Obama knew he could never sell such a far-fetched idea to the American people and the U.S. Congress, his administration used the mostly incoherent Obamabomb Deal as a pretext.

Giving Iran everything it wanted in a nuclear agreement will not lead it to rejoin the community of civilized nations and become a friend of the U.S. All indications from Tehran say the opposite: the regime's character remains unchanged, and if anything it has become a more influential and destabilizing actor in the Middle East since the announcement of the Obamabomb deal.

Renegotiate or Tear Up the Obamabomb Deal?

Given these factors, I believe the most intellectually honest way for a future U.S. president to deal with the nuclear agreement with Iran is to tear it up on his or her first day in office and start over. This agreement is so flawed and sets so many bad precedents for American foreign policy and international diplomacy that our nation should not attempt to salvage it. It should be discarded as an aberration by one of America's worst and most incompetent presidents. Instead, the next president should begin again by working with America's European allies to forge a strategy to pressure Iran to cease all nuclear activities with weapons applications and impose painful new sanctions against Iran for its sponsorship of terrorism, pursuit of weapons of mass destruction, developing ballistic missiles, threats against the state of Israel, and human rights violations.

National Security Deputy Adviser Ben Rhodes said during a June 16, 2016 speech to the Atlantic Council that the nuclear deal was front-loaded with incentives to Iran to make it difficult for a future president to tear up. According to *The Daily Caller*, Rhodes explained that "should a future president tear up the agreement, Iran would restart its nuclear weapons program, meaning future leaders are chained to the agreement, whether the American public likes it or not."[248]

In my view, Rhodes' arrogant statement is another example of abuse of power by the Obama administration and a powerful reason why the next president must discard the nuclear deal on his or her first day in office.

Some have argued, including a few Republican presidential candidates, that it would be inappropriate for the next president to discard the nuclear agreement because it is an international agreement that was negotiated with America's European allies. This argument is wrong for several reasons.

First, the nuclear agreement is primarily the result of bilateral negotiations between the United States and Iran based on the radical ideology of President Obama. The key concessions that led to this Obamabomb deal on uranium enrichment and the possible military dimensions of Iran's nuclear program were negotiated in advance in secret meetings of Iranian and American diplomats.

Second, other nations do not determine the foreign policy of the United States, especially on an agreement that is not a treaty and is not binding on our nation. We need a new president who is prepared to lead an alliance to stop Iran's nuclear program with a new nuclear agreement and who will not be dissuaded by complaints from European leaders, the American left and the news media that the United States has a moral responsibility to abide by the Obamabomb deal because we don't want to offend the Europeans. If President Obama wanted the JCPOA to have the legitimacy of a legally binding international agreement, he could have submitted it as a treaty for Senate ratification. Obama chose not to do so and instead did an end-run around the U.S. Constitution by ramming through a major international agreement which a majority of both houses of Congress voted against.

The Iran Deal Under a Clinton Presidency

If she wins the 2016 presidential election, I see no chance Hillary Clinton will tear up the JCPOA or seek to negotiate a better agreement. Like President Obama, Clinton also "owns" the JCPOA because she assigned the personnel who negotiated it and headed the Department of State in 2011 and 2012 when the key U.S. concessions were made that which to the Obamabomb Deal. I don't give credence to recent claims by Clinton supporters that Clinton is really a "hawk" or that she harbored reservations about the nuclear talks with Iran – I view this as election year posturing. I also believe the Democratic Party is heavily invested in this agreement and that Clinton will not wander far from her party on this issue.

Since I am pessimistic about the chances for throwing out the nuclear deal with Iran during a Clinton presidency, I fear Iran will make enormous gains in its nuclear weapons program if Hillary Clinton wins the 2016 presidential election and will become a more powerful and destabilizing influence in the Middle East. In my view, Iran probably also will use a Clinton presidency to expand its military and the use of the international banking system to finance terror and other illicit activities.

However, despite Clinton's strong support for the Obamabomb deal, I am hopeful she will join growing bipartisan efforts in Congress to reverse some dangerous elements of this agreement with new sanctions. This might be possible if there is a significant uptick in belligerent behavior by Iran.

I call on Mrs. Clinton if she wins the 2016 presidential election to support new sanctions on Iran in response to its ballistic missile tests, human rights violations, threats to shipping in the Persian Gulf, and threats to Israel. Such sanctions would have wide bipartisan support if she backed them. I also hope Clinton will reverse any concessions made to Iran in 2016 giving it greater access to the U.S. financial system and institute new measures to restrict Iran's access to the international financial system until Tehran can demonstrate that its banks are not involved in illicit activities. This should be a no-brainer after recent warnings by the Financial Action Task Force on the threat Iranian banks pose to the global financial system due to financing terrorism, money laundering and other illicit activities. [249]

Finally, I call on Mrs. Clinton if she wins the 2016 election to extend the Iran Sanctions Act of 1996. This is an important law that, due to JCPOA waivers, only targets non-nuclear Iranian WMD programs and Iran's sponsorship of terrorism. This law does not violate the JCPOA. Extending it will send a message to Iran that the United States demands that it cease its sponsorship of terrorism and not develop ballistic missiles, chemical weapons or biological weapons.

The Iran Deal Under a Trump Presidency

Republican presidential candidate Donald Trump has rightly described the JCPOA as a disaster and one of the worst international agreements ever negotiated. However, Trump has not indicated he would not tear up the agreement if he wins the 2016 election. Instead, Trump claims he would attempt to negotiate a better one with Tehran. Although I disagree with this approach, given Trump's condemnations of the nuclear deal, I believe it is likely that his efforts to renegotiate the JCPOA would either scuttle the deal or result in a stronger agreement that comprehensively addresses nuclear and other security threats posed by Iran. Whether or not he chooses to attempt to renegotiate the nuclear deal, I call on him to implement the recommendations listed above for Mrs. Clinton.

How Donald Trump Should Renegotiate the Nuclear Deal With Iran

If Donald Trump is elected president and the JCPOA is renegotiated, this renegotiation effort should rely on the following principles.

1. Make clear to Iran: stop all uranium enrichment and uranium enrichment research or we will stop it for you. Halting Iranian uranium enrichment must be nonnegotiable in a meaningful nuclear agreement with Iran. A Trump administration must repudiate the fiction promoted by the Obama administration that Iran's uranium enrichment effort does not pose a serious nuclear proliferation threat and that there is no way to force Iran to end it. This program has undermined regional and global nuclear nonproliferation. If Iran will not agree to cease all uranium enrichment and research and dismantle all enrichment centrifuges and send them out of the country, the United States should plan to implement strong sanctions and work with Israel and Saudi Arabia to develop a plan to destroy this program with airstrikes.

2. Make clear to Iran: you may not have a heavy-water reactor or a plant to produce heavy-water. The only purpose for Iran's Arak heavy-water reactor is to produce plutonium for nuclear weapons. It was long the position of Western states until 2013 that, given its record of cheating on its nuclear treaty obligations, Iran cannot be permitted to have such a reactor. The United States must return to this position. The JCPOA's provisions to construct a redesigned heavy-water reactor must cease since it will still give Iran a route to a plutonium-fueled nuclear bomb. Iran also must shut down its heavy-water production plant. If Iran does not agree to this, United States should implement strong sanctions and work with Israel and Saudi Arabia to develop a plan to destroy this program with airstrikes.

3. Robust verification. Iran must give IAEA inspectors full access to all declared and suspect nuclear sites, including military facilities. Inspectors must be permitted to perform any-time, any-place surprise inspections. Military sites cannot be off-limits. IAEA inspectors must be given free access to Iranian declared and suspect nuclear sites and be permitted to inspect with whatever equipment they deem necessary.

4. Iran must fully and truthfully answer all questions about its prior nuclear weapons-related work. (The Possible Military Dimensions of Iran's nuclear program or PMDs). Resolving PMD issues is crucial to a meaningful nuclear deal with Iran since this information is necessary to understand what types of nuclear weapons work in which Iran was engaged and where this work was taking place. A December 2015 IAEA report indicated Iran did not fully cooperate with an investigation into this matter and provided the agency with false and misleading answers. By going forward with the nuclear agreement despite Iran's failure to cooperate with this investigation, the Obama administration condoned this behavior and probably emboldened Iran to defy the IAEA and the international community on future investigations and demands about its nuclear program. A Trump administration must insist that the IAEA reopen its PMD file and require Iran to fully and truthfully answer all PMD questions.

5. Iran must curtail and agree to limitations on its ballistic missile program. Iran's missile program is the delivery system for its nuclear weapons program. By continuing to conduct ballistic missile tests after the announcement of the JCPOA – which President Obama has called a violation of the "spirit" of the agreement – Tehran has made a mockery of Obama administration promises that the nuclear deal placed limitations on its missile program and has increased regional tensions. Iran's missile tests in the spring of 2016 with the words written on the sides of them "Israel must be wiped off the earth" was another reminder to Israelis that the nuclear agreement did nothing to reduce the existential threat Iran poses to the State of Israel. If Iran will not end its missile program, the United States should respond with sanctions and by shooting down launches of nuclear-capable missiles. Tehran also must be required to become a member in good standing of the Missile Technology Control Regime and the Hague Code of Conduct against Ballistic Missile Proliferation.

6. **Lift sanctions in stages in response to Iranian compliance.** A new nuclear agreement must give the international community leverage to assure that the Iranian government implies with all of its commitments over time. This means sanctions against Iran (and I am assuming new sanctions will be imposed) must be lifted gradually in response to proven compliance by Tehran.

7. **Iran must agree to end its meddling in regional conflicts and sponsorship of terror.** A nuclear agreement cannot allow Tehran to use fungible billions of dollars in sanctions relief and the release of frozen funds for its ongoing efforts to destabilize the Middle East and sponsor terrorism. Sanctions relief must be tied to a demonstrable improvement in Iranian behavior.

8. **Threats by Iran to ships in the Persian Gulf, U.S. naval vessels and American servicemen and servicewomen must cease.** The United States must inform Iran that America will no longer tolerate such provocations and if they occur again, Iran will pay a price both in terms of new sanctions and a possible U.S. military response.

9. **Iran must cease its hostility toward Israel.** America cannot strike an agreement providing billions of dollars in sanctions relief to a state that explicitly seeks to destroy one of its closest allies. The Iranian government must agree to end its hostility toward Israel – including halting weapons shipments to terrorist groups that threaten Israel such as Hamas, Hezbollah and the Islamic Jihad – as part of any nuclear agreement.

10. **Iran must release all US prisoners.** Iran is known to be illegally holding former FBI agent Robert Levinson who was detained in 2007. Iranian-American

businessman Siamak Namazi and Nizar Zakka, a Lebanese businessman with a permanent U.S. green-card, were arrested in November 2015. Iran has arrested and imprisoned at least six other Western citizens with dual Iranian citizenship since January 2016 during trips to visit their families, including one U.S. dual citizen. Namazi's 80-year old father was arrested in February 2016 after he tried to free his son. Iran may be holding other Americans. The United States must demand the release of these innocent Western citizens unconditionally, not as part of prisoner swaps or in exchange for ransom payments. U.S. officials must tell Iran that the United States will not tolerate the taking of innocent Americans hostage and will make Iran pay a price for this lawless behavior, including sanctions, expelling Iranian UN diplomats from the United States, and possible military action.

.

A Time for Leadership and Truth Telling

Aside from the damage the Obamabomb deal has done and will continue to do to American and international security, a major casualty of this deal is the truth.

The Obamabomb agreement constitutes national security fraud. This was an agreement based on huge U.S. concessions to Iran and the President Obama's radical ideology that he and his senior advisers knew they could never sell to the American people or the Congress. It was negotiated and promoted through a campaign of stealth, deception, and intimidation.

The president's ends-justify-the-means strategy to get a nuclear agreement with Iran has set a dangerous precedent. Mr. Obama abused his office to mislead the American people and defy the constitutional prerogatives of the U.S. Congress to ram through a dangerous nuclear agreement with a rogue state that most Americans and members of Congress opposed. The mainstream media let the president get away with this. Even though congressional Republicans overwhelmingly opposed the nuclear agreement with Iran, they too let Mr. Obama get away with this terrible agreement by not taking more aggressive action to hold him accountable for this disastrous accord.

President Obama's stealthy and deceptive campaign to implement the Obamabomb deal over the objections of Congress has set a dangerous precedent for future presidents who may use this campaign as a blueprint to implement other foolhardy and dangerous international agreements opposed by the American people. It is therefore crucial that Americans speak out against this dangerous agreement and demand that the next president tear up the Obamabomb deal on his or her first day in office and replace it with a much stronger pact that actually addresses the nuclear and security threats posed by Iran.

About the Author

Fred Fleitz is Senior Vice President with the Center for Security Policy. He served in U.S. national security positions for 25 years with the Central Intelligence Agency, the Defense Intelligence Agency, the Department of State and the House Intelligence Committee staff. During the administration of President George W. Bush, Fleitz was chief of staff to John Bolton, then Under Secretary of State for Arms Control and International Security. He is the author of Peacekeeping Fiascoes of the 1990s (Praeger) the editor of the June 2016 book, "Warning Order: China Prepares for Conflict, and Why We Must Do the Same."

In his five years with the House Intelligence Committee staff, Fleitz was a senior aide to Chairman Peter Hoekstra and the committee's expert on the Iranian and North Korean nuclear programs.

End Notes

[1] The acronym ISIS is often mistakenly said to stand for the "Islamic State of Syria and Iraq" when it in fact represents an area of the Middle East known as al-Sham, which roughly represents what the West refers to as the Levant. This discrepancy is probably why the Obama administration and many Western governments refer to this terrorist group as "ISIL" – the Islamic State of Iraq and the Levant. Many in the Middle East and some Western leaders also refer to ISIS as "Daesh" an acronym for "al-Dawla al-Islamiya al-Iraq al-Sham." The term Daesh is preferred by some Western leaders because it is seen as a derogatory term for ISIS used by its enemies since it has negative undertones in Arab. The Western news media usually uses the acronyms ISIS or "IS" (Islamic State).

[2] Joseph Lieberman, "Reject Toothless Iran Deal and Try Again," Hartford Courant, July 19, 2015.

[3] "Obama at the Mosque," *Wall Street Journal* editorial, February 6, 2016, http://www.wsj.com/articles/obama-at-the-mosque-1454632914

[4] Since Rep. Paul has left Congress, his House website is no longer active. However, this statement was posted to the Free Republic blog site on December 21, 2009 and can be accessed at http://www.freerepublic.com/focus/f-rlc/2412613/posts.

[5] Paul Pillar, "We can live with a nuclear Iran," Washington Monthly, March/April 2012 http://washingtonmonthly.com/magazine/marchapril-2012/we-can-live-with-a-nuclear-iran/

[6] Ed Lasky, "Obama keeps hiring anti-Israeli advisors," American Thinker, April 25, 2008. http://www.americanthinker.com/blog/2008/04/obama_keeps_hiring_antiisraeli.html

[7] Kenneth Waltz, "Why Iran Should Get the Bomb," Foreign Affairs, July/August 2012. https://www.foreignaffairs.com/articles/iran/2012-06-15/why-iran-should-get-bomb

[8] Jeffrey Goldberg, "Netanyahu to Obama: Stop Iran—Or I Will," The Atlantic, March 2009, http://www.theatlantic.com/magazine/archive/2009/03/netanyahu-to-obama-stop-iran-or-i-will/307390/

[9] Samuels, op. cit.

[10] Katie Pavlich, "Brutal: Former Defense Secretaries Openly Slam 'Inexperienced' Obama White House War Micromanagement," Town Hall.com, April 7, 2016. http://townhall.com/tipsheet/katiepavlich/2016/04/07/former-defense-secretaries-openly-discuss-war-micromanagent-of-obama-white-house-n2144666

[11] David Samuels, "The Aspiring Novelist Who Became Obama's Foreign-Policy Guru," *New York Times*, May 5, 2015

[12] Leon, "Iran nuclear deal is an opportunity the U.S. should seize wholeheartedly," Los Angeles Times, September 4, 2015.

[13] Jeffrey Goldberg, "A Withering Critique of Obama's National Security Council," The Atlantic, November 12, 2014. http://www.theatlantic.com/international/archive/2014/11/a-withering-critique-of-president-obamas-national-security-council/382477/?single_page=true

[14] Stuart Winer, "Geneva talks a facade, US-Iran worked secretly on deal for past year," Times of Israel, November 18, 2013 http://www.timesofisrael.com/iran-and-us-held-secret-talks-for-over-a-year/

[15] Wanda Carruthers, "Lt. Gen. Boykin: Rice, Jarrett Calling Shots on ISIS, Iran Deal," Newsmax.com, February 10, 2015. http://www.newsmax.com/Newsfront/Jerry-Boykin-ISIS-Iran-Susan-Rice/2015/02/10/id/623868/

[16] Leslie Gelb, "This Is Obama's Last Foreign Policy Chance," Daily Beast, January 14, 2015. http://www.thedailybeast.com/articles/2015/01/13/this-is-obama-s-last-foreign-policy-chance.html

[17] David Rutz, "28 Times Obama Promised Iran Wouldn't Get a Nuclear Weapon," Washington Free Beacon, April 10, 2015. http://freebeacon.com/national-security/obama-promised-iran-wouldnt-get-a-nuclear-weapon-over-and-over/

[18] Mark Landler, "Alter Egos: Hillary Clinton, Barack Obama, and the Twilight Struggle Over American Power" London: WH Allen, 2016, p. 239-242.

[19] Mark Landler, "Alter Egos," p. 242.

[20] David Sanger and Thom Shanker, "Gates Says U.S. Lacks a Policy to Thwart Iran," New York Times, April 17, 2010.

[21] Daniel Dombey, "US senator opens Iran nuclear debate," Financial Times, June 10, 2009.

[22] Jay Solomon, "Secret Dealings With Iran Led to Nuclear Talks," Wall Street Journal, June 28, 2015.

[23] These figures of "reactor-grade uranium" refer to enriched uranium hexafluoride (UF6) which would need to be processed to separate the uranium metal to make reactor fuel rods or further enriched to weapons-grade (about 90% U-235) at which time the uranium metal would be extracted and fabricated into bomb fuel.

[24] The Institute for Science and International Security estimated in a 2009 report that Iran would need 20-25 kg of highly enriched uranium to construct a crude nuclear weapon and that it could produce this by further enriching 1,030 to 1,180 kg of low enriched uranium hexafluoride (UF6). See David Albright, Jacqueline Shire, and Paul Brannan, "Has Iran Achieved a Nuclear Weapons Breakout Capability? Not Yet, But Soon," Institute for Science and International Security, December 2, 2009. In a November 2015 report, the Wisconsin Project on Nuclear Arms Control said Iran would theoretically need 1,053 kg of UF6 to produce a bomb's worth of weapon-grade uranium metal. See "Iran's Nuclear Potential before the Implementation of the Nuclear Agreement," Wisconsin Project on Nuclear Arms

Control, November 18, 2015. http://www.iranwatch.org/our-publications/articles-reports/irans-nuclear-timetable.

[25] "Implementation of the NPT Safeguards Agreement and relevant provisions of Security Council resolutions in the Islamic Republic of Iran" Report by the IAEA Director General, Report GOV/2013/56, November 14, 2013. Annex II, p. 1.

[26] William Tobey, "The Iranian Nuclear-Inspection Charade," *Wall Street Journal*, July 15, 2015.

[27] Wendy Sherman's remarks to a Hearing of the Senate Banking, Housing and Urban Affairs Committee, "Assessing the P5+1 Interim Nuclear Agreement with Iran: Administration Perspectives," December 12, 2013.

[28] "Iran's Nuclear Masters," *Wall Street Journal* editorial, May 27, 2014.

[29] "Implementation of the NPT Safeguards Agreement and relevant provisions of Security Council resolutions in the Islamic Republic of Iran," Report by the IAEA Director General, Report GOV/2011/65, November 8, 2011.

[30] "Final Assessment on Past and Present Outstanding Issues regarding Iran's Nuclear Programme," International Atomic Energy Agency, report GOV/2015/68, December 2, 2015.

[31] "Implementation of the NPT Safeguards Agreement and relevant provisions of Security Council resolutions in the Islamic Republic of Iran," Report by the IAEA Director General, Report GOV/2011/65, November 8, 2011, page 8, paragraph 4.

[32] November 2011 IAEA report, p. 8, paragraph 45.

[33] Ibid, p. 6, paragraph 24.

[34] Julian Borger, "Iran may be researching nuclear warhead, claims watchdog," *London Guardian*, November 8, 2011

[35] November 2011 IAEA report, p. 8, paragraph 43.

[36] In hydrodynamic testing, non-fissile isotopes, such as uranium-238 and plutonium-242, are subjected to enough explosive pressure and shock so they behave like liquids (hence the 'hydro' in hydrodynamic) similar to how fissile nuclear fuel would behave in a nuclear weapon. Radiographs (x-ray photographs) are used to obtain information on the resulting hydrodynamic implosion. Computer calculations based on test results are used to predict how a nuclear weapon will perform.

[37] Jacqueline Shire and Jonathan Karl, "Suspicions Arise About Iran's Nuclear Program," ABC News, September 15, 2004. http://abcnews.go.com/WNT/story?id=131422

[38] Annex to November 2011 IAEA report, pp. 1-12.

[39] November 2011 IAEA report, p. 8, paragraph 41.

[40] November 2011 IAEA report, p. 8, paragraph 35.

[41] David Albright, Paul Brannan, Mark Gorwitz and Andrea Stricker, "ISIS Analysis of IAEA Iran Safeguards Report: Part II - Iran's Work and Foreign Assistance on a Multipoint Initiation System for a Nuclear Weapon," Institute for Science and International Security, November 13, 2011 http://isis-online.org/isis-

reports/detail/irans-work-and-foreign-assistance-on-a-multipoint-initiation-system-for-a-n/

[42] Joby Warrick, "IAEA says foreign expertise has brought Iran to threshold of nuclear capability," *Washington Post*, November 6, 2011.

[43] November 2011 IAEA report, attachment 2.

[44] November 2011 IAEA report, p. 6, pp. 9-10.

[45] Joby Warrick, "IAEA says foreign expertise has brought Iran to threshold of nuclear capability," *Washington Post*, November 6, 2011; Edwin Black, "The Iranians are almost there. This is how they did it." Times of Israel September 4, 2012.

[46] Ibid

[47] November 2011 IAEA report, p. 7, paragraph 33.

[48] November 2011 IAEA report, p. 7, paragraphs 34-35.

[49] David Sanger and William Broad, "U.N. Agency Says Iran Data Points to A-Bomb Work," *New York Times*, November 8, 2011 http://www.nytimes.com/2011/11/09/world/un-details-case-that-iran-is-at-work-on-nuclear-device.html?_r=0

[50] See James Schlesinger, "Stupid Intelligence on Iran," *Wall Street Journal*, December 19, 2007 and Alan Dershowitz, "Stupid Intelligence," Huffington Post, May 25, 2011.

[51] Wendy Sherman testimony to the Senate Foreign Relations Committee on the Iran Nuclear Negotiations, February 4, 2014.

[52] Senator Robert Menendez question to Treasury Under Secretary David Cohen, Senate Foreign Relations Committee hearing, December 2, 2011.

[53] Senator Jon Kyl quoted in John Vinocur, "A Hard Push to Get Tough on Tehran," *New York Times*, May 17, 2010.

[54] Mark Dubowitz testimony before the Senate Committee on Banking, Housing, and Urban Affairs, January 27, 2015. http://www.iranwatch.org/sites/default/files/dubowitz-012715.pdf

[55] Paul Richter, "Obama administration takes back seat on Iran sanctions," LA Times, February 17, 2012. http://articles.latimes.com/2012/feb/17/world/la-fg-us-iran-20120218

[56] Hillary Clinton, "Hard Choices," New York: Simon and Schuster, 2014, p. 439.

[57] U.S. Department of the Treasury, Press Release, "Fact Sheet: New Sanctions on Iran," November 21, 2011. http://www.treasury.gov/presscenter/pressreleases/Pages/tg1367.aspx

[58] Mark Dubowitz testimony before the Senate Committee on Banking, Housing, and Urban Affairs, January 27, 2015. http://www.iranwatch.org/sites/default/files/dubowitz-012715.pdf

[59] "Iranian Senior Officials Disclose Confidential Details From Nuclear Negotiations: Already In 2011," Special Dispatch Number 6131, Middle East Media Research Institute, August 10, 2015. http://www.memri.org/report/en/0/0/0/0/0/0/8700.htm

[60] Landler, "Alter Egos," pp. 250.

[61] Landler, "Alter Egos," pp. 249-252.

[62] Indiria Lakshmanan, "If You Can't Do This Deal ... Go Back to Tehran," *Politico*, September 25, 2015. http://www.politico.com/magazine/story/2015/09/iran-deal-inside-story-213187

[63] Landler, "Alter Egos," p. 416.

[64] William Broad, "For Iran, Enriching Uranium Only Gets Easier," *New York Times*, March 8, 2010.

[65] Maseh Zarif, "The Iranian Nuclear Program: Timelines, Data, and Estimates V7.0," American Enterprise Institute, July 10, 2013. http://www.irantracker.org/nuclear-program/zarif-timelines-data-estimates-july-10-2013

[66] Patrick Migliorini, David Albright, Houston Wood, and Christina Walrond, "Iranian Breakout Estimates, Updated September 2013," Institute for Science and International Security, October 24, 2013. http://www.isisnucleariran.org/assets/pdf/Breakout_Study_24October2013.pdf

[67] Gregory S. Jones, "Iran's Enriched Uranium Stocks Can Produce Enough HEU for 3 to 5 Nuclear Weapons," Nonproliferation Policy Education Center, September 10, 2013. http://nuclearpolicy101.org/wp-content/uploads/2013/09/Iran-Enrichment-Update-09-2013.pdf

[68] Fred Fleitz, "Why Congress Must Repudiate the Nuclear Talks with Iran," Center for Security Policy, November 14, 2015. http://www.centerforsecuritypolicy.org/2014/11/14/why-congress-must-repudiate-the-nuclear-talks-with-iran/

[69] Eli Lake, "Obama Kept Iran's Short Breakout Time a Secret," Bloomberg.com, April 21, 2016. https://www.bloomberg.com/view/articles/2015-04-21/obama-kept-iran-s-short-breakout-time-a-secret

[70] Samantha Stern, "Wendy Sherman recounts Iran nuclear deal negotiations," The Dartmouth, October 28, 2015. http://thedartmouth.com/2015/10/28/wendy-sherman-recounts-iran-nuclear-deal-negotiations/

[71] Foundation for the Defense of Democracies conference, June 1, 2015. Video available at: http://www.centerforsecuritypolicy.org/2015/06/02/senator-lieberman-says-uranium-enrichment-is-a-deal-killer-in-any-nuclear-deal-with-iran/

[72] "Fact Sheet: First Step Understandings Regarding the Islamic Republic of Iran's Nuclear Program," White House press release, November 23, 2015. https://www.whitehouse.gov/the-press-office/2013/11/23/fact-sheet-first-step-understandings-regarding-islamic-republic-iran-s-n

[73] Fred Fleitz, "Iran Deal: Not as Bad as It Could Be, but Still Bad," National Review Online, November 24, 2013. http://www.nationalreview.com/corner/364714/iran-deal-not-bad-it-could-be-still-bad-fred-fleitz?target=author&tid=906156

[74] Jay Solomon, "Saudi Royal Blasts U.S.'s Mideast Policy," *Wall Street Journal*, December 15, 2013.

http://online.wsj.com/news/articles/SB100014240527023039495045792605106449 6826; Steven Erlanger, "Saudi Prince Criticizes Obama Administration, Citing Indecision in Mideast," *New York Times*, December 15, 2013. http://www.nytimes.com/2013/12/16/world/middleeast/saudi-prince-accuses-obama-of-indecision-on-middle-east.html?_r=0

[75] Mark Urban, "Saudi nuclear weapons 'on order' from Pakistan," BBC website, November 6, 2013. http://www.bbc.co.uk/news/world-middle-east-24823846

[76] Landler, "Alter Egos," pp. 250-251.

[77] Landler, "Alter Egos," p. 251.

[78] David Albright and Andrea Stricker, "A Note on Iran's IR-5 Centrifuge Feeding." Institute for Science and International Security, November 20, 2014. http://isis-online.org/isis-reports/detail/a-note-on-irans-ir-5-centrifuge-feeding/8

[79] Louis Charbonneau, "U.S. and Iran: the unbearable awkwardness of defending your enemy," Reuters, July 5, 2015. http://www.reuters.com/article/us-iran-nuclear-usa-awkward-idUSKCN0PF0NL20150705

[80] David Albright and Andrea Stricker, "A Note on Iran's IR-5 Centrifuge Feeding." Institute for Science and International Security, November 20, 2014. http://isis-online.org/isis-reports/detail/a-note-on-irans-ir-5-centrifuge-feeding/8

[81] Indiria Lakshmanan, "If You Can't Do This Deal ... Go Back to Tehran," *Politico*, September 25, 2015. http://www.politico.com/magazine/story/2015/09/iran-deal-inside-story-213187

[82] Michael Gordon, "U.S. Lays Out Limits It Seeks in Iran Nuclear Talks," *New York Times*, November 20, 2014. http://www.nytimes.com/2014/11/21/world/middleeast/us-lays-out-limits-it-seeks-in-iran-nuclear-talks.html

[83] David Sanger, "Fear of Israeli Leaks Fuels Distrust Over U.S. Talks With Iran," *New York Times*, February 17, 2015. http://www.nytimes.com/2015/02/18/world/fear-of-israeli-leaks-fuels-distrust-as-us-and-iran-hold-nuclear-talks.html

[84] Robert Einhorn, "Will Iran Play Ball in Nuke Talks?" National Interest, January 14, 2015.

[85] Armin Rosen, "An Iran nuclear deal is coming into focus, but there's one glaring problem," Business Insider, February 20, 2015. http://www.businessinsider.com/status-of-iran-nuclear-negotiations-2015-2

[86] Michael Morrell comment on The Charlie Rose Show, February 18, 2015.

[87] Adam Kredo, "Nuclear Deal Would Leave Iran With 5,000 Centrifuges," *Washington Free Beacon*, June 30, 2015. http://freebeacon.com/issues/iran-nuke-deal-ensures-iranian-centrifuges-continue-spinning/

[88] Lee Smith, "Has the Obama Administration Become Iran's Lawyer?," Tablet Magazine, July 6, 2015. http://www.tabletmag.com/scroll/192045/has-the-obama-administration-become-irans-lawyer

[89] Ibid.

[90] Bill Gertz, "North Korea Transfers Missile Goods to Iran During Nuclear Talks," *Washington Free Beacon*, April 15, 2015.

[91] Greg Richter, "Iranian Defector: US Working 'On Behalf' of Iran," *Newsmax.com*, March 29, 2015. http://www.newsmax.com/Newsfront/amir-hossein-motaghi-defector-working-behalf/2015/03/29/id/635149/

[92] Carla Anne Robbins, "As Evidence Grows of Iran's Nuclear Program, U.S. Hits Quandary," *Wall Street Journal*, March 18, 2005. http://online.wsj.com/news/articles/SB111111017248183340

[93] Charles Hoskinson, "Iran's ballistic missiles could derail nuke deal," Washington Examiner, June 8, 2015

[94] A. Savyon and Y. Carmen, "Nuclear Negotiations at an Impasse," Middle East Media Research Center," July 11, 2015. http://www.memri.org/report/en/0/0/0/0/0/0/8604.htm

[95] "Top Obama adviser dismisses idea that better Iran deal is possible," Times of Israel, April 6, 2015. http://www.timesofisrael.com/top-obama-adviser-dismisses-idea-that-better-iran-deal-is-possible/

[96] Katie Pavlich, "Top Iranian Nuke Deal Negotiator Admits "Anytime" Inspections Are Pretty Much Bogus," Townhall.com, July 17, 2015. http://townhall.com/tipsheet/katiepavlich/2015/07/17/inspections-of-iranian-nuclear-facilities-at-any-time-are-pretty-much-bogus-n2026864

[97] Herb Keinon, "Top US official: Anytime, anyplace' access to Iranian facilities was rhetorical flourish." *Jerusalem Post*, July 16, 2015. http://www.jpost.com/Middle-East/Iran/Top-US-official-Anytime-anyplace-access-to-Iranian-facilities-was-rhetorical-flourish-409249?utm_campaign=shareaholic&utm_medium=twitter&utm_source=socialnetwork

[98] John Kerry Press conference, June 16, 2015. http://www.state.gov/secretary/remarks/2015/06/243892.htm

[99] Jennifer Rubin, "John Kerry's ludicrous statements on Iran and Syria," *Washington Post*, June 17, 2015. https://www.washingtonpost.com/blogs/right-turn/wp/2015/06/17/john-kerrys-ludicrous-statements-on-iran-and-syria/

[100] Louis Charbonneau and Parisa Hafezi, "Exclusive: Kerry tells Iran foreign minister 'the past does matter' – sources," Reuters, June 25, 2015. http://www.reuters.com/article/us-iran-nuclear-kerry-exclusive-idUSKBN0P51PT20150625

[101] President Barack Obama, "Remarks by the President in a Conversation with the Saban Forum," Washington, DC, December 7, 2013. https://www.whitehouse.gov/the-press-office/2013/12/07/remarks-president-conversation-saban-forum

[102] "Transcript: President Obama's Full NPR Interview On Iran Nuclear Deal," National Public Radio, April 7, 2015. http://www.npr.org/2015/04/07/397933577/transcript-president-obamas-full-npr-interview-on-iran-nuclear-deal

[103] David Albright and Andrea Stricker, "The Nuclear Deal's Procurement Channel: Overcoming Post-Implementation Day Blues," Institute for Science an International Security, April 21, 2016. http://www.isisnucleariran.org/assets/pdf/JCPOA_Procurement_Channel_Post_Implementation_Day_21April2016_Final1.pdf

[104] Testimony of David Albright to the Senate Foreign Relations Committee, August 4, 2015. http://www.isisnucleariran.org/assets/pdf/Albright_SFRC_Testominy_August4_2015_Final.pdf

[105] Olli Heinonen testimony to the House Committee on Financial Services Task Force to Investigate Terrorism Financing, July 22, 2015. http://financialservices.house.gov/uploadedfiles/hhrg-114-ba00-wstate-oheinonen-20150722.pdf

[106] Mark Dubowitz testimony to the House Foreign Affairs Committee, July 23, 2015, p. 25. http://www.defenddemocracy.org/content/uploads/documents/Dubowitz_Testimony_HFAC_Implications_of_a_Nuclear_Agreement.pdf#page=2&zoom=auto,-15,580

[107] "Iran-China discussing Arak reactor," PressTV, January 26, 2016. http://presstv.com/Detail/2016/01/26/447446/IranChina-discussing-Arak-reactor--/

[108] Kelsey Davenport, Daryl G. Kimball, and Greg Thielmann, "Solving the Iranian Nuclear Puzzle: The Joint Comprehensive Plan of Action," The Arms Control Association, August 2015, pp. 17-18. http://www.armscontrol.org/files/ACA_Iran-BB_2015%20Aug6_FINAL.pdf

[109] William Broad, "Plutonium Is Unsung Concession in Iran Nuclear Deal," New York Times, September 7, 2015. http://www.nytimes.com/2015/09/08/science/irans-unsung-plutonium-concession-in-nuclear-deal.html

[110] Mark Dubowitz testimony to the House Foreign Affairs Committee, July 23, 2015, p. 16. http://www.defenddemocracy.org/content/uploads/documents/Dubowitz_Testimony_HFAC_Implications_of_a_Nuclear_Agreement.pdf#page=2&zoom=auto,-15,580

[111] David Kay quoted in "How Iran Could Get Sanctions Relief under the Nuclear Deal Sooner than Anticipated," Wisconsin Project on Arms Control, July 17, 2015. http://www.iranwatch.org/our-publications/nuclear-iran-weekly/how-iran-could-get-sanctions-relief-under-nuclear-deal-sooner-anticipated

[112] Olli Heinonen testimony to the House Committee on Financial Services Task Force to Investigate Terrorism Financing, July 22, 2015. http://financialservices.house.gov/uploadedfiles/hhrg-114-ba00-wstate-oheinonen-20150722.pdf

[113] Rebecca Kheel, "Kerry: Some Iran sanctions relief will go to terrorists." *The Hill* January 21, 2016. http://thehill.com/policy/defense/266619-kerry-some-iran-sanctions-relief-will-go-to-terrorists

[114] Ali Akbar Dareini, "Iran's Defense Minister says his country will sign a contract with Russia for the purchase of fighter jets," Associated Press, February 10, 2016. http://www.usnews.com/news/world/articles/2016-02-10/iran-to-purchase-sukhoi-30-fighter-jets-from-russia

[115] House Foreign Affairs Committee hearing, February 25, 2016. https://foreignaffairs.house.gov/hearing/hearing-strengthening-u-s-leadership-in-a-turbulent-world-the-fy-2017-foreign-affairs-budget/

[116] Jonathan Karl Twitter post, July 14, 2015. https://twitter.com/jonkarl/status/620975713546543104

[117] Transcript of State Department background briefing by unnamed administration officials on JCPOA Adoption Day, U.S. Department of State, October 17, 2015. http://m.state.gov/md248310.htm

[118] Secure America Now national survey of 1,000 likely general election voters by McLaughlin and Associates and Caddell Associates, August 2015.

[119] "Support for Iran Nuclear Agreement Falls," Pew Research Center, September 8, 2015. http://www.people-press.org/2015/09/08/support-for-iran-nuclear-agreement-falls/

[120] John R. Bolton, "Debating the dubious Iran deal," *Washington Times*, August 4, 2015. http://www.washingtontimes.com/news/2015/aug/4/john-bolton-debating-the-dubious-iran-deal/

[121] Senator Chuck Schumer press releases, "My position on the Iran deal." August 6, 2015. https://www.schumer.senate.gov/newsroom/press-releases/my-position-on-the-iran-deal

[122] Senator Robert Menendez, "Menendez Delivers Remarks on Iran Nuclear Deal at Seton Hall University's School of Diplomacy and International Relations," Menendez press release, August 18, 2015. https://www.menendez.senate.gov/news-and-events/press/menendez-delivers-remarks-on-iran-nuclear-deal-at-seton-hall-universitys-school-of-diplomacy-and-international-relations

[123] Congressman Ed Royce press statement on the Iran deal, August 5, 2015. https://foreignaffairs.house.gov/press-release/chairman-royce-reacts-to-president-obamas-iran-deal-speech/

[124] Congressman Eliot Engel press release on the Iran deal, August 6, 2015. https://engel.house.gov/latest-news1/engel-statement-on-iran-deal1/

[125] Hillary Clinton, "Hard Choices," New York: Simon and Schuster, 2014, p. 439.

[126] Ibid, p. 416.

[127] Landler, "Alter Egos," pp. 252-253.

[128] Fred Fleitz, "Kasich's, Bush's Iran Nukes Stance Will Cost Both GOP Nod," *Newsmax.com*, September 17, 2016. http://www.newsmax.com/Fred-Fleitz/Jeb-Bush-2016-Elections-2016-GOP-Media-Bias/2015/09/17/id/692047/

[129] Transcript of Donald Trump's address to AIPAC convention, Time, March 21, 2016. http://time.com/4267058/donald-trump-aipac-speech-transcript/

[130] Aaron Klein, "Eric Trump: Obama's Iran Deal Drove My Father to Run for President," Breitbart.com, May 29, 2016. http://www.breitbart.com/2016-presidential-race/2016/05/29/eric-trump-obamas-iran-deal-drove-father-run-president/

[131] Secretary of State John Kerry testimony to the Senate Foreign Relations Committee, April 8, 2014. http://www.foreign.senate.gov/imo/media/doc/04%2008%202014,%20International%20Affairs%20Budget1.pdf

[132] Andrew McCarthy, "The Corker Bill Isn't a Victory — It's a Constitutional Perversion," National Review Online, April 18, 2015.

[133] House Foreign Affairs Committee hearing on the nuclear deal with Iran, July 28, 2015. http://ribble.house.gov/transcript-house-foreign-affairs-hearing

[134] Letter to Congressman Mike Pompeo from State Department Assistant Secretary for Legislative Affairs Julia Frifield, November 9, 2015.

[135] Todd Beamon, "House panel slams Kerry on "condescending" testimony on Iran deal," *Newsmax*, July 28, 2015.

[136] David Samuels, "The Aspiring Novelist Who Became Obama's Foreign-Policy Guru," *New York Times*, May 5, 2015

[137] Ibid.

[138] Lee Smith, "Ploughshares and the Iran Deal Echo Chamber," Weekly Standard, May 24, 2016. http://www.weeklystandard.com/ploughshares-and-the-iran-deal-echo-chamber/article/2002528

[139] Eli Lake, "The Secret History of the Iran-Deal 'Echo Chamber,'" Bloomberg View, May 24, 2016. https://www.bloomberg.com/view/articles/2016-05-24/the-secret-history-of-the-iran-deal-echo-chamber

[140] "David Albright, Paulina Izewicz, and Andrea Stricker," Iran's Stock of near 20 Percent LEU under the Extension of the Joint Plan of Action," December 8, 2014. http://isis-online.org/isis-reports/detail/irans-stock-of-near-20-percent-leu-under-the-extension-of-the-joint-plan-of/

[141] Bradley Klapper, "Group that helped sell Iran nuke deal also funded media," Associated Press, May 20, 2016. http://bigstory.ap.org/article/7044e805a95a4b7da5533b1b9ab75cd2/group-helped-sell-iran-nuke-deal-also-funded-media

[142] "NPR ombudsman has issues with funding by pro-Iran Group." Associated Press, May 31, 2016.

http://www.bostonherald.com/business/business_markets/2016/05/npr_ombudsman_has_issues_with_funding_by_pro_iran_deal_group

[143] Congressman Mike Pompeo press release, June 1, 2016.
http://pompeo.house.gov/news/documentsingle.aspx?DocumentID=399013

[144] Congressman Mike Pompeo press release, May 27, 2016.
http://pompeo.house.gov/news/documentsingle.aspx?DocumentID=399008

[145] Adam Entous and Danny Yadron, "U.S. Spy Net on Israel Snares Congress," *Wall Street Journal*, December 28, 2015.

[146] Rep. Ron DeSantis letter to President Obama, January 4, 2016.
http://desantis.house.gov/sites/desantis.house.gov/files/Rep.%20DeSantis%20Letter%20to%20Obama%20Regarding%20the%20NSA.pdf

[147] Chaffetz letter to NSA Director Rogers, December 30, 2015.
http://desantis.house.gov/sites/desantis.house.gov/files/2015-12-30%20Letter%20to%20Rogers.pdf

[148] Jay Solomon, "The Iran Wars," New York: Random House, 2016, pp. 291-292.
http://desantis.house.gov/sites/desantis.house.gov/files/Rep.%20DeSantis%20Letter%20to%20Obama%20Regarding%20the%20NSA.pdf

[149] Chairman Ed Royce letter to State Department Inspector General Steve Linick, June 3, 2016. House Foreign Affairs Committee website.
http://foreignaffairs.house.gov/sites/republicans.foreignaffairs.house.gov/files/Royce%20to%20Linick%206-3-16.pdf

[150] Congressman Mike Pompeo and Senator Tom Cotton press release, July 21, 2015.
http://pompeo.house.gov/news/documentsingle.aspx?DocumentID=398509

[151] Ibid

[152] George Jahn, "UN to let Iran inspect alleged nuclear work site," Associated Press report via The Military Times, August 19, 2015.
http://www.militarytimes.com/story/military/2015/08/19/un-let-iran-inspect-alleged-nuclear-work-site/32003359/

[153] Fred Fleitz, "The Plot Thickens: Iran-Deal Backers Claim AP Side Deal Document Is a Forgery," National Review Online, August 21, 2016.
http://www.nationalreview.com/corner/422915/plot-thickens-iran-deal-backers-claim-ap-side-deal-document-forgery-fred-fleitz?target=author&tid=906156

[154] "Support for Iran Nuclear Agreement Falls," Pew Research Center, September 8, 2015. http://www.people-press.org/2015/09/08/support-for-iran-nuclear-agreement-falls/

[155] Jeremy Diamond, "Iran missile test sparks concern over nuclear deal implementation," CNN.com, December 17, 2015.
http://www.cnn.com/2015/12/17/politics/iran-missile-test-un-resolution-violation/

[156] Andrew McCarthy, "Delusional White House on Iran Missile Test: UN Resolution Implementing Iran Deal 'Altogether Separate' from Iran Deal," National Review Online, October 13, 2015.

http://www.nationalreview.com/corner/425507/delusional-white-house-iran-missile-test-un-resolution-implementing-iran-deal

[157] Jay Solomon, "Obama Administration Preparing Fresh Iran Sanctions," *Wall Street Journal*, December 30, 2015. http://www.wsj.com/articles/obama-administration-preparing-fresh-iran-sanctions-1451507921

[158] Yigal Carmen and Ayelet Savyon, "Iranian Supreme Leader Khamenei's Letter Of Guidelines To President Rohani On JCPOA Sets Nine Conditions Nullifying Original Agreement Announced July 14, 2015," Middle East Media Research Institute," October 22, 2015   http://www.memri.org/report/en/print8813.htm

[159] Parisa Hafezi, "Iran's Khamenei conditionally approves nuclear deal with powers," Reuters, October 21, 2015. http://www.reuters.com/article/us-iran-nuclear-khamenei-idUSKCN0SF18720151021

[160] Blake Seitz, "Gen. Campbell: Iran is Arming the Taliban," *Washington Free Beacon*, October 6, 2015. http://freebeacon.com/national-security/gen-campbell-iran-is-arming-the-taliban/

[161] Jay Solomon, "U.S. Detects Flurry of Iranian Hacking," *Wall Street Journal*, November 4, 2015. http://www.wsj.com/articles/u-s-detects-flurry-of-iranian-hacking-1446684754

[162] Secretary of State John Kerry speech to the Council on Foreign Relations, New York, NY, July 24, 2015. http://www.state.gov/secretary/remarks/2015/07/245253.htm

[163] U.S. Department of State, "Background Briefing on the JCPOA Adoption Day," October 17, 2015. http://m.state.gov/md248310.htm

[164] Francis Murphy and Shadia Nasralla, "Report on whether Iran sought nuclear bomb will not be clear cut - U.N.," Reuters, November 26, 2015 http://www.reuters.com/article/iran-nuclear-iaea-idUSKBN0TF1L420151126

[165] "Final Assessment on Past and Present Outstanding Issues regarding Iran's Nuclear Programme," International Atomic Energy Agency, Report GOV/2015/68. December 2, 2015. http://isis-online.org/uploads/isis-reports/documents/IAEA_PMD_Assessment_2Dec2015.pdf

[166] Olli Heinonen testimony to the House Committee on Financial Services Task Force to Investigate Terrorism Financing, July 22, 2015. http://financialservices.house.gov/uploadedfiles/hhrg-114-ba00-wstate-oheinonen-20150722.pdf

[167] David Albright, Andrea Stricker, and Serena Kelleher-Vergantin, "Initial Reactions to the IAEA's PMD Report," Institute for Science and International Security, December 2, 2015. http://isis-online.org/isis-reports/detail/initial-reactions-to-the-iaeas-pmd-report/

[168] Jay Solomon, "Obama Administration Welcomes IAEA Report on Iran's Nuclear-Weapons Work," *Wall Street Journal*, December 2, 2015. http://www.wsj.com/articles/obama-administration-welcomes-iaea-report-on-irans-nuclear-weapons-work-1449085109

[169] "Iran reacts to IAEA chief report on PMD," Iranian Republic News Agency, December 2, 2015. http://www.irna.ir/en/News/81863238/

[170] David Albright, Andrea Stricker, and Serena Kelleher-Vergantini, "Analysis of the IAEA's Report on the PMD of Iran's Nuclear Program," Institute for Science and International Security, December 8, 2015. http://isis-online.org/isis-reports/detail/analysis-of-the-iaeas-report-on-the-pmd-of-irans-nuclear-program/8

[171] Fred Fleitz, "James Schlesinger and Alan Dershowitz Were Right About 'Stupid' Iran Intelligence," TohnHall.com, December 21, 2015. http://townhall.com/columnists/fredfleitz/2015/12/21/james-schlesinger-and-alan-dershowitz-were-right-about-stupid-iran-intelligence-n2095968

[172] Karen Delong, "IAEA concludes Iran had active nuclear weapons program until 2003," *Washington Post*, December 2, 2015. https://www.washingtonpost.com/world/national-security/iaea-concludes-iran-had-active-nuclear-weapons-program-until-2003/2015/12/02/e242bc68-993f-11e5-8917-653b65c809eb_story.html

[173] Fred Fleitz, "Report: Iran was researching nukes in 2009," National Review Online, December 2, 2015. http://www.nationalreview.com/article/427899/-iran-nuclear-weapon-research?target=author&tid=906156

[174] Olli Heinonen, "Next Steps in the Implementation of the JCPOA," Foundation for the Defense of Democracies, December 8, 2015. http://www.defenddemocracy.org/media-hit/next-steps-in-the-implementation-of-the-jcpoa/

[175] Jay Solomon, "Uranium Provides New Clue on Iran's Past Nuclear Arms Work." *Wall Street Journal*, June 19, 2016.

[176] "Final Assessment on Past and Present Outstanding Issues regarding Iran's Nuclear Programme," International Atomic Energy Agency, Report GOV/2015/68, paragraphs 47-47, December 2, 2015. http://isis-online.org/uploads/isis-reports/documents/IAEA_PMD_Assessment_2Dec2015.pdf

[177] Olli Heinonen, "Next Steps in the Implementation of the JCPOA," Foundation for the Defense of Democracies, December 8, 2015. http://www.defenddemocracy.org/media-hit/next-steps-in-the-implementation-of-the-jcpoa/

[178] Fred Fleitz, "Congress must release the report on Iran's mistreatment of U.S. sailors," Fox News.com, June 9, 2016. http://www.foxnews.com/opinion/2016/06/09/congress-must-release-report-on-irans-mistreatment-u-s-sailors.html

[179] Congressman Mike Pompeo press release, May 26, 2016. http://pompeo.house.gov/news/documentsingle.aspx?DocumentID=399006

[180] Shima Shahrabi, "Who is Nosratollah Khosravi-Roodsari? The Story of the Fourth American Prisoner," Iran Wire, February 1, 2016. https://iranwire.com/en/features/1600

[181] Jay Solomon and Carol Lee, "U.S. Sent Cash to Iran as Americans Were Freed," Wall Street Journal, August 3, 2016.

[182] Saeed Abedini interview on "The Intelligence Report with Trish Regan," Fox Business Channel, August 4, 2016. http://www.foxbusiness.com/features/2016/08/04/freed-american-hostage-waited-all-night-at-airport.html

[183] Andrew McCarthy, "President Obama Violated the Law with His Ransom Payment to Iran," National Review Online, August 6, 2016. http://www.nationalreview.com/article/438744/iran-ransom-payment-president-obama-broke-law-sending-cash-iran

[184] Carol Morello, "Money paid to Iran was 'leverage' not ransom, State Department says," Washington Post, August 18, 2016.

[185] Devon Barrett, "Justice Department Officials Raised Objections on U.S. Cash Payment to Iran," Wall Street Journal, August 3, 2016.

[186] Claudia Rosett, "Riddle of $1.3 Billion for Iran Might Relate to 13 Outlays Of Exactly $99,999,999.99," New York Sun, August 22, 2016. http://www.nysun.com/foreign/riddle-of-13-billion-for-iran-might-be-solved-by/89692/

[187] Jay Solomon and Carol Lee, "U.S. Transferred $1.3 billion More in Cash to Iran After Initial Payment," Wall Street Journal, September 6, 2016.

[188] Senator Ted Cruz, Fox News Sunday transcript, Fox News.com, January 17, 2016. http://www.foxnews.com/transcript/2016/01/17/ted-cruz-speaks-out-about-his-approach-to-foreign-policy-paul-ryan-lays-out-his/

[189] Charles Krauthammer, "The GOP gets the Iran prisoner swap wrong," Washington Post, January 21, 2016. https://www.washingtonpost.com/opinions/the-gop-gets-the-iran-prisoner-swap-wrong/2016/01/21/58a38eb6-c071-11e5-83d4-42e3bceea902_story.html

[190] Stephen Kruiser, "Colbert Hilariously Deals with Iran Ransom in Monologue," PJ Media, August 4, 2016. https://pjmedia.com/video/colbert-hilariously-deals-with-iran-ransom-in-monologue/1

[191] David Albright and Andrea Stricker, "JCPOA Exemptions Revealed," Institute for Science and International Security, September 1, 2016. http://www.isisnucleariran.org/reports/detail/jcpoa/

[192] James Rosen, "Deal granted exemptions to Iran in order to meet deadline," Fox News Channel, September 1, 2016. http://video.foxnews.com/v/5108999453001/deal-granted-exemptions-to-iran-in-order-to-meet-deadline/?#sp=show-clips

[193] "Annual Report on the Protection of the Constitution," Bundesamt für Verfassungsschutz (Federal Ministry of the Interior) report, June 2016, p. 30.

[194] Benjamin Weinthal, "Exclusive: Iran sought chemical and biological weapons technology in Germany," Jerusalem Post, July 9, 2016. http://www.jpost.com/printarticle.aspx?id=459905

[195] David Albright and Andrea Stricker, "Iranian Atomic Energy Organization Attempted Carbon Fiber Procurement," Institute for Science and International Security, July 7, 2016. http://www.isisnucleariran.org/assets/pdf/AEOI_Attempted_Carbon_Fiber_Procurement_7Jul2016.pdf

[196] David Albright and Andrea Stricker, "Previously Sanctioned Iranian Entities Doing Business in China," July 7, 2016, http://www.isisnucleariran.org/assets/pdf/Previously_Sanctioned_Iranian_Entities_Doing_Business_in_China_7Jul2016_Final.pdf

[197] Olli Heinonen, "The IAEA's Latest Report Falls Short," Foundation for the Defense of Democracies, March 4, 2016. http://www.defenddemocracy.org/media-hit/olli-heinonen-the-iaeas-latest-report-falls-short1/

[198] Ibid.

[199] Barbara Slavin, "What's behind IAEA's change in reporting?," al-Monitor, March 9, 2016. http://www.al-monitor.com/pulse/originals/2016/03/iran-nuclear-deal-officials-jcpoa-information.html

[200] David Albright, Serena Kelleher-Vergantini, and Andrea Stricker, "IAEA's Second JCPOA Report: Key Information Still Missing," Institute for Science and International Security, May 31, 2016. http://isis-online.org/isis-reports/detail/iaeas-second-jcpoa-report-key-information-still-missing/

[201] David Albright and Andrea Stricker, "Analysis of the IAEA's Third Iran Deal Report: Filling in Missing Details," Institute for Science and International Security, September 9, 2016.

[202] Laurence Norman and Sam Dagher, "EU Presses Iran for Help in Syria Peace Talks," *Wall Street Journal*, April 17, 2016.

[203] Ari Soffer, "Iran pledges $70 million to Palestinian Islamic Jihad," Arutz Sheva 7, May 26, 2016. http://www.israelnationalnews.com/News/News.aspx/212833#.V1widf32buQ

[204] Jon Boone, Death of Mullah Mansoor highlights Taliban's links with Iran," *London Guardian*, May 23, 2016, http://www.israelnationalnews.com/News/News.aspx/212833#.V1widf32buQ

[205] "Yemen's Shiite rebels retake ground from government forces," Associated Press, June 2, 2016, http://www.foxnews.com/world/2016/06/02/yemen-shiite-rebels-retake-ground-from-government-forces.html

[206] Bozorgmehr Sharafedin, "Iran could send military advisers to Yemen: official suggests," Reuters, March 8, 2016. http://www.reuters.com/article/us-yemen-security-iran-idUSKCN0WA1PM

[207] Russ Read, "US Tax Dollars Will Help Subsidize Iran's Massive Military Build Up," Daily Caller, June 9, 2016. http://dailycaller.com/2016/06/09/us-tax-dollars-will-help-subsidize-irans-massive-military-build-up/

[208] U.S. Department of State, "Country Reports on Terrorism 2015." http://www.state.gov/j/ct/rls/crt/2015/257517.htm

[209] Bill Gertz, "Iran Conducts Space Launch," *Washington Free Beacon*, April 20, 2016. http://freebeacon.com/national-security/iran-conducts-space-launch/

[210] Rod McGuirk, " Iran's foreign minister says he deliberately negotiated the wording of the latest United Nations resolution restraining his country's nuclear program to ensure that the test-firing of nuclear-capable Iranian missiles would be legal," US News and World Report, March 15, 2016. http://www.usnews.com/news/world/articles/2016-03-15/iran-foreign-ministers-denies-missile-tests-breach-un-rules

[211] Louis Charbonneau, "Exclusive: Iran missile tests were 'in defiance of' U.N. resolution - U.S., allies," Reuters, March 30, 2016. http://www.reuters.com/article/us-iran-missiles-idUSKCN0WV2HE

[212] Ibid.

[213] "Iran should pay a price for its ballistic missile tests." *Washington Post* editorial, April 6, 2016. https://www.washingtonpost.com/opinions/iran-should-pay-a-price-for-its-ballistic-missile-tests/2016/04/06/a85ef152-fc1c-11e5-80e4-c381214de1a3_story.html

[214] Yousef Al Otaiba, "One Year After the Iran Nuclear Deal," *Wall Street Journal*, April 3, 2016. http://www.wsj.com/articles/one-year-after-the-iran-nuclear-deal-1459721502

[215] Senator Kelly Ayotte press release, March 17, 2016. https://www.ayotte.senate.gov/?p=press_release&id=2545

[216] Babak Dehghanpisheh, "Iran parades new weapons at time of Gulf tension with U.S.," Reuters, September 21, 2016.

[217] Ibid.

[218] Adam Kredo, "Iran 'Blackmailing' U.S. for Greater Nuke Concessions," *Washington Free Beacon*, May 24, 2016. http://freebeacon.com/national-security/iran-blackmailing-us/

[219] Bradley Klapper, "The Obama administration is leaving the door open to new sanctions relief for Iran, prompting increased concern from Republican opponents of last year's nuclear deal," US News and World Report, March 24, 2016.

[220] "Remarks of Secretary Lew on the Evolution of Sanctions and Lessons for the Future at the Carnegie Endowment for International Peace." March 30, 2016.

[221] Aaron Kliegman, "Kerry: Iran 'Absolutely' Deserves Access to U.S. Dollars as Part of Sanctions Relief," *Washington Free Beacon*, April 5, 2016. http://freebeacon.com/national-security/kerry-iran-absolutely-deserves-access-american-dollars/

[222] Barbara Slavin, "Central Bank governor: Iran expects access to US financial system," al-Monitor, April 15, 2016.

[223] United Against a Nuclear Iran press release, March 28, 2016.
http://www.businesswire.com/news/home/20160328005764/en/UANI-Gravely-Concerned-Reported-Plan-Iran-Access

[224] Mark Dubowitz and Jonathan Schanzer, "Dollarizing the Ayatollahs," *Wall Street Journal*, March 27, 2016.

[225] Financial Action Task Force statement, February 19, 2016. http://www.fatf-gafi.org/publications/high-riskandnon-cooperativejurisdictions/documents/public-statement-february-2016.html

[226] Jay Solomon, "U.S. Moves to Give Iran Limited Access to Dollars," *Wall Street Journal*, April 1, 2016

[227] "Remarks After Meeting Iranian Foreign Minister Zarif," U.S. Department of State, April 19, 2016.
http://www.state.gov/secretary/remarks/2016/04/255977.htm?Source=GovD

[228] Congressman Ed Royce press release, April 19, 2016.
https://foreignaffairs.house.gov/press-release/chairman-royce-introduces-bill-to-deny-iran-access-to-u-s-dollar/

[229] Stuart Levey, "Kerry's Peculiar Message About Iran for European Banks," *Wall Street Journal*, May 12, 2016

[230] JCPOA, p. 15, paragraph 25.

[231] Jo-Anne Hart and Sue Eckert, "Most U.S. states have sanctions against Iran. Here's why that's a problem," *Washington Post*, June 1. 2016.
https://www.washingtonpost.com/news/monkey-cage/wp/2016/06/01/most-u-s-states-have-sanctions-against-iran-heres-why-thats-a-problem-2/

[232] Ibid

[233] Letter from State Department Ambassador Stephen Mull to North Carolina Governor Pat McCrory, April 8, 2016. https://www.patmccrory.com/wp-content/uploads/2016/04/NC_Federal_Letter_Sanctions.pdf

[234] Letter from Texas Governor Greg Abbott to President Obama, May 16, 2016.
http://gov.texas.gov/files/press-office/ObamaIran_05162016.pdf

[235] Letter by Governor Douglas Ducey et al to President Obama, September 8, 2015.
https://www.scribd.com/doc/279462795/Republican-Governors-Iran-Letter-to-President-Obama

[236] David Albright and Andrea Stricker, "JCPOA Exemptions Revealed," Institute for Science and International Security, September 1, 2016.
http://www.isisnucleariran.org/reports/detail/jcpoa/

[237] Congressman Paul Ryan, "Statement on the Administration's Purchase of Heavy Water from Iran," Office of House Speaker press release, April 22, 2016.
http://www.speaker.gov/press-release/statement-administrations-purchase-heavy-water-iran

[238] Congressman Ron DeSantis press release, May 26, 2016.
https://desantis.house.gov/media-center/press-releases/house-adopts-desantis-amendment-prohibiting-using-taxpayer-dollars-to

[239] David Albright and Andrea Stricker, "The Iran Nuclear Deal's Procurement Channel: Overcoming Post-Implementation Day Issues," Institute for Science and International Security, April 21, 2016.
http://www.isisnucleariran.org/assets/pdf/JCPOA_Procurement_Channel_Post_Impl ementation_Day_21April2016_Final1.pdf

[240] Steven Mufson, "Boeing nears landmark deal to sell airliners to Iran," *Washington Post*, June 14, 2016

[241] Congressman Peter Roskam press release, May 3, 2016.
https://roskam.house.gov/Boeing-Should-Not-Support-Iranian-Terror

[242] Letter to The Boeing Company from Congressmen Peter Roskam and Jeb Hensarling, June 16, 2016.
https://hensarling.house.gov/sites/hensarling.house.gov/files/Boeing_Letter_6_16_20 16.pdf

[243] Patricia Zengerle, "U.S. lawmakers have 'grave concern' over Boeing, Airbus Iran licenses," Reuters, September 23, 2016. http://www.reuters.com/article/us-iran-aviation-usa-congress-idUSKCN11T1TS

[244] AIPAC press release: "Congress Must Reauthorize the Iran Sanctions Act," March 29, 2016. http://www.aipac.org/-/media/publications/policy-and-politics/aipac-analyses/issue-memos/2016/congress-must-reauthorize-the-iran-sanctions-act.pdf?la=en

[245] Rebecca Kheel, "Kerry: Some Iran sanctions relief will go to terrorists." *The Hill,* January 21, 2016. http://thehill.com/policy/defense/266619-kerry-some-iran-sanctions-relief-will-go-to-terrorists

[246] Nicholas Fondacaro, "Nets Blackout State Department Admitting Ineffectiveness of Iran Deal," Media Research Center, September 14, 2016.
http://www.mrctv.org/videos/nets-blackout-state-department-admitting-ineffectiveness-iran-deal

[247] Frank Gaffney interviews Richard Perle on Secure Freedom Radio, January 19, 2016
http://www.centerforsecuritypolicy.org/2016/01/19/reagan-v-obama/

[248] Russ Read, "Ben Rhodes Admits Iran Deal Written So Future Presidents Could Never Tear It Up," Daily Caller, June 17, 2016.
http://dailycaller.com/2016/06/17/ben-rhodes-admits-iran-deal-written-to-prevent-future-presidents-from-tearing-it-up/
Read more: http://dailycaller.com/2016/06/17/ben-rhodes-admits-iran-deal-written-to-prevent-future-presidents-from-tearing-it-up/#ixzz4ByhkIOX6

[249] Financial Action Task Force statement, February 19, 2016. http://www.fatf-gafi.org/publications/high-riskandnon-cooperativejurisdictions/documents/public-statement-february-2016.html

Index